ANTISEMITISM AND RACISM

PSYCHOANALYTIC HORIZONS

Psychoanalysis is unique in being at once a theory and a therapy, a method of critical thinking and a form of clinical practice. Now in its second century, this fusion of science and humanism derived from Freud has outlived all predictions of its demise. **Psychoanalytic Horizons** evokes the idea of a convergence between realms as well as the outer limits of a vision. Books in the series test disciplinary boundaries and will appeal to scholars and therapists who are passionate not only about the theory of literature, culture, media, and philosophy but also, above all, about the real life of ideas in the world.

Series Editors
Esther Rashkin, Mari Ruti, and Peter L. Rudnytsky

Advisory Board
Salman Akhtar, Doris Brothers, Aleksandar Dimitrijevic,
Lewis Kirshner, Humphrey Morris, Hilary Neroni,
Dany Nobus, Lois Oppenheim, Donna Orange, Peter Redman,
Laura Salisbury, Alenka Zupančič

Volumes in the Series:
Mourning Freud edited by Madelon Sprengnether
*Does the Internet Have an Unconscious?: Slavoj Žižek and
Digital Culture* edited by Clint Burnham
In the Event of Laughter: Psychoanalysis, Literature and Comedy
edited by Alfie Bown
On Dangerous Ground: Freud's Visual Cultures of the Unconscious
edited by Diane O'Donoghue
*For Want of Ambiguity: Order and Chaos in Art, Psychoanalysis, and
Neuroscience* edited by Ludovica Lumer and Lois Oppenheim
Life Itself Is an Art: The Life and Work of Erich Fromm edited by
Rainer Funk

ANTISEMITISM AND RACISM

Ethical Challenges for Psychoanalysis

Stephen Frosh

BLOOMSBURY ACADEMIC
NEW YORK • LONDON • OXFORD • NEW DELHI • SYDNEY

BLOOMSBURY ACADEMIC
Bloomsbury Publishing Inc
1385 Broadway, New York, NY 10018, USA
50 Bedford Square, London, WC1B 3DP, UK
29 Earlsfort Terrace, Dublin 2, Ireland

BLOOMSBURY, BLOOMSBURY ACADEMIC and the Diana logo
are trademarks of Bloomsbury Publishing Plc

First published in the United States of America 2023

Cover design by Daniel Benneworth-Gra
Cover image: Untitled, 2019 © Jacqueline Nicholls

Library of Congress Cataloging-in-Publication Data
Names: Frosh, Stephen, author.
Title: Antisemitism and racism : ethical challenges for
psychoanalysis / Stephen Frosh.
Description: New York : Bloomsbury Academic, 2023. |
Series: Psychoanalytic horizons | Includes bibliographical references and index. |
Summary: "A psychoanalytically-informed examination of the relations between
antisemitism and racism more broadly, especially antiblack
racism"– Provided by publisher.
Identifiers: LCCN 2022058805 (print) | LCCN 2022058806 (ebook) |
ISBN 9798765104712 (hardback) | ISBN 9798765104705 (paperback) |
ISBN 9798765104729 (ebook) | ISBN 9798765104736 (pdf) |
ISBN 9798765104743 (ebook other)
Subjects: LCSH: Antisemitism. | Racism. | Psychoanalysis–Moral and ethical aspects.
Classification: LCC DS145 .F76 2023 (print) | LCC DS145 (ebook) |
DDC 305.892/4–dc23/eng/20230103
LC record available at https://lccn.loc.gov/2022058805
LC ebook record available at https://lccn.loc.gov/2022058806

ISBN: HB: 979-8-7651-0471-2
          PB: 979-8-7651-0470-5
          ePDF: 979-8-7651-0473-6
          eBook: 979-8-7651-0472-9

Series: Psychoanalytic Horizons

Typeset by Integra Software Services Pvt. Ltd.
Printed and bound in the United States of America

To find out more about our authors and books visit www.bloomsbury.com
and sign up for our newsletters.

CONTENTS

ACKNOWLEDGEMENTS

Several chapters of this book have been published in earlier versions but have been developed or reworked for this book. I am grateful to the editors and publishers for permission to use the material here.

Chapter 1: An earlier version of this chapter was originally published as Stephen Frosh (2022) Psychoanalytic Judaism, Judaic Psychoanalysis. *European Judaism, 55*(1), 71–85 – Berghahn Books. Reproduced and adapted with permission.

Chapter 2: An earlier version of this chapter was originally published as Stephen Frosh (2009) Promised Land or Permitted Land: a Consideration of Jewish Fundamentalism in the light of Levinasian Ethics. *Psychoanalysis and History, 11*, 209–24. Reproduced and adapted with permission.

Chapter 3: An earlier version of this chapter was published as Stephen Frosh (2020) Psychoanalysis as Decolonial Judaism. *Psychoanalysis, Culture and Society, 25*(2), 174–93. Reproduced and adapted with permission from Springer Nature.

Chapter 4: This chapter is adapted from a longer article that was published as Stephen Frosh (2017) Primitivity and Violence: Traces of the Unconscious in Psychoanalysis. *Journal of Theoretical and Philosophical Psychology, 37*, 34–47. Copyright © 2017 by American Psychological Association. Reproduced and adapted with permission.

Chapter 5: An earlier and much shorter version of this was published as Stephen Frosh (2022) Diversity or Exclusion? Psychoanalysis 'Explains'. *Free Associations, 86*, 9–20. Reprinted and adapted with permission of the editors. Some of this material also appears in Frosh, S. (2022) Psychoanalysis, Race and Colonialism. In A. Govrin and T. Caspi (eds) *The Routledge Handbook of Psychoanalysis and Philosophy*. London: Routledge. Reprinted and adapted with permission of the editors.

Chapter 8: An earlier version of this chapter was published as Stephen Frosh (2021) Psychoanalysis in the Wake. *Psychoanalysis, Culture and Society, 26*(4), 414–32. Reproduced and adapted with permission from Springer Nature.

Many thanks to Dr Ruth Sheldon for permission to use a long quotation from her fieldnotes in Chapter 1. The notes were from her work on the project *Ethical Monotheism*, funded by Dangoor Education, on which I was the grant holder.

INTRODUCTION

Psychoanalysis, antisemitism and racism

Let me start with my personal position. As a Jewish academic, usually situated ethnically as 'white' (though this is something I increasingly contest for reasons discussed later in this book), I am uncomfortable with many things. I do not want to claim that I am the victim of racialized aggression, and my relatively privileged life attests to this. Yet there it is: rising rates of antisemitism in Europe, the UK and the United States, places where we thought it was over and done with after Nazism revealed where it might lead (Community Security Trust, 2020), growing 'insecurity' in Jewish communities (Kahn-Harris and Gidley, 2010) and the political manipulation of antisemitism by right-wing populism, reflected for example in the 'alt-right' movement in the United States but also in Hungary, Poland and elsewhere. The historical continuities are powerful and depressing. Antisemitism remains a presence haunting the whole world, fulfilling all its old functions as well as several new ones. Jean-Luc Nancy (2020), in a tendentiously Eurocentric work on antisemitism, puts at least one finger on this:

> Today an antisemitism circulates all around the Mediterranean – and, more widely, throughout the world – that has become banal again; that is, it feeds on beliefs and images produced over the course of a very long history, in which modern forms have mostly taken over from ancient ones. The latter – often labeled 'anti-Judaism' – emerged first and foremost out of religious condemnations and their consequences (exclusion from many sectors, social statutes, professions). Modern forms – bio-ethnological racism and global conspiracy theories – come together in what Hannah Arendt characterizes as the making of an abstract figure, 'the Jew,' bearer of all flaws and perpetrator of all evils.
>
> (Nancy, 2020, p.12)

This makes antisemitism the core mode of racism in which the Jew, as 'bearer of all flaws and perpetrator of all evils', acts as the paradigm for other racisms. This view is shared by some other commentators such as Slavoj Žižek (1994, p.74), who sees racism as a '*universalized anti-Semitism* – that is, every ethnic "otherness" is conceived of as an *unheimliches* double that threatens our enjoyment; in short, "normal", non-exceptional, non-anti-Semitic racism is no longer possible.' Just as Jews are imagined as infiltrating 'our' (i.e. white) society to poison it or steal its riches, so are other groups with their 'alien' ways – black people, Muslims, 'Orientals' and so on. Others, however, see the concern with antisemitism as heavily politicized. This does not mean that they necessarily deny the reality of antisemitism (though some do), but rather are concerned about the uses to which it is put by those who make it the key manifestation of racism, potentially obscuring, or even being used in the service of, other significant kinds of racist activity.

Alana Lentin (2020, p.135), for example, argues that 'The political utility of antisemitism today is not to illuminate the operations of race, but rather to obscure them.' According to Lentin, this is especially tied up with attitudes to Israel, where the conflation of anti-Zionism and antisemitism (which few people deny sometimes occurs) is taken by some critics as indicating how opposition to antisemitism can be used to perpetrate racism against other groups, especially (as emphasized by Lentin) right-wing Islamophobia. In recent history, it is sometimes claimed that this is a widespread problem: antisemitism is identified in the rhetoric or actions of racialized groups (for example, statements by some who have affiliated themselves with Black Lives Matter), with the effect (and quite probably the intention) of splitting the antiracist conjunction in which antisemitism, anti-Black racism, Islamophobia and other forms of racism are all understood and confronted together. In this context, recovering an alliance between those who oppose antisemitism and those who fight against other forms of racism becomes an urgent task, before this split becomes unbridgeable and the broader antiracist struggle becomes part of a reactionary process that pits racially oppressed groups against each other.

Even if it is the case that opposition to antisemitism is sometimes a cover for racism, one does not have to look too far for ways in which hatred of Jews and hatred of other racialized groups are tethered firmly together in racist discourse and action. For example, in the current moment, antisemitism and anti-Black racism are linked by conspiracy theories making Jews responsible for the 'flood' of migrants – that is, people of colour – into Europe, and of 'terrorist' Muslims into the

United States as part of a phantasmatic Jewish plot to destabilize the West. All this is poisonous, and one might assume should lead to an assertion of Jewish and Black solidarity against antisemitism and anti-Black racism. Yet despite many examples of productive reaching-out between Jewish, Black and Muslim organizations, the situation is unstable and the presence of antiracist 'rivalries' is very evident.

In my own case, for instance, having been open and active about my Jewish identity and affiliations throughout most of my academic career, I now feel wary (though this has not stopped me continuing to be open about it), unsure about what the consequences could be and often feeling that I have to justify myself – and this not just because of the endless array of heated disputes about Israel-Palestine to be found in academic and student communities. Perhaps the most painful aspect of this has been the way Jewishness has become an issue even within the antiracist movement with which I would identify, especially in the decolonizing campaigns but also, at times and not univocally, within supposedly mainstream political groups as well as broader activist communities such as Black Lives Matter. 'Jews don't count', David Baddiel (2021) asserts, addressing the leftist antiracist movements with which he too would like to identify; that is, antisemitism too often does not register as racism and so is neglected or even denied by those movements. To make matters worse, this situation has been leveraged by right-wing forces (for instance the UK Government of the early 2020s) to drive a wedge between different parts of the antiracist campaign so that, under the general rubric of 'free speech', it is possible for racist statements to be made in the guise of 'white replacement theory' and attacks to be pursued on 'critical race theory', whilst universities are compelled to sign up to an impoverished and confused agenda in which anti-Zionism is merged with antisemitism and 'free speech' actually gets restricted. To be clear, if possible, I am not saying here that anti-Zionism is never antisemitic or that antisemites should be allowed free rein to say what they like; rather, I am pointing to a situation in which on both left and right, antisemitism is becoming separated from anti-Black and other forms of racism with negative effects on the potential for solidarity between those who suffer from either – or both.

Under these conditions, it is hard not to feel increasingly alienated from the struggles around us, and to watch with a kind of detached cynicism as the dynamics of antiracism play themselves out. If Jews are not wanted, why should we get involved? We have enough difficulties in looking after ourselves in a world situation in which ethnic nationalism and racialized cultural identities seem central for both left and right, and in which the traditions of internationalism and collaborative affiliation and alliance are under constant attack. Is it even possible to speak about another's experience, for example, for a white person to advocate for the Black voices emerging so powerfully from Black Lives Matter and, more academically, Black Studies? Or is this a repetition of colonialism in the guise of 'cultural appropriation', in which these voices are taken over and ventriloquized with the effect of nothing really changing? These issues will recur throughout this book and not be fully resolved because I think the tensions are real and the questions of location, identity and appropriation have genuine substance. Nevertheless, I want to make my opening statement here: alliances are essential, a solidarity of the oppressed is necessary; and if we cannot imagine the experience of people other than ourselves and respond to the demands that are made on us by those experiences and by their articulation, then we are lost. It is probably obvious that a white person cannot know *from the inside* what Black experience is, or indeed that a non-Jew cannot *fully* know what it is about Jewish life that is distinctive and emotionally powerful; lived experience is particular to those who live it. But we can know *something*, maybe a lot, by encountering others in what they write and say, in how they represent themselves and in the demand for recognition and acknowledgement that they place upon us. This is a theme that I work with throughout the book, claiming that it is linked to a Jewish ethic oriented towards relationality (an ethic that is of course not *exclusive* to Jews or Judaism) that means that people like myself – strongly identified as Jewish – are pressed to try to form alliances in the work we do and in our personal lives. Still, turning the screw a little more, we also have to be *allowed* to do so since antisemitism and anti-Black racism actively interfere with efforts to resist them, and thrive when such attempts at alliance are rejected.

The third part of my interest, psychoanalysis, comes into play here as a discipline or practice that has always been embroiled with Jewishness and antisemitism and has its own uncomfortable history in relation to 'race' and racism. Psychoanalysis has numerous sources, for example, in nineteenth-century neurology, in romanticism and in occultism. The most relevant, however, is its origins in the Jewish lives of Freud and its other first-generation progenitors, and for that matter its continuing intersection with Jewishness that exists even today, if less markedly so than previously. The insistent pressure of antisemitism was something that Freud was deeply aware of and directly reacted against, and his last major work, *Moses and Monotheism* (Freud, 1939), can be seen in part as an assertion of the resilience of Jewishness in the face of the monstrous upsurge in annihilatory antisemitism in the 1930s. This is a crucial element in the history of psychoanalysis, in which antisemitism has played a significant role (Frosh, 2005a), and consequently in the ways in which psychoanalysis has impacted upon emancipatory struggles that establish its 'progressive' credentials, despite a fair amount of conservatism within the psychoanalytic movement and at times its conforming to authoritarian regimes in places such as Latin America and Germany (e.g. Frosh and Mandelbaum, 2017).

The role of the 'Jewishness' of psychoanalysis in creating links with antiracist struggles is noticeable. For instance, Daniel José Gaztambide (2019) sets the scene for his tracing of the relations between psychoanalysis and Latinx liberation psychology by commenting that 'The history of the Jewish people in Europe is in tragic and important ways intricately tied to the history of the Indigenous people of the Americas and Black people kidnapped from Africa – each [of] their subjectivities were distorted and rendered subhuman under the gaze of European Whiteness' (p.6). The argument here is that this shared history of racialized minoritization has also meant a shared history of anticolonial and antiracist opposition to which psychoanalysis has contributed, a tradition that, to the degree that it has been lost, merits recovering and reinstating. This is not to take away from the specificity of either antisemitism or anti-Black racism. The positions of Jews and people of colour are nowadays quite radically distinct in many societies, including within the psychoanalytic movement where, notwithstanding the re-emergence of antisemitic tropes at various times (Frosh, 2012), the Jewish presence has been marked and powerful. The point, however, is that the history of antisemitism that has dogged psychoanalysis is one reason to claim its relative openness to awareness of the reality of anti-Black racism, and to hope that this potential openness can become more marked as the need to combat racism becomes ever more pressing.

For the present, however, the failure to fully address racism is a running sore in the psychoanalytic movement. There are institutional reasons for this, to do with the creation of psychoanalytic societies around a kind of guild framework that promotes a Eurocentric vision and tends to judge the adequacy of candidates for training through the lens of those already 'in' (Winograd, 2014). The location of psychoanalysis in mainly high-fee private practice militates against its availability within Black communities too. There are also conceptual reasons, notably the focus that psychoanalysis has on the individual's so-called 'inner world' and its relative neglect of the 'external' social environment. The degree to which this is the case obviously varies according to school of thought and historical and social location, but it remains a strong tendency that neglects the racialized conditions of a person's life, making them subsidiary to the psychological *perception* of those conditions (Davids, 2011). The result can be a turning away from the social, as if it is not the legitimate concern of the analytic encounter, as if entering into what feels like the politics of a situation can be a betrayal of psychoanalytic neutrality. The result, however, is not to preserve the purity of psychoanalysis but rather to reproduce its colonialist mentality, or maybe to induce its growing irrelevance in the face of the enormous impact that social oppression has on psychic life. Within a racist social structure, how can anything, including the clinical situation, be 'neutral'? Without attending to how racism operates in people's lives, it seems likely that the reality of those lives – including their psychodynamic reality – is being missed.

These issues have always been important, and there is a long history of psychoanalytic discussion of anti-Black racism, perhaps beginning seriously (as so many postcolonial critiques do) with Frantz Fanon (1952) but including significant contributions from many more recent authors, both from within and outside the psychoanalytic movement (e.g. Rustin, 1991; Seshadri-Crooks, 1994; Kovel, 1995; Abel, 1997; Dalal, 2002; Davids, 2011; Frosh, 1989, 2013a; Hook, 2013). The somewhat hidden history of mid-twentieth-century American Black engagement with psychoanalysis has also lately gained some recognition in accounts of progressive psychoanalysis, as has the emergence of psychoanalysis in postcolonial contexts (Khanna, 2004; Zaretsky, 2015; Gaztambide, 2019). Furthermore, in the last thirty years there has been a powerful influx of psychoanalytic work from writers of colour that challenges many of the absences in the literature to date, including Hortense Spillers' (1996) wide-ranging 'All the things you could be by now if Sigmund Freud's wife was your mother' through Kimberlyn Leary's delicate and extensive writings on 'race' and clinical psychoanalysis (e.g. Leary, 2007, 2012) and Kathleen Pogue White's (2002) sensitive elaboration of personal and clinical issues in her paper, 'Surviving hating and being hated'. Some of this material will be discussed later in this book. It can perhaps be seen as part of a broader engagement with social and political issues that itself has a long history (Frosh, 2018); but it is also a specific response to an awareness of the importance of racism in governing the lives and mental health of analytic patients (and analysts) as well as reflecting the use made of psychoanalysis by some committedly antiracist social theorists (e.g. Butler, 2020).

Recently, there have been significant social and intellectual developments that make the issues even more pertinent and that have encouraged a response from some psychoanalysts that is questioning and outward-looking in relation to their own practices and theories. Amongst these developments, two related strands stand out: the decolonizing movement, with its emphasis on the legacies of Empire, particularly in relation to British and European imperialism; and the antislavery movement that has had a very powerful manifestation in Black Lives Matter and that has more of an American focus but is also deeply relevant to British involvement with slavery, and indeed to that of other European colonial powers. These two strands have slightly different emphases and spheres of action, but they make some similar points: the continuing effects and ideologies of colonialism, observable in discriminatory practices in every social sphere, including education and health; perpetuation of the legacy of slavery, observable especially in violence towards people of colour on the part of the State, as well as the radically reduced life chances of many Black communities; and a demand that the haunting of the present by these supposedly past, but in fact current, oppressions needs to be addressed finally and firmly, through acts of genuine acknowledgement, reparation and justice. For psychoanalysis, the injunction is at least twofold: first, to examine its own history of implication in colonialism and racism and to disentangle from this, and develop, the emancipatory practices with which it has long been associated (for example, the Free Clinic movement, the ameliorating of biologizing or regulatory psychiatric practices and the use of psychoanalysis in social welfare and critical psychotherapy centres – e.g. Ernst and Maguire, 1987; Danto, 2005; Russo, 2012a); and secondly, to develop further psychoanalytic ideas that can be used to reflect critically on the spread of racist and antidemocratic practices in contemporary society (for one recent example, see Pick, 2022, and for a survey, Frosh, 2018). Psychoanalysis is not special in having a mixed past and being made up of contrary tendencies, some conformist and some progressive, to use a crude binary. But both because of its specific history in conjunction with a Jewishness that was deeply anathematized in the half century after psychoanalysis' birth, and because of psychoanalysis's commitment to an ethic that promotes personal and social well-being (even if the definition of this might be debated), it can be argued that it has a special responsibility to confront the damage being wrought by the continuation of racism and the resurgence of antisemitism in contemporary times.

Jews, antiracism, psychoanalysis

These considerations produce my felt need to think through ways in which the Jewish heritage within psychoanalysis can be articulated and developed as an ethics of antiracist practice, despite the complexities produced by antisemitism and colonialism and the difficulty of speaking across different experiences of oppression. I have been doing this thinking, in fits and starts and with plenty of setbacks, for some time, and the current book can be understood as a record of this and as a provisional, unfinished set of attempts at a psychoanalytically informed examination of the relations between antisemitism and anti-Black racism. Its starting point is a claim that the Jewish origins and implications of psychoanalysis fuel its capacity to interrogate racism of all kinds; in addition, the shared experience of exposure to (albeit different kinds of) racism raises prospects for renewed alliances between Jewish and Black communities. The book is written from my point of view as a Jewish writer drawing on Jewish sources to establish an ethical position that can be used to build alliances around antiracism, and in so doing create a 'solidarity of the oppressed' that includes progressive Jews. This means that it does not strive to present antisemitism and anti-Black racism equally, but rather to use an understanding of the former to work on responses to the latter. The further claim, or at least 'wager', is that there is in Jewish thought a set of ideas that can be mobilized within antiracist practice, and that these ideas both challenge and are expressible through psychoanalysis. The direction of the argument is therefore from Jewish ethics, through psychoanalysis to antiracism, and then back again to the challenge that antiracist work presents to psychoanalysis itself.

After this Introduction, the book presents two chapters co-locating psychoanalytic and Jewish ethics. The book then develops an argument that Jewish consciousness of antisemitism can feed into psychoanalytic perspectives on racism generally, promoting a possibility of Black-Jewish alliance around opposition to oppression. Along the way, it has to contend with the implications of the notion of 'primitivity' as used by Freud and some post-Freudian psychoanalysts, suggesting that this reflects *both* a colonial impulse (in which some 'others' are relegated to the position of the 'savage' or 'primitive') *and* a potentially decolonizing trajectory in which the civilized-primitive dichotomy is subverted by the psychoanalytic understanding of the unconscious. The question of Jewish 'whiteness' is addressed and the warning voice of the Jewish Tunisian decolonial writer Albert Memmi is reflected upon through an account of two of his major works from just before and just after Tunisian independence, both of which reflect the fraught position he found himself in as a Jewish anti-colonialist. The book ends with a chapter that asks psychoanalysis itself to respond to some of the challenges emerging from Black and decolonial movements. To facilitate navigation across these chapters, here is a brief guide.

Chapter 1: Psychoanalytic Judaism, Judaic psychoanalysis

In this chapter I briefly review some thinking on the relationship between Judaism and psychoanalysis before making the claim that there is something about Jewish 'lived ethics' that is responsive to otherness – and that this speaks to a progressive mode of psychoanalytic consciousness that is relevant for antiracist practice. The chapter begins with a summary account of some major trends in research on psychoanalysis and Judaism, relating particularly to the origins of psychoanalysis; antisemitism directed towards, and within, psychoanalysis; links between Jewish mysticism and psychoanalysis; hermeneutics and interpretation; and the transmission of knowledge through intense personal relationships. The chapter then offers an account of Jewish life as rooted in relational connections and, because of that, having a distinctive appreciation of the importance of others in people's lives, even if these others might raise uncomfortable feelings and complex emotions. I give an example of this from a recent ethnography in a strictly orthodox Jewish community and try to show how this complicated relationality is constitutive of Judaism and of psychoanalysis as well. As such, it is a powerful ethical claim to say that 'Jewish' psychoanalysis may speak to a broader agenda of alliance across communities subjected to racism.

Chapter 2: Promised land or permitted land: A consideration of Jewish fundamentalism in the light of Levinasian ethics

One problem with the argument about Jewish ethics being other-directed is the existence of Jewish insularity and even, in some places, Jewish fundamentalism. At its most extreme, for example, amongst some orthodox Jews in Israel, literalist readings of the Bible are used to justify continued agitation for a 'greater Israel', accompanied by hostility not only towards Palestinians but also towards secular and politically more liberal Jews. This kind of inward-lookingness stems in part from antisemitism (exclusion of Jews leads to insularity), from particularist readings of 'sacred' texts and from a mode of Jewish exceptionalism to be found in the notion of 'chosenness'. In the context of my argument in this book, it is problematic because it suggests that Jewish ethics may not be concerned with relationality and the 'other', but rather with self-preservation and *non-recognition* of non-Jewish others, exactly the opposite of what might be needed for the building of resistive solidarities.

There is, however, another tradition within Judaism that emphasizes the moral responsibility Jews have and the requirement to exemplify ethical practices. This chapter approaches this topic 'sideways' (and hence psychoanalytically) through tracking a remarkable reading by the philosopher Emmanuel Levinas of the Talmudic passage dealing with the biblical account of the spies sent by Moses to Canaan, who were then punished for dissuading the Israelites from conquering the land. Levinas's ambivalent shifts between understanding these spies as motivated by an ethical refusal to see themselves as having a right to the land and seeing them (more conventionally) as having too little faith, perhaps reflect the operations of a 'guilt' about which psychoanalysis may have something to say. It also suggests that it might be possible to disrupt religious literalism through an alternative legitimate religious tradition – the multifarious commentaries of the Talmud – establishing that Jewish culture, history and ethics are always contested. Levinas here offers a way to think about notions of responsibility that are intensely relevant for the question of how Jews might draw on their own traditions to contest oppression in general, and racism in particular.

Chapter 3: Psychoanalysis as decolonial Judaism

In some recent work on decolonization, there has been an attempt to claim some Jewish writers of the twentieth century as participating in a rethinking of 'barbarism' that aligns Jewish thought with the decolonial movement. This is problematic, especially because post-Shoah and Zionist discourses have positioned Jews normatively as part of a European 'civilization' opposed to barbarism. Nevertheless, the reclaiming of a radical Jewish tradition allied with other movements of the oppressed may provide resources for 'barbaric thinking,' using 'barbaric' here in the *positive* sense to mean that which confronts the hegemony of European colonial thought. The relative absence of psychoanalysis from this discussion is striking. Given the place of psychoanalysis both as a colonial discipline and as a contributor to critical and postcolonial thought, can it be seen in the positive tradition of Jewish barbarism? This chapter offers an account of Jewish barbaric possibilities and suggests ways in which psychoanalysis might connect with them.

Chapter 4: Primitivity and violence in psychoanalysis

Psychoanalysis, the theory and practice of the 'unconscious', has an unconscious of its own, in the sense of containing unacknowledged assumptions that continue to affect it. The unconscious of psychoanalysis can be seen in the implicit models that it holds of the nature of the human subject, and particularly in the manner in which psychoanalytic 'knowledge' is disrupted by persistent assumptions and recurrent blind spots that are at best partially recognized. These operate especially strongly in relation to 'otherness' and so are directly relevant to the question of alliance or solidarity.

In this short chapter, I explore some lingering effects of psychoanalysis's 'unconscious' assumptions. I argue that the colonial elements of psychoanalysis' heritage are visible in its conceptualization of violence and 'primitivity', and specifically in thinking of violence as an atavistic reproduction of a foundational savagery that, in its imagery and in its substance, is caught up with divisions between civilization and barbarism with very particular sociohistorical resonances. Recognizing this tendency and thinking through its origins and the alternatives that might push us towards more progressive thought are crucial if the radical potential of psychoanalysis is to be developed in ways that promote antiracist practice.

Chapter 5: Racialized exclusions, or 'Psychoanalysis Explains ...'

This chapter is concerned with how racialized boundaries and exclusions are made and can be overcome. For Jews, psychoanalysis has been a kind of 'home': familiar, sharing in certain assumptions and practices, but also marginal, subjected to prejudice and antisemitism and consequently not (exactly) 'white'. For Black communities, psychoanalysis has often been pathologizing and colonial, yet also at times emancipatory either as a practice of socially reformist mental health intervention or as a set of concepts that offer potential leverage for self-emancipation. In this chapter, I develop a more detailed account of the relationship between Blackness and Jewishness to be found in Freud's writings, examine ways in which psychoanalysis has been used to 'explain' racism and describe one important Black engagement (that of Hortense Spillers,

1996) with psychoanalytic ideas. My suggestion is that we start to see in this material both the difficulties for psychoanalysis in emerging from a colonialist mindset and, on the other hand, the possibilities it offers for emancipatory thought.

Chapter 6: Whiteness with Jewishness

The issue of Jewish 'whiteness' has become a contested one as Jews come gradually to appreciate the presence of Black Jews amongst them, as well as the diversity of Jewish 'ethnicities' that cannot be regarded as white. Indeed, the assumption that Jews are white can itself be seen as an aspect of antisemitic discourse, in that it leads to obscuring anti-Jewish racism on the grounds that Jews share in white privilege and therefore cannot be seen as oppressed. The antisemitic imaginary of the Jew as scheming, conspiratorial, anti-nationalist and corrupting is core to racism even though it is by no means its sole element. This is because it embodies the scheme of envy of the other's enjoyment: the Jew has what the white subject wants. From the other side, Jewish expositions of the importance of approaching others as having the same rights and standing as oneself fuel the drive to oppose racism from the position of being an outsider – in this context, from the non-white position. Absorbing Jews into whiteness denies this possibility and loses the specificity both of antisemitism and of Jewish antiracism; it also, perhaps just as significantly, obscures the dynamic of racism by denying Jewish otherness. Jewish suffering and other forms of racialized oppression relate to one another; Jews receive projections and envious attacks just as obviously and destructively as do other groups subjected to racist abuse and genocidal assault. Jews also have a tradition that opposes this, however fraught and contested it might be at times. Activating this opposition requires that Jews both own their white privilege where it is in operation and separate themselves from it; and it also needs other antiracists to recognize that Jewish solidarity with them can be a positive phenomenon with specifically Jewish roots.

Chapter 7: Being ill at ease

If there is to be an alliance across different oppressed groups, then the issue of whether each group can find its own way towards this inclusive, capacious attitude needs to be addressed. This chapter explores this question from the more 'pessimistic' end, using some of the writing of the Tunisian Jewish decolonial thinker Albert Memmi as a case study.

In *The Colonizer and the Colonized*, Memmi (1957) gives a striking portrait of both sides of the colonial relationship that acknowledges his own position as a Jew and consequently as someone who does not quite belong in either camp, yet also – or possibly because of this – demonstrates an ability to think through the characteristics of both. Memmi notes his psychosocial links with the French colonialists yet leaves no doubt as to his sympathies or his understanding of colonialism as something to be resisted and overthrown. A few years later, in *Portrait of a Jew*, Memmi (1962) maintains a sensitivity towards the suffering of all oppressed groups, yet is clearly overwhelmed by the experience of antisemitism, which is the central concern of the book, as well as the consequences of post-coloniality in Tunisia, which found no place for Jews like himself. The aspiration to a universal alliance of the oppressed now looks far-fetched, as antisemitism permeates all elements of the social world. Is there a way out of this? Can Memmi's universalist vision be preserved against his despair?

Chapter 8: Psychoanalysis in the wake

Psychoanalysis has a long history of engagement with racism, often through theorizing racism's sources. It has nevertheless been criticized for its neglect of Black experience and its narrowness in relating to the social realities of racism as lived in the wider black community. Very recently, there have been attempts by psychoanalytic institutes and practitioners to respond positively to the emergence and strengthening of the Black Lives Matter and decolonizing movements. In this final chapter, the possibility of this response is examined through the lens of one particular text that has had a substantial impact and offers one of the clearest and most potent articulations of black lives in the wake of slavery. This is Christina Sharpe's (2016) book *In the Wake: On Blackness and Being*. This chapter draws out some of the issues from *In the Wake* that seem to have most potential for challenging psychoanalysis to rethink some of its assumptions and practices in relation to the ongoing violence of anti-Black racism. In doing so, it draws together the main themes of the book, articulated in a short conclusion concerning, once again, the three-way partnership of Jewishness, antiracism and psychoanalysis.

Chapter 1

PSYCHOANALYTIC JUDAISM, JUDAIC PSYCHOANALYSIS

'Jewish' Psychoanalysis

My argument throughout this book is that psychoanalysis inherits and reworks some important ethical principles, derived in part from Judaism and from Jewish life (including the experience of antisemitism), and that these principles warrant an engagement with broader antiracist practices. In this chapter I sketch out some of the background to this by exploring some thinking on the relationship between Judaism and psychoanalysis – a relationship that has produced a voluminous if unsteady literature – to eventually stake a claim that centres on the identification of a particular kind of Jewish 'lived ethics'. This ethics is *relational* in nature, in the sense that it is concerned with the impact and response to other people, especially in the guise of 'neighbours' – which means they are not necessarily 'othered' as strangers but rather recognized as subjects with whom one is in a relationship of co-existence. I offer an example of this from an encounter between different branches of the Jewish community in the UK as the beginning of an exploration of the nature of this ethics that also has to be explored with regard to non-Jewish neighbours, specifically those subjected to anti-Black racism. This ethics is by no means unproblematic, any more than relations with actual neighbours usually are; as my example will show, it has undertones of violence and exclusion as well as of hospitality. Nevertheless, it lays some of the groundwork for the claim that there is an ethical thrust towards identification with suffering others, and that this can be a springboard for antiracist alliance. The involvement of psychoanalysis in this is crucial in that the implication of Jewishness in psychoanalysis provides, through this ethics, one route towards a progressive mode of psychoanalytic consciousness that is relevant for antiracist practice.

The Jewish origins of psychoanalysis are well recognized and widely rehearsed and are a clear sociological fact. However, this does not mean quite the same thing as it might have done if the origins of psychoanalysis were, for instance, Christian. In that case, we might be talking specifically of a *religious* source for psychoanalysis, perhaps related to Christian notions of grace and forgiveness, or something embedded in the confessional relationship – a wiping clean of the bad conscience in the conviction that one has been forgiven by a divine power. To claim that psychoanalysis has Jewish origins is not a statement of this kind, or at least not necessarily so; it might simply mean that the person who invented it, Sigmund Freud, was Jewish and that so were most of the early European psychoanalysts. Though of course this is insufficient as well. Saying that psychoanalysis was Jewish is no more neutral than saying it was 'European' or 'German-language' in origin, both true statements and both relevant to understanding psychoanalysis's history and core concepts. The assumptions of European colonialism and of science, and the traditions of German philosophy, literature and romanticism, were themselves powerful influences on how psychoanalysis emerged and the form it took when it did. One could even argue that it had 'occult' origins, given the intense interest in forms of hypnosis, suggestibility, 'spirit-possession' and telepathy that surrounded and to some degree permeated early psychoanalytic thought (Frosh, 2013b). Without the notion of the occult, would a mysterious 'unconscious' be imaginable, even in the material form that psychoanalysis gives it? The point here is that there are many sources for psychoanalysis and many justifiable claims that can be made for their influence on it. Jewishness arguably could be seen as only one of those sources, sometimes working alongside and sometimes in tension with others.

Despite all this, there is something peculiar and especially complex about the Jewish connection to psychoanalysis. In part this is because, even more than the relationship with the German language or bourgeois Europe of the period, it was especially strongly emotionally and politically loaded. For Nancy (2020, p.19), antisemitism is foundational in European Christian society generally: 'Antisemitism must be called "historical" and "spiritual" because the hate that animates it is rooted in the spiritual and historical (one might say, awkwardly, civilizational) configuration where the West took shape.' Whatever the truth of this, throughout Freud's lifetime and since, Jews and Jewishness were targets more for denigration than approbation; antisemitism was rife and grew rather than faded with the advances of scientific rationality (which turned out to be all too precarious, at least in terms of the uses to which it has been put); Jewish identity was a prominent marker of difference; and the negative associations of Jewishness (for instance, deceitful, poisonous, sexualized, secretive …) were easily connected with the products of Jewish thinkers – especially when, as was the case with psychoanalysis, what they produced was in many people's view unsavoury. In particular, the fascination of psychoanalysis with sexuality, and its tendency (by no means universal, but real) towards social criticism that placed it on the side of 'progressive' politics, fed the association with Jewishness as contaminating, unpatriotic and corrupting. The classic antisemitic trope of Jews 'poisoning the wells' and the more modern notion of poisoning the mind are not unrelated ideas, at least emotionally. The scandalous effect of Freud's postulation of infantile sexuality as well as the early trauma theory represented in his so-called 'seduction hypothesis' was a sign of the repressive sexual hypocrisy of his period (something that he seems to have enjoyed exposing) but was also easily assimilated to fantasies of Jewish depravity. This negative set of associations of psychoanalysis applies also in relation to some of its other sources, especially occultism (though this might also have been tainted by fantasies of Jewish connections, for example, through the fictional figure of Svengali (Pick, 2000)) and sexology. But it is especially relevant to psychoanalysis because of psychoanalysis's context in the lives of emancipated Jews, always positioned as on the margins of a deeply antisemitic society. This implies that although there are many genuine 'origins' to psychoanalysis which have effects and are of importance, its Jewish origins are uniquely significant because of the political, historical, social and emotional baggage that they brought with them, and which psychoanalysis has never been able to escape.

A lot of work has been done by many scholars tracing the connections between Jewishness and psychoanalysis, from David Bakan's (1958) *Sigmund Freud and the Jewish Mystical Tradition* through Martha Robert's (1974) *From Oedipus to Moses: Freud's Jewish Identity* and onwards to twenty-first-century writings (Frosh, 2005a; Slavet, 2009). This work has compellingly established not just the connections between Freud's 'Jewish identity' and psychoanalysis (even if some of the wilder claims are tenuous) but also resonances between psychoanalytic assumptions and Jewish ones – or perhaps *Judaic* notions, if this term can be used to apply specifically to the traditions of Judaism, the religion of the Jews. Sorting through some of these claims is part of the ambition of this chapter, but one difficulty worth marking out at the start is the complicated signifier 'Jewish' itself. It refers to an ethnicity, or maybe multiple ethnicities (Ashkenazi, Sephardi, Mizrachi …); it is often cast as 'peoplehood', implying a shared sense of identity and possibly of culture, yet the variations in Jewish traditions and attitudes are pronounced; it is internally designated through a matriarchal line of descent with the possibility but relative infrequency of inward conversion (i.e. it is mostly defined by birth but not necessarily so); it is characterized even religiously as a set of practices more than of beliefs.

This last point is crucial in the context of Judaism: being Jewish does not depend on holding any particular beliefs or even solely on self-definition, but rather it is a matter of community acknowledgement of one's belongingness and heritage. In this way it diverges from the predominant assumption of a (secular-)Christian way of thinking that religious affiliation is a matter of belief and spirituality, freely entered into as a kind of choice (though it may *feel* impelled and inarguable). Indeed, from a Jewish point of view, the idea that the sphere of the religious is a solely spiritual one, constituted by beliefs and an actual or aspired-to experience of the divine, is oddly limited and fails to take account of the many ramifications of what is nowadays termed 'lived religion' – the set of personal and communal practices and affiliations characterizing individuals and groups that may have little or nothing to do with belief at all.

Freud himself played into this confusion by not always being especially alert to the importance of differentiating between religions. Even though he clearly retained his self-identity as a secular Jew, opposing conversion when it was an accepted route to social advancement, he tended to unite Judaism and Christianity under the general heading of 'religion'. Celia Brickman (2009) describes this clearly:

> Because Judaism has always held a particular and necessary place within Christianity – what from a Christian perspective would be called the place of superseded origins – Judaism has often been subsumed as part of so-called 'Judeo-Christian' religious culture, which is then shortened to the seemingly universal term 'religion' ... With this common and general use of the term religion, Freud – and his followers – obscure the structural differences between the two religions, as well as what we might call the political differences between them – the vast differences in the social and political locations of Christian and Jewish communities and their experiences in European countries leading up to and including the times in which Freud wrote.
>
> (pp.25–6)

Whilst Brickman has a point about Freud's use of the term 'religion' in such texts as *Totem and Taboo* and *The Future of an Illusion*, I do not think she is quite fair to his arguments, especially in *Moses and Monotheism* (1939), about the advances in civilization produced by Judaism's monotheism and, in contrast, Christianity's retreat from this intellectual and social 'maturity'. It is also relevant that Freud continued to assert his own non-religious Jewishness throughout his public life. One can be, as Isaac Deutscher (1968) famously put it, a 'non-Jewish Jew', meaning someone who has no religious beliefs or observances yet could feel themselves drawing on their Jewishness to inform their view of the world and their actions within it. Deutscher's elaboration of this is compelling and has considerable resonance both for thinking about Freud and for some of the arguments later in this book. 'The Jewish heretic who transcends Jewry belongs to a Jewish tradition', he writes (1968, p.26); and discussing the likes of Spinoza, Marx and Freud, he comments (p.27), 'I think that in some ways they were very Jewish indeed. They had in themselves something of the quintessence of Jewish life and of the Jewish intellect. They were *a priori* exceptional in that as Jews they dwelt on the borderlines of various civilizations, religions and national cultures.' For Deutscher, who was extremely knowledgeable about Judaism, there is an ethic at work here, one of a universalism born out of this experience of being 'in society and yet not in it, of it and yet not of it' (1968, p.27), resulting in a particularist solidarity with one's people that merges into a universalist solidarity with all the oppressed of the world. 'Religion?' Deutscher writes (1968, p.51), 'I am an atheist. Jewish nationalism? I am an internationalist. In neither sense am I therefore a Jew. I am, however, a Jew by force of my unconditional solidarity with the persecuted and exterminated. I am a Jew because I feel the pulse of Jewish history; because I should like to do all I can to assure the real, not spurious, security and self-respect of the Jews.'

Freud was also exemplary here, even though his Jewish knowledge was less detailed than that of Deutscher, who had been a Talmudic prodigy in his youth. Deutscher certainly included Freud in his list of great secular Jews with universal ideals, perhaps overlooking the actual cultural specificity of Freud's practice: 'the man whom he analyses is not a German or an Englishman, a Russian or a Jew – he is the universal man ... whose desires and cravings, scruples and inhibitions, anxieties and predicaments are essentially the same no matter to what race, religion, or nation he belongs' (Deutscher, 1968, p.35). Freud's own self-descriptions of his relationship with his Jewish identity are well known (Frosh, 2005a). I will restrict myself here to the most famous quotation,

drawn from his 1930 preface to the Hebrew edition of *Totem and Taboo*,
where he describes himself as:

> an author who is ignorant of the language of holy writ, who is
> completely estranged from the religion of his fathers – as well as from
> every other religion – and who cannot take a share in nationalist
> ideals, but who has yet never repudiated his people, who feels that
> he is in his essential nature a Jew and who has no desire to alter that
> nature. If the question were put to him: 'Since you have abandoned
> all these common characteristics of your countrymen, what is left to
> you that is Jewish?' he would reply: 'A very great deal, and probably
> its very essence.' He could not express that essence in words, but
> some day, no doubt, it will become accessible to the scientific mind.
>
> (Freud, 1930, p.xv)

Jacqueline Rose's (2003, p.71) comment on this is that 'Freud offers
here one of the most striking self-definitions of the modern secular
Jew – that is, the Jew for whom shedding the trappings of linguistic,
religious and national identity ... does not make him less Jewish, but
more'. This 'more Jewish' status resides in something that Freud finds
hard to express, yet it is clear that it centres partly on what he terms his
'essential nature' or, as he describes it in a well-known letter to the Bnai
Brith in Vienna responding to their congratulations on his seventieth
birthday, 'many dark emotional powers all the stronger the less they
could be expressed in words, as well as the clear consciousness of an
inner identity, the familiarity of the same psychological structure' as
other Jews (Freud, 1926, p.367). But it is also an *ethical* statement,
because in the same letter Freud goes on to say that whilst he was
brought up 'without religion', it was 'not without respect for the so-called
"ethical" demands of human civilisation' (Freud, 1926, p.27). That is,
Freud's identification with his Jewishness was specific; and he registered
a strong link between the religious values of the Jews embodied in
Judaism and ethical ideals that he saw as universal. This is a hint of
where we might look for Jewish solidarity with other oppressed groups.
Something speaks at the formation of psychoanalysis about its Jewish
ethics, which as Deutscher writes is connected with 'the pulse of Jewish
history' and as Freud adds is a specific inheritance of Judaism, yet is
also universal in its outlook. But whilst this might be a real motivator
of psychoanalytic ethics, is it enough to claim psychoanalysis as having
a link with Judaism itself? A Judaic psychoanalysis might be possible,
but is it *necessary*?

As noted at the start of this chapter, there are many sources to psychoanalysis, however central the Jewish one might be; and some of these sources (for example, in the medicine or politics of the period) might themselves fuel the kind of universalist ethics that Freud and Deutscher, in rather different ways, call upon. And in any case, if we are to argue for a specific link between Judaism and psychoanalysis via the prism of ethics, what exactly might that mean? Freud seems to have pursued the version given by the Bnai Brith itself through the mouthpiece of Ludwig Braun, to whose 1926 letter of appreciation Freud's own letter was a response. Braun, defining psychoanalysis as 'genuinely Jewish', 'went on to define the meaning of Jewishness as being comprised of an independence of spirit, the willingness to do battle with an unjust society, and a vision of the whole of nature and humanity' (Diller, 1991, p.170). These social democratic ideals are indeed, arguably, linked with some aspects of the Jewish tradition; but in that tradition can also be found elements that are insular, reactionary, patriarchal and intolerant – not exactly the scientifically rational values that Freud wished to adopt. To claim certain aspects of Judaism as mobilizing ethical thought is fine and there is no reason to avoid doing this, as Judaism is capacious enough to offer powerful guidelines for living. But to argue for an intrinsic link between Judaism and psychoanalytic ethics is a more difficult thing to do. Nevertheless, in what follows in this chapter I am going to make an attempt at it; and in the rest of the book I am also going to try to develop Deutscher's claim that Jewish history produces an anti-oppressive orientation towards others; that, as he puts it, 'I am … a Jew by force of my unconditional solidarity with the persecuted and exterminated' (1968, p.51).

Psychoanalysis (not) as Judaism

Perhaps at this point one thing is clear: one might accept (we should accept) that psychoanalysis has a Jewish heritage, but this says nothing specific about any religious connection it may or may not have – even though it is to religion that one might expect to look for an ethical impulse. The 'religious' works of early psychoanalysis, again with Freud's as exemplary, are at best suggestive rather than drawing directly on Jewish or any other religious thought. *The Future of an Illusion* (Freud, 1927) is an examination of religion as a psychological phenomenon that takes for granted its illusory status, its function as a wishful fantasy. Religion is to be overcome by science; its appeal is understandable given the exigencies of life and people's need for consolation and protection, and yet it has not provided the happiness it promises precisely because it is founded on wishfulness and not on reality. There is no *religiously* ethical message in this book of Freud's; its stance is rather the secular-ethical assertion of the need to ensure that our lives are founded in truth and not in illusion. In that sense, indeed, but only in that sense, it is a 'therapeutic' intervention into the religious neurosis of humankind. Freud is explicit on this. Framing religion as 'infantile', he grants psychoanalysis the role of liberating people from their illusions: 'But surely infantilism is destined to be surmounted. Men cannot remain children for ever; they must in the end go out into "hostile life". We may call this "education to reality". Need I confess to you that the sole purpose of my book is to point out the necessity for this forward step?' (Freud, 1927, p.48). *Moses and Monotheism* (Freud, 1939) is different, resolving into a rather surprising affirmation of Judaism even as it universalizes and secularizes it, and best understood as a critique of identity and/or a vigorous response to the emerging barbarism of Nazism. In this book, there is a defence of a certain kind of religion – abstract monotheism, identified mainly with Judaism – against other religious approaches (especially Christianity, seen as a 'regression' away from the symbolic to the concrete), but once again there is little to recommend it as a *religious* text, profound though it is in many other ways. Instead, it presents a speculative history of monotheistic religion in order to account for the perpetuation of religious belief over time and to explain its transgenerational appeal. Freud nowhere posits the actual existence of God or the *rationality* of spiritual belief; he explains religion as a vestige of ancient historical events and superstitious or animistic belief systems that have continued into the present through unconscious modes of reproduction and the absence of a full orientation of humans to reality.

None of this has stopped many commentators, myself I am afraid included (Frosh, 2006a), from exploring the possible links between Judaism – the religion of the Jews – and psychoanalysis. I will go over this very briefly here, leaving aside some highly speculative work on the possible religious influences on Freud himself, especially in relation to Jewish mysticism in which it is occasionally claimed he was steeped. Some of this sees him as a 'hidden Jew' (Berke, 2015), bringing to mind associations with the conversos or crypto-Jews hiding from the Inquisition; except that as noted earlier, Freud's Jewishness was never hidden even if he was indisputably atheistic and opposed to any Jewish religious practices. Quite a lot of the discussion has centred on the idea that there are parallels between Judaism and psychoanalysis and that, given the obvious timeline, this indicates how the former infiltrated the latter (though as Levinas (1990) suggests, only half-jokingly, there is evidence that the rabbis of Talmudic time knew their psychoanalysis in that some of their textual interpretations are redolent of an appreciation of unconscious motivations). One example of this is the claim that '*tikkun olam*', the doctrine of 'healing the world' that arises with the emergence of Lurianic mysticism (named after its originator, Isaac Luria of Safed) after the expulsion of the Jews from Spain at the end of the fifteenth century, parallels the Kleinian psychoanalytic notion of *reparation* in that it makes destruction primordial and sees humans (or Jews in the kabbalistic case) as being responsible for restoring the brokenness that this fundamental state creates. The parallels can indeed be made striking and Lurianic imagery is extremely powerful, especially as mediated by Gershom Scholem's (1941) ground-breaking account, taken up in discussions of Messianism and political liberation in the twentieth and twenty-first centuries by secular Jewish writers such as Walter Benjamin and Judith Butler (Butler, 2012). The Lurianic vision is that during the original creation the vessels built to contain the divine light were broken by the strain, dispersing the light throughout the universe; this breach can only be repaired through the actions of humans, whose good deeds gradually repair the vessels and integrate the broken shards of light.

For Kleinian psychoanalysts, a similar model of brokenness and restoration can be found in the account of normal development processes. Psychic fragments characteristic of the early paranoid-schizoid position, in which the destructive impulses of the death drive are managed through projection into the external world, are brought together into a whole through reparative actions as it becomes possible for people to understand and feel their capacity for doing damage and to overcome this through practices of loving gratitude. The general model at work here is basically one of destruction, mourning and repair and is certainly characteristic of both Jewish mysticism and psychoanalysis; it is, however, a very widespread and prominent one, so to say that it demonstrates a causal link between the two approaches is stretching things. I would rather argue that just as Jewish mysticism responded to the devastating event of the fifteenth-century Spanish exile by interrogating how evil can exist and what might be done to restore hope, so psychoanalysis responded to the enormous destruction in Europe of the two twentieth-century world wars by examining the effects of violence and loss and developing a moral account of what might be required to do restitution for these – to make good the damage that we do to ourselves and to one another. Both these are deeply felt responses to terrible suffering and could be said to have a 'religious' element to them – though the psychoanalytic variety might better be called an ethical impulse rather than a religious one, with its implication of divinity and spiritual belief, features absent from the psychoanalytic vision. I am sure they draw on the same human impulse to keep on going in the face of pressure to despair, but I doubt that Melanie Klein had Lurianic kabbalism in mind when she developed the theory of the depressive position and of reparation.

A somewhat more convincing set of parallels seems to me to derive from the Jewish emphasis on textual study and hermeneutics, which might arguably have helped shape psychoanalysis's conviction that the stories told by its patients could not be taken at face value but had hidden meanings that should be subjected to interpretation. This is of course the characteristic Jewish approach to the texts of Judaism, from the Bible with its supposed 'seventy faces' to the study of Talmud and commentaries that can – and indeed, according to orthodox Judaism, should – take a lifetime and still remain unfinished at the end. In Judaism, this is a divinely ordained task: studying the Torah is the purpose of life and the way one comes close to God. The texts themselves are imbued with divine meaning, which makes them inexhaustible given the limitations of human understanding. This is not quite the psychoanalytic version of things, but the notion of an inexhaustible unconscious, the interpretation of which is the central task of an analysis, is not far-fetched; and the idea that the 'good life' is one governed by, and dependent upon, this kind of continuous self-examination is present in the psychoanalytic literature. Religiously, this hermeneutic approach is bound by belief in the existence and unity of God, and more prosaically by the law as outlined in the Torah and promulgated in the interpretations of the rabbis. That is, faced with complex material one is encouraged to think freely, considering alternative readings, but always to come back to a particular source and set of authoritative renderings of the text. The same might not be true of psychoanalysis: there is no absolute set of laws that one must in the end obey. And yet … there is certainly pressure to find confirmation of all readings in Freud, and a reluctance to move outside the agreed parameters of psychoanalytic interpretation, as developed over a century and more of practice and argumentation. Even transference has its place here: loyalty to the rabbis of the past, loyalty to one's supervisors and one's analyst. It is doubtful that this is due simply to the Jewish influence on psychoanalysis, but maybe the hermeneutics-bound-by-law tendency of psychoanalysis felt familiar to those who came from a religious culture where the same approach applied.

The impulse to bring psychoanalysis and Judaism closer together might also be linked to a wider move in psychoanalysis itself towards greater tolerance of religion than was the case in Freud's day. Rachel Blass (2004) has described how psychoanalysis has gradually accommodated itself to religious belief, tolerating it in its patients and resisting the earlier temptation to see it as a sign of continuing neurosis and hence of psychotherapeutic failure. Now, it seems, religion is a private realm that cannot be challenged but must only be respected – perhaps a sign of times in which religion is a sensitive and even dangerous issue, or possibly an indication that there is less certainty amongst analysts that they know what is real or true or can believe in scientific progress as reliable and a force for good. Blass comments (p.618), 'While psychoanalysis is, perhaps, one of the most atheistic professions in terms of official religious affiliation and practice of its members, there has nevertheless evolved a prevalent analytic attitude that considers religious belief and practice to be not beyond interpretation, but something not to be questioned by analysis – a kind of private, personal decision, which may be positively regarded if it allows for growth and well-being.' If this is the case, psychoanalysis has drifted a long way from the position in which nothing is unquestionable; how can there be a 'private, personal decision' that is not subject to the workings of the unconscious and hence open to psychoanalytic inquiry and challenge? The 'private and personal' is precisely the area on which psychoanalysis focuses, its field of discovery and action, so abandoning any part of it is giving up the analytic campaign for truth. Blass goes on to identify four sources of this shift: a change in the valuing of illusion, now seen (due to the influence of Donald Winnicott) as a positive source of creative functioning; appreciation of how religion satisfies basic self and relational needs, something Freud understood but criticized as a regression into wishfulness; a reinterpretation of *religion* in terms of broad spiritual experience, which Blass suggests is inadequate to most religious people's understanding of religion as founded in the truth of the existence of a divinity outside the self; and a reinterpretation of *psychoanalysis* as a spiritual experience, again something at odds with Freud's brutally materialist view of what psychoanalysis might seek to achieve. This critique seems well founded and significant; referencing some recent thinking on the topic, Blass (2004, p.621) comments,

the ideal religion becomes more of a personal, self-determined mysticism, devoid of history, ritual, authority, obligation and mediation, a kind of westernised Buddhism, while strong words are levelled at the dogmatism, fundamentalism, primitiveness and wrong-mindedness of religion that does not fit this mould ... Experience becomes central and truth, in the original sense of corresponding to something real, is no longer particularly relevant.

This 'ideal religion' thus misreads most religions as well as reducing the range of application of psychoanalysis itself; both religion and psychoanalysis have more substance than this. We need to be wary, Blass implies, of the attempt to reconcile what were once opposed entities in order to bring comfort to believers and avoid conflict; in backing away from *critical* engagement, we may be doing no favours either to psychoanalysis or to religion itself.

Jewish and psychoanalytic relational ethics

So far I have been arguing that whilst the connection between psychoanalysis and Jews is real, pervasive and significant in terms of the history, sociology and possibly the general 'attitude' of psychoanalysis, the links between psychoanalysis and Judaism as a religion are more tenuous, with the claims made being mostly unsustainable except as indications of parallel solutions to the question of human suffering and perhaps a proclivity towards interpretive versatility that comes from generations of work on 'sacred' texts. That said, however, there are grounds to link Jews, Judaism and psychoanalysis not in the sense that psychoanalysis is to be understood as a religious phenomenon, or specially applicable to Judaism, but as a characterization of a shared ethical project, one in which psychoanalysis reveals some of its Jewish origins. It is in this that we may find the possibility for links with anti-oppressive and consequently antiracist practices. Judaism is of course much more than a system of ethics; it is a set of practices bound by law and ritual as well as a focus for communal identification and cultural life, with beliefs and spiritual experiences part of the package, though not solely constitutive of it. Nevertheless, it is *also* an ethical system, permeating the everyday practices of Jewish people and offering a sense of meaning and guidelines for action. Psychoanalysis, too, is more than a system of therapeutic work or a scientific exploration of the mind; it is also a 'moral' practice, to adapt Philip Rieff's (1959) characterization of Freud, attached to a conceptualization of the human subject that is rigorous and at times harsh, avoiding what Freud (1930) called false 'consolation' in the face of suffering.

Both Judaism and psychoanalysis maintain a powerful ethical dimension based in the apparent contradiction that each human subject is to be understood as part of a social world *and* to be valued as singular. In the Jewish tradition, according to the Talmud (tractate Sanhedrin 37a), 'Whoever saves a single life is considered by scripture to have saved the whole world'; in psychoanalysis, a single individual might have many years of intensive psychotherapy because this is what they need, however 'inefficient' it might seem. This implies a model in which the individuality of each person is indissoluble. Yet each of us is also characterized by ambiguities and ambivalence, which never allows for a settling of the human subject into an integrated whole. The singularity of being is therefore a continuing struggle; the ethical approach to this is to accompany it and acknowledge its painful reality whilst also seeking a way towards more openness of mind – a kind of 'difficult freedom', to use the title of one of Emmanuel Levinas's collections of essays on Judaism (Levinas, 1963/1990). More specifically, as relational practices both psychoanalysis and Judaism see the human subject as incomplete in itself because it is fundamentally *interrupted by otherness*. I will say a bit about this now, making some obvious references but also developing an example from a research study that on the face of it has little to do with psychoanalysis, but which offers an illustration of how Jewish 'lived religion' and psychoanalytic ethics might come together, sometimes as adversaries and sometimes in alliance. There is a risk here of slipping back towards identifying Jewishness with Judaism as if there is no Jewish identity without religion; but part of my case is that this is characteristic of Jewish religiosity (i.e. that it does not reduce to a theology), that Judaism is the *lived life* of Jews and not a separate order of experience or belief. The same, it might be claimed, goes for psychoanalysis.

If we are to construct a model of practical ethics that opposes discrimination, oppression and racism, then an inviting route through to it is the one that is associated in general but by no means exclusively with Levinas: that the ethical relationship with the 'other' is primary, facing every human subject with the challenge of recognizing and acknowledging that other as a subject of concern (Levinas, 1991). The argument here is that the closed mind of Western ontology is displaced by the more transgressive and open possibilities of the 'Jewish' emphasis on the interruptive presence of the other – something which Levinas regards as the necessary core of human subjecthood. Reading Levinas 'Jewishly' in this way, which is an open invitation given his absorption in Jewish as well as secular philosophical writings, this becomes part of an assertion that ethical relationality is key to what we could tendentiously call 'progressive' Jewish thought – a point that has been worked up by several Jewish philosophers of the twentieth century prior to or coincident with Levinas, and in the twenty-first century can be seen in the ethical writings of Judith Butler (Butler, 2005, 2012). What links this with psychoanalysis is an appreciation found within both Jewish and psychoanalytic thought that openness to otherness means encountering the complexity of the psyche, the way it is cut across by affective engagements that disrupt the evenness of life and make humans much more than rational actors. Attempts at clarity and rationality are always obscured by the interruptions caused by our relations with others; this is a perception of psychoanalysis that is also central to Jewish culture and religious life. *Psychoanalytically*, it is not difficult to make this claim. The unconscious disrupts everything, in the sense that our relationships with ourselves and with others are mediated by impulses, wishes and desires that have the quality of coming from 'somewhere else', somewhere that is 'unconscious' yet also deeply inscribed in our subjectivity. Where is this elsewhere from which they come? Whatever might be the supposedly 'constitutional' elements of the unconscious, for instance as envisaged in classical Freudian drive theory, the observation that *relational* or *intersubjective* encounters fuel the formation of supposedly 'inner' realities is broadly accepted across the range of contemporary psychoanalytic approaches. From so-called 'British School' object relations theory to American relational psychoanalysis, and in a different way from the French Lacanian idea of 'extimacy' – the external scaffolding of unconscious life – to Jean Laplanche's (1999) unremitting focus on the decentring of the subject, the 'other' (as other person, or more generally as the experience of something coming from outside oneself) has found a place as primary in the foundations of the unconscious.

It is worth explaining this a little more. Without re-describing object relational, Lacanian and Laplanchian theory here (see Frosh, 1999, 2010), what should be stressed is this idea that each of us as a human 'subject' is dependent on others from the first and thereby formed in response to others and to what they 'put into' or around us. Our being is forged in the light of our vulnerability to others and is constructed both through practices of care and the desire of others that we should align ourselves with their often unconscious expectations and wishes. In this sense, to use the Lacanian slogan crudely, we are subjected to the 'desire of the other'. Stated more forcefully, the subject is, to adopt Butler's (2005) phrase, '*interrupted prior to the possibility of any continuity*,' always inhabited by something from outside that predates what we might call our 'identity'. The immediacy of the other is therefore both an ethical demand and an ontological claim: there is no subject without the other, no 'me' without 'you', or in Winnicott's famous phrase 'there is no such thing as an infant' – meaning, 'that whenever one finds an infant one finds maternal care, and without maternal care there would be no infant' (Winnicott, 1960, p.587). No baby will be found alive and thriving on its own. This immediacy of the other then translates into a kind of *intrusion*, mostly benign in cases of parental care, but nevertheless introducing the sense of something from outside that inhabits each of us at our unconscious core. Butler (2005) writes, 'I find that my very formation implicates the other in me, that my own foreignness to myself is, paradoxically, the source of my ethical connection with others' (p.84). It is worth noting one echo that Butler's emphasis on 'foreignness' has with Otto Fenichel's (1940, p.31) account of antisemitism. Fenichel makes a poignant identification between the Jew as foreign and uncanny, and the site of foreignness within: 'It can be expressed in one sentence: one's own unconscious is also foreign. Foreignness is the quality which the Jews and one's own instincts have in common.' This is not only part of the explanation of antisemitism – the inability of antisemites to tolerate this 'foreignness' in themselves – but also an astute observation about the link between psychoanalysis and antisemitic emotion. Psychoanalysis, identified with the discovery of the unconscious, is a 'Jewish science' not just because it was invented by a Jew, but also because it deals specifically with what an antisemitic culture frames as the 'Jewish' aspect of the psyche, the 'foreign unconscious'. When the one is unbearable, so is the other.

My suggestion is that this outward-directedness of psychoanalysis that understands the so-called 'inner world' to be constructed in the context of intrusions from the external social world of others connects with a Jewish ethics that also emphasizes relationality. In this sense, the 'Jewishness' of psychoanalysis, framed religiously as well as culturally, has an ethical dimension that lies in the promotion of a relationally muddied vision in which it is the impact of others, marked by our deep involvement and emotional connections with them, that constructs us as human subjects. In opposition to what is essentially a narcissistic, antisemitic and racist vision of a uniform society founded on ethnically 'pure' identities (as well as in opposition to other types of homogeneity, for instance around sexuality), Judaic ethics recognizes that we are always 'unsettled' by our relations with others. This can be found in some fundamental Jewish texts (see, for example, Frosh, 2005b; Zornberg, 1995) but also in everyday interaction and attitudes in which what forms the centre of concern are the emotional ties and acts of loving responsibility towards others – and the disruption these relationships produce. This claim is of course complex, with the insularity of some parts of the Jewish community arguably acting against it, a point to which I return in the next chapter: how can one establish an ethics based on the other if the only other one recognizes is ethnically similar to oneself? Yet the contradictions here are themselves informative, marking out an area of struggle within Jewish communities to make the 'outsider' welcome, and to align themselves with those who resist the damaging refusal of ethical relationality that characterizes racism.

To dramatize the problems and possibilities here, I want to turn briefly to some research that I worked on with my colleague Ruth Sheldon in the London Haredi (strictly orthodox) Jewish community. Ruth, a secular Jewish sociologist, was the ethnographer on this project, which involved developing quite close connections with some of the women in the community. Ruth's fieldnotes contain many encounters around food. Amongst them, her links with Esther, a member of the Satmar sect (one of the largest strictly orthodox Hassidic groups) show a very conscious awareness on the part of both participants of the function of *eating* in constructing families and communities, both 'symbolically' and in concretely relational terms. Ruth notes, 'my relationship with Esther unfolded explicitly against what was inscribed as a horizon of hunger, emptiness and lack'.

> Despite being from what is often presented as one of the most 'insular' groups, Esther was somehow very receptive towards me, and quick to adopt the role of 'feeder'. After our first meeting, she asked me if I was planning to learn Hebrew and I responded enthusiastically 'yes'. She smiled and said, 'you're really hungry aren't you' (just as a mother would say to her baby guzzling milk). Then after we had arranged another time to eat [sic], she said to me, 'take care, you seem like in starvation mode, don't try to do everything at once.' We began to meet weekly, so that she could 'teach' me and one of the ways she began was by teaching me the blessings for the drinks (and sometimes food) that she gave me during our meetings. I found myself taking up a very obedient role, wanting to remember these (checking what I had written as I went to visit her), and also gradually internalizing other laws (e.g. my consciousness of my prawn sandwich on Pesach [Passover]; my ways of holding my body in public space, choosing not to use the tape recorder when I was with her). Esther did not 'command' me to do anything, she gave me the choice, yet she felt

like a very powerful presence. I wanted to please her – it wasn't just about her authority, it was about expressing a kind of trust in, and appreciation of, her emphasis on a kind of moral project which worked through the unquestioning observation of mitzvoth [laws] – blessings for example, which she described as deepening a relationship with food as nourishment rather than just something you consume.

Yet while Esther exerted a kind of authority, she also shared what seemed like a still-raw sense of vulnerability, struggling with experiences of lack, emptiness, depression – and known in the neighbourhood as someone who had struggled with her mental health. She talked about how this was linked to her experiences of growing up with parents who were very damaged by the Holocaust – very detached and, as she described, unable to feel. Spending time in her kitchen, she was showing me how to make bread and told me that her mother 'didn't really know how to teach' – she had not passed this down. Gradually, I learned about the violence in her family, how she used to hate it when her father would bless her, because he had been violent against her mother. She told me how relieved she was that her parents had not been 'that' religious, because this didn't turn her against religion. This had led to some difficult conversations between us, in which she articulated a narrative which linked Jewish failures of observance (assimilation, reform) to the Holocaust – a framing through which the 'loving' and joyful insistence on obedience to Jewish law and tradition was shadowed by a darker historical-theological narrative.

Eating is used metaphorically in this observation, when Esther refers to Ruth's desire to learn as being 'hungry' and 'in starvation mode' – terms which seem to 'feed forward' to the Holocaust reference in the piece. But it is also clear how much food provides the site for the relationship between these very different Jewish women to emerge. Ruth's orthographic slip ('eat' for 'meet') and the centring of Esther's teaching on the blessings over food and drink confirm that meals are the obvious place, the default setting, for a pedagogic encounter of this kind. It is also something that produces a sense of shame: Ruth is aware of carrying a prawn sandwich with her on Passover, which is probably the most 'treyf' (unkosher) combination one can imagine – prawn not being kosher and bread being banned on Passover! Her 'disobedience' is thus very explicit, yet for a while at least Ruth prefers to adapt and conform, to obediently respond to the instructions of how to behave in an orthodox Jewish way. Ruth's understanding of this is that she is responding to something in Esther that is not just her 'authority' as self-appointed religious instructor, but which is also *spiritual* – the food changes as a result of Esther's approach, which requires blessings and therefore thoughtfulness, introducing a domain of depth into the everyday, unthinking practice of eating.

Yet this encounter is also a fraught one. The resonant emotions incited by the kitchen, as Esther prepares bread, throw her back into a history that is dissatisfying and alienating, a history of coldness and violence in her family. This re-emerges as violence directed towards Ruth herself, who, Esther knows, comes from the kind of secular background characterized by 'failures of observance (assimilation, reform)' that Esther links with the cause of the Holocaust. Ruth's experience of this was of being made to submit to violence, in which the kind of secular Jewish life that Ruth embodies is made responsible for the destruction of the Jewish people. The context given in the observation makes it clear how she is the recipient of an enactment of violence projected from Esther's own inner experience and history. The 'darker historical-theological narrative' that the ethnographic report refers to is brought to life in the physicality of the food preparation: the associational chain is from bread to warmth to intergenerational coldness to violence, all reappearing in the space of this orthodox Jewish kitchen. Perhaps Ruth's purported personal and research 'hunger' here, observed by Esther and coded as being 'in starvation mode,' creates an associational matrix in which the pleasures of food screen deeper anxieties about violence and rejection. Esther responds to this at an unguarded moment by a rather bitter (another food metaphor) intergenerational response to Ruth's 'daughterly' desire.

Food can thus be spiritualized through acts of thoughtful blessing, as in Esther's teaching of Ruth, whilst also carrying a very complex psycho-historical burden around intergenerational suffering, disappointment (the mother who fails to teach her daughter baking skills) and possibly unworked-through hostility. In this instance, the act of teaching Ruth about orthodox Judaism seems to provoke in Esther a complex set of feelings about the differences between them, and a reminder of the 'failed' teaching by her own mother and the possible cause of this in the mother's suffering. Esther, in the process of teaching Ruth about spirituality as well as religious practices and laws, seems to have experienced a set of ambivalent 'maternal' emotions or associations. These leave her open to feelings of care and even willingness to talk about the difficulties of her personal history, but also provoke a kind of violence in which – knowing of Ruth's secular Jewish background – she articulates a view of secularism that almost equates it with murder.

How does this relate to the psychoanalytic points I have been raising? Esther perhaps exemplifies how Judaism as a set of practices is bound up with religious law, obviously, but is also saturated by the emotional and relational contexts out of which these practices have emerged. These are not always conciliatory and reassuring; sometimes the context is one of brutality and violence, sometimes of loving interchange and sometimes a combination of both. In Esther's case, there is a form of reaching-out to Ruth which is also resonant with the ambivalence of her personal history, all framed by a mode of Judaism that is both formidable (the law, the rituals, the moralistic judgement) and warmly inclusive (feeding). Psychoanalysis, it seems to me, appreciates this combination, not, one hopes, by reducing it to a family (Oedipal) scenario, but rather in noting how our lives are never straightforwardly one thing or another, but are always structured in and through relations with others that haunt us both negatively, as modes of trauma and unsettledness, and positively, as filling out the practices we take on with the intensities of our losses and our loves.

My suggestion is to link psychoanalysis and Judaism through their parallel insistence on interruption by the multiplicities and muddles of one's attachments and loves as well as one's anxieties and troubles. To me, this is an important ethical point, and one consonant with both Jewish tradition and with psychoanalysis, despite the investment both these systems of thought also have in reason. In some other work (Frosh, 2019), I engaged with Rebecca Goldstein's (1992) reading of the biblical story of Lot's Wife, in the course of which she describes her exchange with her father about the value of Western philosophy, which she has immersed herself in, with its emphasis (at least in certain strands) on lucidity. She compares this with what she identifies as the densely emotional context of the Judaic world. She explains,

> my father never could work up any enthusiasm for the luminous vision of the life of pure reason I tried to paint for him. I argued that it was the life that was the most consistent and thus right. He agreed with me that it was consistent, but he wouldn't agree that it was right. In fact, he thought it was all wrong. He thought it was right for human life to be subject to contradictions, for a person to love in more than one direction, and sometimes to be torn into pieces because of his many loves.

(p.41)

The idea of being 'subject to contradictions,' 'loving in more than one direction' and 'sometimes being torn into pieces because of one's many loves' is precisely what we see being dealt with in psychoanalysis, and it is also core to Jewish tradition, identification and religious practice. Finding ways to live with contradictions is the usual way of thinking about this, but it raises the question of how we might deal with contradictions that never cease tearing us apart. This must have to do with loss and with the wish to hold together all one's 'loves', to 'love in more than one direction' even when that puts other loves at risk. Judaism, with its insistence on the relational nexus in which religion exists – its formation in the history and its preservation in the culture of a people – has a lot to say about such loves. Maybe, though I would not want to claim this too grandly, that is a genuine way in which Judaism as well as Jewishness is at the source of psychoanalysis.

We might ask, can this openness to relationality be extended outside the Jewish community in the patterns of alliance and solidarity that might link Jews and others in the task of opposing racism? How imaginatively can this ethical imperative be embraced? What lessons might be learnt from this 'Jewish' experience that can enrich anti-oppressive practice, within and outside psychoanalysis? It is to these questions that the next few chapters turn.

Chapter 2

PROMISED LAND OR PERMITTED LAND

Insularity and solidarity

The question of what can be drawn on in Judaic thought that might fuel antiracist alliances, and their conjunction with psychoanalysis, runs up against the issue of Jewish 'insularity'. This is often simply an antisemitic smear, sliding into conspiracy theories that are as ubiquitous as they are long-held: Jews stick together, help each other, conspire together to undermine Christian civilization. In fact, to the extent that there is some truth in the claim that Jews focus in on themselves, devoting themselves more to their own community than to others, it is in large part in *response* to that antisemitism that posits this insularity as its cause. Albert Memmi, who will be discussed more fully later, notes that this supposed self-centredness is a characteristic of isolated and oppressed groups and can be seen as necessary self-sufficiency in the face of a hostile environment. He calls it 'Jewish solidarity' and, using the terminology of his time, compares it with the solidarity to be found in other racialized communities.

> Jewish solidarity is in the first place one example of the vast solidarity of all oppressed persons, a defense reaction of a particularly vulnerable group. On these grounds mutual aid and active intervention are not peculiar to Jews. One finds them mentioned frequently in the works of Negro novelists or of North African writers at the same time as one finds other clearly contradictory manifestations ... solidarity includes more than cases of stated oppressions. It is also the way all isolated peoples, all minorities, defend themselves against solitude and danger.
>
> (Memmi, 1962, p.280)

This is a somewhat different point from that made by Deutscher and quoted in the last chapter concerning his 'unconditional solidarity with the persecuted and exterminated' (1968, p.51), which moves beyond particularist solidarity with one's own group to assert an internationalist vision (though Memmi does use the word 'vast', which hints at links with 'all oppressed persons'). But Deutscher too felt committed to his Jewishness and wished to 'assure the real, not spurious, security and self-respect of the Jews'. Both these writers are almost certainly correct in identifying ethnic and cultural solidarity as a characteristic of oppressed groups and therefore Jewish solidarity as flowing from this. There is also, at times, something joyful about the connections that can be made between Jews in this way. As Freud (1926, p.367) put it in his letter to the Bnai Brith, solidarity is derived from 'the clear consciousness of an inner identity, the familiarity of the same psychological structure', or as Memmi (1962, p.282) stated, 'In a world that is too often stifling and restrictive, Jewish solidarity allows Jews that release of self, that resonance.'

The idea that people with things in common – even experiences of oppression – should gather together is not a strange one. Yet there are exaggerations of this insularity with which Jews are familiar and sometimes by which they are troubled, even if their source in antisemitism is recognized. The most obvious example of this is in the 'enclave' lifestyles of most 'Haredi' or other strictly orthodox Jewish groups. These groups include extreme religious Zionists, ultra-orthodox Ashkenazi anti-Zionists, Sephardi fundamentalists and various Hassidism and non- or anti-Hassidic orthodox Jews. Many of them are isolationist communities with their own inward-looking structures and strong community ties, 'traditionalist' patriarchal values and a suspicious, largely arms-length attitude to the rest of the 'modern' world – of which, of course, they are part. These types of Jewish community are by no means restricted to Israel (in the UK, approximately 25 per cent of the Jewish community is Haredi as is about 12 per cent of the US Jewish population – that is, approximately 700,000 Jewish Americans (Staetsky, 2022)), and their social and political significance in some geographical areas should not be underestimated. They show very little interest in the world outside their communities, except sometimes when they feel threatened by the encroachment of its values, or where it is necessary to vote as a bloc in order to gain resources. In the case of extreme religious Zionists (who are not usually Haredim), especially in Israel, they also promote a belligerent version of nationalism combined with a justification of conquest of the Land of Israel (a somewhat disputed geographical notion, but usually extended to mean what the settlers call 'Judea and Samaria') in the light of what are seen as biblical statements of the God-given Jewish ownership of this land. Indeed, fundamentalist religious Zionists might go further to argue that there is a special covenant of the Jewish people with God that includes the founding of a Jewish, or perhaps *Judaic*, society in the Holy Land, which because of its religious-historical significance is also a spiritually special place, a higher order of location lifted above its material reality, but nevertheless rooted in it. This is one instance of an inward-looking cultural disposition dictated to a considerable degree by traditional interpretations of foundational texts, a mode of lived religion that shuts out the external world and prioritizes Jewish concerns over relations with others.

This issue of the Torah justification for occupation of the Land of Israel cannot just be dismissed as the irrational or bad faith rhetoric of a colonizing group; nor is it helpful to simply write off the religious impulse within these broader groups as an irrelevance in contemporary times. It should be understood as an outgrowth of the orthodox Jewish religious tradition in which sacred texts have a living impact on people's everyday worlds. Indeed, the broad understanding of 'fundamentalist' as in 'taking the Bible literally' could be said to have been the dominant feature of pre-emancipation Judaism, if one makes the very important move of including in the idea of 'taking literally' acceptance of the 'oral law' codified in post-biblical texts (notably the early rabbinic literature, encompassing Talmudic and midrashic texts and later commentaries). However, these texts are not unmediated, but rather take their place within a structure in which (as in other religions) sacred texts require interpretation, and it is the authority of the interpretation that fixes it in place as the legitimate way to read the text.

Members of religious Jewish sects rely on ancient rabbinic interpretations of the written texts, constantly reapplied to the demands of contemporary life by the leaders of these sects, albeit based firmly in hermeneutic precedents. The texts do not speak straightforwardly: not only are they always amenable to alternative interpretations but, at least in the Jewish tradition, what one might term a variety of 'subjugated narratives' are retained within the holy texts themselves, as a kind of 'trace', sometimes explicit, sometimes more akin to what one might call 'unconscious' residues. We should not be too relativistic here: Jewish religious scholarship, for example, in the Talmud, is based around argument and dispute, but in most instances such dispute resolves itself into an agreed halacha or legal ruling, which is what the orthodox will follow. (There is, however, a group of unresolved disputes left by the Talmud to the prophet Elijah to sort out when he arrives to announce the coming of the Messiah.) Nevertheless, the existence of debate – indeed the promotion of argument 'for the sake of heaven', that is, in order to explore the Torah more deeply – is a key aspect of Jewish life that, with the caveat just given, marks out a space of resistance to fundamentalism. There is no single absolute reading that can be given, no certainty without an undercurrent of doubt. This is therefore a *religious* justification for pluralism of at least a limited kind. The reason why the Talmud codifies argument is that humans do not have the capacity to fully understand the Torah, which itself can always be subject to 'seventy interpretations', seventy here being shorthand for infinity. For reasons of community cohesion and religious order, certain readings of the Torah are seen as more legitimate than others, so it is not correct to say that any ruling is only provisional or relativistic. Nevertheless, the Talmud preserves evidence of its debates and uncertainties; these offer leverage for those who are troubled by the apparent definitiveness of the religious world.

If insularity is a product of antisemitism and also a feature of some aspects of orthodox Jewish life, there is also the issue of the supposed 'chosenness' of the Jewish people. This chosen status is usually understood in relation to the injunction to be a 'light to the nations', a 'kingdom of priests', promoting Torah and its values, and leading the world in understanding God's moral vision: the first monotheism, the first democratic approach to justice ('Justice, justice shall you follow' [Deuteronomy 16: 20]) and so on. This is an uplifting vision, and one that carries with it a continuing tension within Judaism and amongst many of its most sophisticated thinkers, between a universalistic view of the good of all humanity (after all, Judaism is not evangelical and acknowledges that all people have their own route to God) and a particularist notion of the Jews as having a special role – not one amongst many, but a leading one, giving the Jews special responsibilities and maybe special rights. Even in the sophisticated work of some major philosophers, this point about chosenness can become contentious. Freud had this idea in relation to Jewish intellectuality, but for him it was produced by the history of the Jewish people which forced them to adopt the values of the mind as a way of managing survival: 'The pre-eminence given to intellectual labours throughout some two thousand years in the life of the Jewish people has, of course, had its effect', he wrote (Freud, 1939, p.114). 'It has helped to check the brutality and the tendency to violence which are apt to appear where the development of muscular strength is the popular ideal.' In the case of the thinker with whom the rest of this chapter is concerned, Emmanuel Levinas, the issue is more complex.

Linking this together, we have a push towards insularity within orthodox Judaism, legitimized by particularist readings of sacred texts, and the idea that these texts are amenable to various interpretations, not an 'infinite' number perhaps, but still to what might in more modern terms be called resistant reading or 'reading against the grain'. This kind of reading, taking the texts seriously yet offering something subversively different from the received version, is given by Levinas in his *Talmudic Readings* (Levinas, 1990), described more fully below. Levinas is in most respects an exponent of a non-insular Judaism, an activist Judaism that turns its attention to the world around, bringing the deep insights of the philosophy of what he calls 'Jerusalem' to bear on that of 'Athens'. As noted in the previous chapter, Levinas's profound influence on contemporary philosophy (including psychoanalysis and psychosocial studies) lies largely in his articulation of the foundational status of the 'other' in the construction and ontology of human subjecthood. Levinas makes it clear that a relationship of responsibility towards the other – an *ethical* relation – is in his view primary for the human subject, rather than following on from something pre-existent. It is not the case that the human subject exists and then engages in ethical relations; rather, ethics is the defining feature of subjectivity itself:

> I speak of responsibility as the essential, primary and fundamental structure of subjectivity. For I describe subjectivity in ethical terms. Ethics, here, does not supplement a preceding existential base; the very node of the subjective is knotted in ethics understood as responsibility. I understand responsibility as responsibility for the Other, thus as responsibility for what is not my deed, or for what does not even matter to me; or which precisely does matter to me, is met by me as face.
>
> (Levinas, 1985, p.95)

Levinas insists that responsibility for the other comes before the subject can even know what the other is; it is, consequently, an absolute given, and the recognition which is part of it is as non-contingent as can be. This is caught up, famously and controversially, in Levinas's account of suffering and persecution: the other's actions make demands on the subject, and these demands put the subject in a kind of 'persecuted' position which still produces a requirement of responsibility. That is, the intrusion of the other requires the subject to set aside an egocentric response of self-preservation, creating a demand that the subject maintains an awareness of responsibility for the other, even if and when that other is persecutory. As Judith Butler (2005) points out, this is a troubling philosophy, made even more so when Levinas elides it with a view of 'Israel' (which means both the people and the State, it seems) as especially persecuted: 'The ultimate essence of Israel derives from its innate predisposition to involuntary sacrifice, its exposure to persecution' (Levinas, 1990, p.225). Butler argues that, in making this move, Levinas extracts the 'Jew' from history, presenting the Jew's fate as timelessly one of suffering, and then reads this as also the fate of Israel, making a special case for the position of the Jew, spiritually and politically, and, as Butler puts it (in what is otherwise a rather sympathetic critical analysis of Levinas's philosophy), providing 'an implausible and outrageous account of the Jewish people problematically identified with Israel and figured only as persecuted and never persecuting' (Butler, 2005, p.95). This critique will be returned to in Chapter 3 where the complications of Levinas's attitude to the Palestinians will be noted. Yet the philosophy itself seems to compel an outward-looking vision: if it is the case that the other always makes a demand on us, this can hardly be restricted to the other Jew. This paradox will be explored again in a later chapter, but it reflects what is an ever-present tension between the universalistic and particularistic elements in Jewish identity and in the Jewish religious impulse. It might also gesture towards both an unconscious sense of guilt and an insistence on an ethics of responsibility that can be discerned in various Jewish textual traces.

Levinas the Jew

The choice of Levinas here is not accidental. He was one of the most significant and influential philosophers of the twentieth century, whose work is currently heavily referenced not only in philosophy but also in social theory, the social sciences and psychoanalysis (e.g. Alford, 2007; Marcus, 2007), and whose undertaking provides a foundation for a philosophy of ethics that can be seen as deeply universalist. On the other hand, as already noted, there are particularist tendencies in Levinas that have provoked controversy, especially in relation to his often outspoken defence of the State of Israel in the face of post-1967 criticism (Caygill, 2002). But what is useful here in Levinas's work is his deep engagement with Jewish religious texts and his attempt to explore this material in such a way as to derive meaning from it in a contemporary context that can form the basis for reaching out towards those other 'oppressed persons' to whom Memmi and Deutscher refer. Orthodox Jews ground the legitimation for their actions, their moral and ethical ideas, their understanding of history and culture, and their Jewish identity in texts. Study of the Torah and its interpretation in the rabbinic literature is a core component of Jewish religious life, every bit as important as – perhaps even more important than – prayer. It is from these texts that the orthodox derive the axes that govern their personal and their public lives, including their politics. From a religious point of view, therefore, intervention in the interpretation of these texts is a highly significant way of debating within Judaism, of not only doing what Levinas claimed to be doing, translating the Jewish sources into 'Greek', but of reflecting back ideas and principles for living to Jews themselves.

Levinas's engagement with the Talmud was deep and has probably not been given due attention, although it is by no means unknown. First it is worth recollecting how immersed Levinas was in Jewish life. Born in 1906 into an orthodox family in Kovno, Lithuania, he was brought up reading Hebrew, even though his first spoken language was Russian. In the 1920s and 1930s in France, when he was at his greatest distance from Judaism, he was nevertheless a member of the Alliance Israélite Universelle, an organization with a largely assimilationist programme based on enlightening backward Jews in secular knowledge. However, in the 1930s Levinas was already reconsidering this outlook, seeking means of returning Jews to their own heritage as a way of accessing the inner sources of their creativity, whilst retaining the orientation towards an emancipatory future. Annette Aronowicz comments:

> For Levinas, the rethinking of the relation of Jewish to 'Greek' sources would have to include the vision of *universality*, of *one* humanity in which all related as equals and in which all participated responsibly, the ideals of the Alliance. The difference now was that in order for this *one* humanity to come into being, Western sources of spirituality, Western wisdom, would no longer suffice. In order for a genuine human community to emerge, it was *Jewish* wisdom, the *Jewish* vision of the human being, which must be understood and made available to everyone else.
>
> (Aronowicz, 1990, p.xiii)

This is the beginning of the strand of Levinas's thought that makes the particularity of Judaism essential for the well-being of the world; the world is read through a Jewish frame and perhaps with a Judaic mission in mind. After the Second World War, this task became yet more urgent and also ambivalent, and was informed by the deep study that Levinas made of the Talmud with his mysterious teacher, 'Monsieur Chouchani' (also a huge influence on Elie Wiesel), during the period

1947–51. In 1946, Levinas took on what was to be his day job for much
of the rest of his life, becoming Director of the École Normale Israélite
Orientale, an Alliance teacher training college; his professional activity
became dedicated to developing an approach which took seriously
both the requirements of the world (his 'secular' philosophy) and of
Judaism. Jews would need to be open to the world, as Levinas was; Jews
would also need to know their culture, their sources and to utilize this
knowledge in the service of the world.

Levinas's Talmudic commentaries reflect this dual aspect. They
were not confined to the religious seminary, but instead were given
to the annual gatherings of French Jewish intellectuals, the 'Colloques
d'intellectuels juifs de langue française' in which he participated from
the early 1960s. These readings of Talmudic texts are a considerable
achievement. As I have described elsewhere (Frosh, 2013b), Levinas
follows what on the surface looks like a traditional route of exegesis
of Talmudic passages, taking them a step at a time. Yet by omitting the
major commentaries and instead concentrating on the contradictions
and excesses of the texts and 'surreptitiously' putting them in a modern
context, he draws out a kind of subversive or 'subjugated' narrative
within them – lines of thought hinted at in the text, lying behind its
message as usually understood. Levinas reads the texts retrospectively,
through 'afterwardsness' as psychoanalysts might say (Laplanche,
1999), which means that the originals come to have new significance
in the face of contemporary concerns – in the case we shall look at,
fundamentalist religious Zionism. In this way, they are true to a certain
tradition not just of Jewish reading, but of *psychoanalytic* reading,
in which texts are treated as the site of a struggle that leaves behind
traces, that still contains, in what might be thought of as a 'melancholic'
fashion, the unresolved or unmourned possibilities that have been left
behind. Freud gives a suitably dramatic account of this process in one
of his own 'religious' tracts, *Moses and Monotheism*, where he describes
biblical texts as a kind of covering-over, embodying evidence of an act
of violence, even of a crime. Focusing on the hidden history of Moses,
he writes:

> The text, however, as we possess it today, will tell us enough about
> its own vicissitudes. Two mutually opposed treatments have left
> their traces on it. On the one hand it has been subjected to revisions
> which have falsified it in the sense of their secret aims, have mutilated
> and amplified it and have even changed it into its reverse; on the
> other hand a solicitous piety has presided over it and has sought to

preserve everything as it was, no matter whether it was consistent or contradicted itself. Thus almost everywhere noticeable gaps, disturbing repetitions and obvious contradictions have come about – indications which reveal things to us which it was not intended to communicate. In its implications the distortion of a text resembles a murder: the difficulty is not in perpetrating the deed, but in getting rid of its traces.

(Freud, 1939, p.43)

It is in these 'traces' that the 'unconscious' of the text resides; whether in subtle distortions or visible undercurrents of dispute, religious texts commonly reveal the uncertainties and ambivalences that go into their construction but are then repressed ('murdered') to produce an acceptable mode of orthodoxy. Reading resistively means finding ways to release these repressed possibilities; and a psychoanalytic way of doing this will always be to notice gaps, slips or contradictions and to examine where investigation of them might lead. This kind of sleuthing is a mode of literary psychoanalysis, but it was also familiar to the Talmudic rabbis who used exactly such a method when interrogating biblical texts.

In relation to Levinas's Talmudic explorations, the power of such an interpretive endeavour is perhaps nowhere more palpable than in the reading concentrated on below, holding in mind the claim of Zionist religious fundamentalists that there is textual proof of their absolute right to the Land of Israel. The text is from Levinas's November 1965 seminar on the section from *Tractate Sotah* concerning the episode of the spies, which is given the title *Promised Land or Permitted Land* (Levinas, 1990). My suggestion here is that, albeit in some ways reluctantly and uncertainly, Levinas reveals an undercurrent of doubt in this Talmudic passage that calls into question fundamentalist fervour. In doing so, he also asserts the ethical responsibility that Jews might have in considering relationships with dispossessed others and hence lays open the possibility of alliance with these others, of not only Jewish solidarity but of solidarity with all the oppressed.

Spying out the land

The biblical text with which the Talmudic passage is concerned is the account in Numbers and Deuteronomy of the men sent by Moses to spy out the land of Canaan, prior to the planned invasion by the Israelites.

The relevance of this to the concerns of Zionism should be obvious, not just in its general subject matter (conquest of the Land of Israel), but in the way the spies are punished for their lack of faith – an early example, one might think, of Jewish self-hatred. The story in brief is that a year after leaving Egypt, and on the borders of Canaan, God tells Moses to send spies into the land, either as a test or simply because the people have been clamouring for this (the version of the story in Deuteronomy has Moses acquiescing to the *people's* demand, with God approving). Twelve spies are sent, one representing each tribe; they go up and down the land, observing its inhabitants and picking its fruits, and come back mightily impressed. It is indeed, they say, a 'land of milk and honey'; the problem is that the people within it are fierce, are giants, and there is little chance of the Israelites overcoming them. Only Joshua and Caleb stand out against this dismal scene, and they are nearly stoned for their trouble until an appearance of the cloud of God saves them. God then threatens to destroy the people because of their ingratitude, which Moses dissuades him from doing, but the ten critical spies are killed by a plague, and the people are punished by being condemned to wander in the wilderness for a further thirty-nine years, until all the men (with the exception of Joshua and Caleb) have died out and been replaced by a new generation, more doughty and muscular in its approach to battle, less full of slave mentality.

These are the bones of the story, but as ever the Talmud fleshes it out and introduces numerous issues which are derived from a close, speculative reading of the text. One has to remember here that if this is genuinely Holy Writ, as it was for the Talmudic rabbis, then every nuance will have meaning, nothing is accidental or reducible to mere noise; every element of the message is ripe for decoding. In their enthusiastic response to the challenge of opening out the text for associations and disputatious readings, the rabbis are engaging in a *religious* act, as is Levinas in his own analysis. Characteristically, the Talmud moves back and forth between different textual allusions, draws on myths and received opinions, and constructs a narrative which is consciously polysemic, even though it also presents itself as an authoritative rendering of what the Torah means. Levinas has his own take on this, and one can justifiably claim that it is 'just one view'; the argument here is that doing this his way, philosophically one might say, produces a disruption of set or automatic meaning that makes fundamentalist arguments untenable. Levinas states:

> What seems so simple in the biblical text, the fear which seizes the children of Israel when they are just about to reach their goal, will

become problematic in the Talmudic text we are reading. In the great fear of the explorers, we may discover anxieties more familiar to us ... You will see ... that in the course of history, Jewish thought, like Jewish conscience, has known every scruple, every remorse, even when it came to the most sacred rights of the people troubled by this thought.

(Levinas, 1990, p.54)

This is indeed what happens.

The Talmudic text that Levinas extracts starts with a play on words, a conventional rabbinic as well as psychoanalytic ploy. In Deuteronomy, it states that the spies were sent: 'That they may explore the land for us', using the Hebrew word '*veyachperu*'. The text quotes Rav Hiyya bar Abba as associating this word with the word '*vechapra*', used in the book of Isaiah to mean 'ashamed' ('The moon will be ashamed and the sun will be confounded'), and on the basis of this, he concludes: 'The explorers sought only the shame of the land.' Levinas reads this as a link with the idea of confounding idolaters (those who worship the sun and moon), and from there those who idolize the earth, the land. He concludes (and recall that this was in 1965, before the criticisms of Israel after the Six-Day War):

The explorers go toward this land so that the land will be shamed, so that the worshipers of this land – for example, the Zionists of that time – will be shamed. They have decided, in the name of truth, to confound the Zionists.

(Levinas, 1990, p.56)

The introduction of 'Zionists' at this moment is something of a shock, suggesting that Levinas is speaking more to his audience than from his material, wrestling it into becoming a contemporary resource. He clarifies his point immediately, after an apology for intellectualism ('The intellectual has been defined as the one who always misses the mark but who, at least, aims very far' (Levinas, 1990, p.56)). Levinas claims that in this passage: 'We are informed of the intention of a few men to put to shame all those who want and hope for the Promised Land. The Promised Land would not be allowed.' This is a central idea in Levinas's reading of the Talmudic passage, and he develops it as he goes along, bringing it into tension with the more traditional notion that the spies suffered a crisis of faith, but also seeing a deliberate, even ironic undercurrent to the rabbis' discussions, one which supports the subversive reading more than it does the orthodox one.

The next part of this has to do with names. The list of names of the spies is famously ironic – sons of horse and camel being amongst them – but the Talmudic text claims (in the name of Rav Isaac) that: 'We have a tradition according to which the explorers are named after their actions, but we only know how to interpret one name, that of Sethur, son of Michael' (p.56). According to Rav Isaac, he is named Sethur because 'he has given the lie to [*sathar*] the words of the Holy One Blessed be He' and his father, Michael, was so called 'because he has weakened him [*mak*]' (p.51). Rav Jonathan adds another interpretable name: 'Nahbi, son of Vophsi, because he hid [*hihbi*] the words of the Holy One. Son of Vophsi because he jumped over [*pasa*] the attributes of the Holy One, Blessed be He.' Levinas points out several things about this passage. First its surface meaning: the fault of the spies includes that they disdain the power of God, who is in their eyes a 'weak God' who cannot do anything or deliver on his promises, and in any case he promises nothing, 'He has promised nothing and does not care at all if virtue is rewarded and vice punished' – this being the essential attribute of God that the spies 'jump over' (p.51). But, more importantly, Levinas shows how the Talmudic discussion of the names is so blatantly misleading that one is led to ask what truth is being hidden *in order that* it might be discovered – what trace is there in the text (the closest we can get to a 'textual unconscious') of something else it might be wanting to say?

> Read these names. Does one need a tradition to understand the virtues registered in these names? One need only think about the roots of these words and show less imagination than that which drew from Vophsi 'he-who-jumped-over!' Shammua ben Zaccur: he who listens, son of he who remembers; Shaphat ben Hori: he who judges, son of he who is free; Igal ben Joseph: the redeemer, son of Joseph; Palti ben Rafu: he who spares, son of he who was healed. I cannot indulge in this etymological game on all twelve names, but I understand why those who upheld that our explorers were corrupt from birth preferred to forget the tradition! What a lucky amnesia! They found *mak* in Michael but forgot that Michael means 'Who is like God' ... All the noble meanings of the names of the guilty were miraculously lost! Don't we have here an effort to remove the suspicion that this whole hateful conspiracy was a plot of the righteous?
>
> (Levinas, 1990, p.58)

So the Talmud resists or represses the honourable elements of the spies, but does so with such blatant dissimulation that it actually draws attention to the counter-narrative, one in which righteous men go down to explore the land, and see something there that makes them fear to become settlers. What might determine this 'failure of the righteous' is examined in the next remarkable group of passages, but even here one must remember the end of the story, as Levinas does: the spies, whether righteous or not, were punished, the strong rabbinic view is that they should have encouraged the people to invade the land. Yet, at what cost, with what ambivalence and uncertainty?

The following section of the Talmudic passage deals with Caleb and his visit to Hebron. It begins with a classic Talmudic worry about an apparent grammatical error in the biblical text, which states (Numbers 13: 22): 'They went toward the South and *he* came to Hebron.' The rabbis' interpretation of this is that the different spies went to different places, and specifically Caleb went to Hebron, where he prayed at the graves of the patriarchs for protection from the guiles and persuasions of his compatriots, or, as Levinas puts it: 'God, preserve me from my friends' (p.58). Hebron, we know today as well as then, is and was a place of great contestation, one of the flash-points of the Israel–Palestine conflict, a scene of tragedy on all sides. Here, Caleb is placing himself in the tradition of his ancestors, of Abraham, Isaac and Jacob who are buried there, and seeking support from them for the holy project of conquering the land. Can anything be clearer as a signal from the Talmud of the value given to the tradition that makes the Land of Israel Jewish? As Levinas points out, the next section of the Talmud, which emphasizes the hugeness of the inhabitants of the land, that they were 'descendants of Anak', that is, giants, supports the standard reading of the passage as revealing the fear of the slave-people confronted with the armed might of the native population. How could a people so recently oppressed believe that they could ever defeat such a powerful enemy? Caleb pleads that the faith of his ancestors will sustain him in the face of this political and military reality. His view, apparently approvingly indexed by the Talmud, is that the religious and moral superiority of the Jews, their direct connection with God through the act of choosing and being chosen, entitles them to pursue the fulfilment of what was already by then an age-old promise to Abraham that his descendants will inherit the land, and that it is fear alone that one should fear.

But nothing is unequivocal here. In this moment of the insistence of moral entitlement, it is not clear who occupies the high ground. Levinas comments: 'Perhaps the explorers had moral qualms' (p.61). The Talmud takes an apparently innocent biblical line and worries away at it, as it always does when faced with the question of explaining why something that seems to be unnecessary has been included in the text: 'Hebron was founded seven years before Zoan' (Numbers 13: 22). So what? Again, the issue is peculiarly Talmudic: how could Hebron, in Canaan, have been founded before Zoan, in Egypt, when a father will always provide for his elder son before his later son; and it states clearly in the Bible in Genesis 10:6: 'The descendants of Ham: Cush, Mizraim, Put and Canaan'. That is, Ham's son Mizraim (Egypt) is listed before Canaan and so was older than him, so Zoan must have been founded before Hebron. Perhaps it means that Hebron was more cultivated than Zoan; yet again this is contradicted by biblical texts, which teach clearly that Hebron is full of rocks (which is why we find a burial place in a cave there) whilst Egypt was fertile ('Like the garden of the Lord, like the land of Egypt', the Talmud quotes from Genesis 13:10). Hebron, indeed, has one physical claim – because it is barren, it is full of sheep and the Talmud quotes from the book of Samuel (2 Samuel 15:7) that Absalom, King David's son, went there to find sheep for his sacrifices. But this is hardly enough to establish Hebron's precedence, so it must mean that the superiority of Hebron, its status as 'before Zoan', is given not by its antiquity or ecology – not, that is, by something physical – but by the special *spiritual* nature of the place. That is, the Holy Land is on a different level, its priority is clearly a religious one, it has a potential which, once realized, is transformative, and because of this: 'Despite the rocks, despite the vast quantity of sand, this country holds more possibilities than Zoan, which is located in the midst of Egypt, in the midst of civilization; it calls upon those who are capable of realizing these potentials. Aren't some rights conferred through moral superiority?' (pp.62–3). This would be the textual justification for settling the land. However, Levinas undermines the claim immediately ('But one can also doubt that moral superiority, of whatever kind, permits an expropriation' [pp.62–3]), and then goes on to show how delightfully and seditiously the Talmud has subverted its own apparently clear moral justification for colonization. The trick lies in the exact examples picked by the rabbis in justifying the special status of Hebron. First, the choice of Ham as the authoritative father who does the right thing by his children, placing them in order. Surely this is ironic: Ham and Canaan were damned for shaming Ham's father Noah, after the flood. Then, of all people, Absalom, who went to Hebron not solely to worship, but to plot, to unite people in a revolt against his father King David. Levinas draws the conclusion:

> Earlier, we had said: We, the Israelites, have a right to this land because we have the Bible. The objection consists in reminding us of the very teaching of this Bible and the deeds it relates. People of the

Book? Nothing but sons who honour their fathers? Children who obey all the moral principles? What about Absalom? The example is wonderfully well chosen. Bad lots are not lacking in the Bible, but isn't Absalom in a certain sense the counterpart of Ham, the founder of the land of Canaan? Remember what Ham did. He made fun of his father's nakedness. And Absalom? Here a euphemism is in order, even in the presence of intellectuals: he cohabited with all his father's concubines on the roof of the royal palace. So much for the superiority of Judaism! Which obviously gives it the right to conquer a country! One can understand the explorers, one can understand the revolt of the pure. They asked themselves ... By what right are we going into this land? What moral advantage do we have over the inhabitants settled in this country?

(p.63)

This is a very strong and clear statement, both on behalf of the Talmud, which slips in its own harmonics, its own associative network, to block a fundamentalist reading of the right-to-the-Land variety, and by Levinas, who reinstates doubt in the modern context of the debate over Palestine.

In the rest of the commentary, Levinas heightens this still further, examining what it means to be involved in a moral crusade and identifying the quandary of the spies as 'those of an overly pure conscience. It begins to doubt God because God's command asks us either what is above our strength or what is beneath our conscience' (p.64). Like the spies, caught in the dilemma of how to obey God whilst also obeying their conscience, Levinas revolves between the positions that there is a moral entitlement to the land given by the 'chosen' status of the Jews and that this kind of entitlement does not actually entitle one to anything. On the one hand, he uses some of the text to argue for the 'disproportion that exists between messianic politics and all other politics' (p.65) and that the act of founding a 'just' community 'sacralizes' the earth, so the pursuit of Torah is its own legitimating performance. This is understood in relation to a universalism present in the Torah, which is drawn on to justify the Jews' claim to occupation of the land:

What we call the Torah provides norms for human justice. And it is in the name of this universal justice and not in the name of some national justice or other that the Israelites lay claim to the land of Israel.

(p.66)

This would be a Judeo-centred reading, with the Jews possessing the truth, their special position legitimizing their acts. On the other hand, Levinas also argues for the limits of this view. Quoting his own translation, he notes that the Talmudic passage states in the name of Rav Hanina bar Papa (and hence, approvingly): 'Even the Boss, so to speak, cannot remove his tools from there' (p.53). That is, in contemporary terms:

> The right of the native population to live is stronger than the moral right of the universal God. Even the Boss cannot retrieve the tools entrusted to them; as long as the tools correspond to their needs, there would be no right on earth that could deprive them of them, one cannot take away from them the land on which they live, even if they are immoral, violent, and unworthy and even if this land were meant for a better destiny.
>
> (p.67)

This is another strong claim, but one has to remember the end of the story and of the commentary before hailing the Talmud as a pro-Palestinian text and calling on Levinas as one of its greatest recent interpreters. In the former case, the Talmud reminds us that the spies died of the plague, an 'unnatural death', in which 'their tongue was elongated and reached down to their navel and ... worms issued from the navel to the tongue and from the tongue to the navel' (p.54). Or maybe it was 'diphtheria'. They should have obeyed and encouraged the people to conquer. In Levinas's case, too, despite his exploration of the undercurrent in the Talmud, he comes down in the end to the question of faith: 'What matters is the idea of two punishments' reflecting the two possible reasons for their 'fault': they might have thought they were too weak, or that the Promised Land was not permitted to them. 'In both cases,' he writes, 'they were wrong ...' (p.69).

A final ambivalence

Levinas's reading of the Talmudic passage is both revelatory and symptomatic. It convincingly plays the rabbis at their own game, using the clues they give to find the 'unconscious' traces in the text through associations and harmonics, through word-play and memory, to find another track in their argument to the one that might have been expected. Rather than a clear admonition of the religious weakness of the

spies and a justification of their punishment – a straightforward, literal
rendering of the biblical verses – we are offered a subtle examination
of human uncertainty, of fear perhaps mixed with a moral sensibility
that is rehearsed constantly today amongst many Jewish supporters of
Israel: with what right does this or that occur, what are the limits of
what is permitted and what is justifiable? In the end, the rabbis do their
job and plump for religious authority and acceptance, but at times it is a
close run thing, and the beauty of the Talmud is that it allows its readers
access to the other version, to the alternatives, the paths less taken, as
it were, the undercurrent that does not justify, but questions whether
what occurred – and occurs daily – was and is right. For Levinas, too,
one might hazard, this was a complex, ambivalent enterprise. On the
one hand, he held a belief in the special position of the Jew and the
Torah, and a political and personal commitment to the preservation of
the State of Israel. On the other hand, his was a universalist philosophy
in which ethics is the founding of ontology, in which the relationship
with the other comes first, and in which one has the most responsibility
for the other with whom one has no particular connection, or even the
other against whom one is opposed.

How does one reconcile this particularism and this universalism,
this wish to have security and this desire to be an outward-facing
ethical being? The analysis of 'ethical violence', of the degree to which
others are recognized in their singularity, is significant here (e.g. Butler,
2005), and is in part a struggle over whether ethics is embedded in a
relational domain or answers to some kind of external truth. In general,
Judaism seems to place itself in the latter camp, answering to a 'call'
that comes from God and dictates its responsibility to the other. Indeed,
Jean-Luc Nancy (2020) sees this as a distinguishing feature of Judaism
and a source of Christian antisemitism: 'the heteronomy of the Hebrew
people,' he writes (p.43),

> bestows upon it a singular autonomy: an independence from any
> belonging or membership other than that of its response, that is, of its
> faithfulness. One could say that Revelation – as well as the revelation
> of a god – is the revelation to themselves of the ones who respond
> to the call. In this revelation, they are excluded from belonging in
> general: they belong to that which withdraws from belonging.

In this reading, the accountability of the Jews to God separates them
from belonging with other people. Levinas's more detailed theory of
the Other confirms something of this. And even in the reading given

here, in Levinas and maybe also in the Talmud, the question of ethics is forced shut through a final acceptance of the truth of God's word. Nevertheless, quite a lot of light is let in, too, to suggest that there is plenty of room for doubt.

What might be the source of this doubt, psychoanalytically speaking? If the insular impulse is interpretable at times as a response to anxiety, to the fragmentation or assault on selfhood that comes from the uncertainties endemic to modernity, then the security given by a direct and firm reading of the sacred texts can be understood as a way of bolstering this response, of securing the stability of boundaries and boundedness – itself also a link with the security offered by an obsession with the land. But for a certain kind of modern sensibility, perhaps definable as humanistic or even 'liberal', with all the difficulties of both those words, adoption of this defence itself produces anxiety and, alongside it, guilt. It is not possible to move from the textual traces of the Talmud to suggest that the rabbis felt guilty about the displacement of other people from the land; in any case, this seems unlikely, even if the reading that finds guilt feelings amongst the spies is a supportable one. It is also not possible to label the modern, post-Shoah consciousness of the universalist but Jewish-identified Levinas as feeling 'guilty' on the basis of his Talmudic argument; one has to be cautious about sweeping psychoanalytic claims based only on textual and not on face-to-face encounters (and Levinas is the great philosopher of the face-to-face, as Freud – despite his aversion to being looked at – was its great psychologist). Still, in his to-ing and fro-ing, in his choice of an obviously colonizing passage to find an emancipatory ethical stance, in finding a meaning under the meaning, and in speaking out publicly but slightly hiddenly about the *religious* problem of identification with Zionist fundamentalism, one might think that Levinas is putting his finger on the specifically Jewish problem of how to make claims for something whilst also renouncing those same claims, of how, that is, to live with ambivalence without being overwhelmed by guilt. The ethical stance that Levinas pushes for thus perhaps mirrors the ethical claims of Judaism, all too easily swamped by the stridency of its equally strong, but less productive, isolationist tendencies.

Something else is made impossible by this reading. The fundamentalist claim that the Land of Israel is God-given, that the right to it is established beyond doubt by the Bible and reinforced by the inspired texts of Judaism, is made much more muddy and less tenable when one realizes that even the rabbis were not sure. Is it weakness to resist the colonizing impulse, is it a mode of Jewish self-disbelief or even self-hatred? Or is it a moral stance that doubts one's own worthiness and wonders if even the conviction of having *a* right to the land, or possibly of being 'chosen' for a specific role, is sufficient to justify attacks on 'the right of the native population to live?' From a religious perspective, that is, in which one accepts as true some fundamental principles of belief, in our context specifically acceptance of the truth of the Torah and its interpretations through the sages of old, it is still wrong to adopt a fundamentalist position that brooks no opposition. The opposition is there *in the sacred texts themselves* and in the equally sacred activity of interpreting them; one's religious duty, that is, is in part to live in awe of the complexity of reasons and motivations, of justifications and legitimations, which give rise to the actions that we take. This is not so far, of course, from a psychoanalytic sensibility, which also, one might hope, opposes fundamentalism through its awareness of the subversive disruptions that any 'text' might allow.

Finally, this brings us back to the question of solidarity. At the start of this chapter, Jewish solidarity was presented as a response to antisemitism constituted in legitimate self-care in and by the Jewish community. But if it is also the case that Jewish ethics requires a stance of responsibility to the other, then this cannot be restricted only to the other Jew. It must also be directed outwards, if not universally at least to what Memmi (1962, p.280) refers to as the 'vast solidarity of all oppressed persons'. Some of these 'oppressed' might not always be friendly to Jews, a point that Memmi dwells on in his writings on colonialism, as we shall see in a later chapter. But if the subversive reading offered by Levinas is to have traction, this in itself is not a reason to withdraw from the stance of responsibility. The 'failings' of the spies might have been failings of faith, but they were also what psychoanalysts could possibly refer to as depressive anxieties – the awareness that one's actions are likely to do damage. Stepping back from this brink, they were punished; but that is not the whole story. The Israelites did not have the moral right to assert their ownership of the land because they were not secure in their ethical position; and there is also acknowledgement of the pain of dispossession ('The right of the native population to live is stronger than the moral right of the universal God'). Clearly, this is ambiguous and can be argued back and forth. However, it also reels in the self-aggrandizing assuredness of religious truth to ask some difficult questions: do our actions make us worthy; do we have the courage not just to fight, but to see further into the difficulties of others and respond to them? One strand of Jewish ethics – and perhaps it is no more than that, despite the way in which many Jewish movements have argued for the centrality of '*tikkun olam*' ('healing the world') to assert the responsibility of Jews for social action – is to challenge any assumptions that might be made about moral superiority. Pushing this further, it suggests that the solidarity we should seek is based in an ethics of responsibility that is not limited to fellow Jews, however understandable an attitude that might be; it stretches, rather, to all those whose 'tools' *should* 'correspond to their needs' – but because of violence, oppression and discrimination, do not.

Chapter 3

PSYCHOANALYSIS AS DECOLONIAL JUDAISM

Ambivalences

A repeated difficulty in writing about antiracism from a Jewish perspective is the reticence produced by coming at it from what can seem to be the 'outside'. In particular, there is a potential (self-)criticism that drawing on experiences of antisemitism to develop a commentary on racism in general represents a retreat from an engagement with contemporary progressive ideas, particularly around postcolonial and decolonial interventions in the academy. Instead, it can be seen as reiterating a rather tired trope in which Jewish intellectualism stands in for radical thinking and occludes the new, vibrant and necessary voices from the so-called 'periphery'. But in developing this book I have become ever more aware of the extraordinary prominence of concern over antisemitism both in the UK and (possibly with different dynamics) in Europe and America – a concern justified by the actual increase in antisemitic rhetoric and attacks, especially from the authoritarian political Right. This suggests once again that racism and antisemitism go together, or perhaps that 'racism' includes antisemitism just as it does anti-Blackness and anti-Muslim 'Islamophobia'. Could my initial reticence be construed as a kind of 'internalized antisemitism', an apologetic attitude that reads Jewishness through the eyes of those who disparage it rather than through its own rich resources? My reticence or even embarrassment would therefore be shameful, failing to appreciate the creativity of Jewish tradition, including that of some of the major Jewish critical thinkers of the twentieth century (Walter Benjamin, Max Horkheimer and maybe Theodor Adorno) as well as, in the contemporary scene, Judith Butler (2012, 2020).

Partly to establish a credential here, it is worth noting that Frantz Fanon (1952) – more or less ubiquitous in postcolonial and decolonial writings – was quite clear on the parallels and necessary alliances amongst victims of different forms of racism:

> It was my philosophy professor, a native of the Antilles, who recalled the fact to me one day: 'Whenever you hear anyone abuse the Jews,

pay attention, because he is talking about you.' And I found that he
was universally right – by which I meant that I was answerable in
my body and in my heart for what was done to my brother. Later
I realized that he meant, quite simply, an anti-Semite is inevitably
anti-Negro.

(p.92)

Admittedly, the last sentence of this quotation gives pause in that it
suggests that the alliance between Black people and Jews might be merely
contingent – the same people hate them. Indeed, it is clear that Fanon
himself, however universally minded he might have been in *Black Skin,
White Masks,* held ambivalent views about the relationship between
the victims of what he called 'Negrophobia' and those of antisemitism.
On the one hand, the oppression of the Jew demands solidarity: 'Anti-
Semitism hits me head-on: I am enraged' (p.65). On the other, whilst
Fanon sees parallels, he notes the differences in the phenomenology of
these different forms of racism. Jews are discriminated against because
of their assumed intellect and the plotting they supposedly do to
support one another to gain leverage; Black people, on the other hand,
are feared sensually. Even though it has resonance in the contemporary
appreciation that different discriminatory acts and prejudicial attitudes
need to be understood in their specificity as well as in what they share
(Young-Bruehl, 1996), this set of associations has some problematic
consequences. For instance, it feeds into Fanon's (1952) rather dubious
notion that Jews are hated in a 'general' or even 'rational' way ('Anti-
Semitism can be rationalized on a basic level. It is because he takes
over the country that the Jew is a danger') whilst 'Negrophobia' is 'to
be found on an instinctual, biological level' (pp.123–4). The 'biological'
nature of anti-Black racism means that the Black person is attacked
in 'his corporeality' (p.126) – lynched, for instance – whereas 'the Jew
is attacked in his religious identity, in his history, in his race, in his
relations with his ancestors and with his posterity' (pp.125–6), though
this too can also involve the Jew being 'killed or sterilized' (p.125),
which certainly sounds corporeal.

In the end, for Fanon, the Jew might be white, or at least he can pass
as such, whereas the Black subject is trapped in the skin of one who will
always attract attention.

He is a white man, and, apart from some rather debatable
characteristics, he can sometimes go unnoticed. He belongs to the
race of those who since the beginning of time have never known

cannibalism. […] Granted, the Jews are harassed – what am I thinking
of? They are hunted down, exterminated, cremated. But these are
little family quarrels. The Jew is disliked from the moment he is
tracked down. But in my case everything takes on a new guise. I am
given no chance. I am overdetermined from without. I am the slave
not of the 'idea' that others have of me but of my own appearance.

(p.87)

Describing being 'exterminated, [and] cremated' as 'little family quarrels'
does not invite solidarity amongst different oppressed groups, even
allowing for Fanon's sometimes ironic tone. And the distinction between
Jews being the slave of the 'idea' others have of them and Black people of
their own 'appearance' does not really hold either, as the choice of skin
colour as a marker of human value is itself an 'idea'. As Bryan Cheyette's
(2013) explains, however, there is more to Fanon's wavering position
(alliance versus differentiation) than ironic provocation. 'The references
to Jews and anti-Semitism in *Black Skin, White Masks*,' Cheyette argues,
are 'part of a wider tension concerning the relationship between a
particularist anti-colonial nationalism (which excludes "the Jew") and
more universalist or cosmopolitan theories of racial oppression (which
include "the Jew")' (p.61). This may be one of the most significant areas
of uncertainty around Jewish incorporation into the decolonial struggle
and also raises a general question about the multidimensionality of that
struggle. Is every specific group defined through a process of national
self-determination, or is the core revolutionary, decolonial move that
of banding together all people aiming to overthrow colonialism? If the
former, then we need to acknowledge that, despite fervent and often
antagonistic debates about the nature of Zionism in the period up
until the Second World War amongst critical intellectuals (Gershom
Scholem, Martin Buber and Walter Benjamin amongst others), as well
as religious versus secular Jews (the former often being anti-Zionist),
plus the continuing presence today of non-Zionists and anti-Zionists
who nevertheless identify as Jews, the route most Jews have taken is
towards attachment to the State of Israel (e.g. Cohen and Kahn-Harris,
2004) – sometimes wholly supportively, sometimes critically in relation
to the policies of Israeli governments. This has posed huge obstacles to
their incorporation into the decolonial movement, which has been very
strongly aligned with the Palestinian cause and is often anti-Zionist.
And if, alternatively, decolonization focuses on the solidarity of the
oppressed, what about the issue of 'whiteness'? Are Jews 'white' and
can they pass as such in the way Fanon imagines, or does the periodic

recrudescence of antisemitism suggest that assimilation to whiteness is unstable and insecure? Fanon wavers, but the wavering is not just his issue; the supposed whiteness of Jews will be discussed in a later chapter. Maybe all that can be said at this point is that the assertion that anti-Black racism is distinct from antisemitism is well founded, just as is the recognition that 'an anti-Semite is inevitably anti-Negro'.

For its reciprocation of the compliment that Fanon, the hero of decolonial thought, possibly saw Jews as his co-persecuted compatriots, Emmanuel Levinas's (1978) famous French dedication to his book *Otherwise than Being* is relevant. This has been translated as 'to the memory of those who were closest among the six million assassinated by the National Socialists, and of the millions on millions of all confessions and all nations, victims of the same hatred of the other man, the same anti-semitism'. The same hatred, the same antisemitism applied to victims of 'all confessions and all nations' – unity in suffering, and hence, one might hope, in opposition to oppression. In some ways, this is accentuated by the book's second dedication, which Annabel Herzog (2005) presents as untranslatable by those outside the comity of the Jewish people: a Hebrew language dedication that is specific and personal, that names the 'closest among the six million' as six individuals from Levinas's family killed by the Nazis. Herzog explains:

> The Hebrew sentences follow a traditional phraseology and dedicate [*Otherwise than Being*] to the memory of Levinas's father, mother, brothers, and father and mother in-law, who are all recalled by their names in the following order: Yehiel, son of Avraham Halevi; Devorah, daughter of Moshe; Dov, son of Yehiel Halevi; Amminadav, son of Yehiel Halevi; Shemuel, son of Gershon Halevi; and Malka, daughter of Hayyim. The National-Socialists are not mentioned, as are neither the millions of victims of all nations, the hatred of the other man, or anti-Semitism. The second dedication expresses a particular and intimate remembrance of people and events that we, the readers, cannot share.
>
> (p.342)

Herzog suggests that what is taken to be an 'immemorial' memory of the general is more accessible than the personal memory that Levinas gives us – we cannot know exactly what these names mean, nor to whom they refer in the detail of their lives. Still, is it really the case that we cannot enter into the particularity of another's experience in this way, whether or not we share their background or social identity?

Knowing the Jewish liturgy, I recognize Levinas's use of the traditional forms of memorializing to honour his family members. But, even if I did not know this, and even if I required a translation from the Hebrew to make the text accessible (just as I might require a translation of the first dedication from the French) – and granted that I can never fully know the lives of these people in the way that Levinas himself might have done – it is surely possible and ethically essential to respond to something here. These personal losses are neither unique nor unimaginable and might have fuelled Levinas at moments when he moved away from the particularity into which he sometimes fell (the Jewish people as singularly chosen) and saw every one of the oppressed, of all faiths and all nations, as victims of 'the same antisemitism'.

There is also the striking comment to consider by Edward Said, scholar, polemicist and author both of *Orientalism* and of *Zionism from the Point of View of its Victims* (Said, 1978, 1979), to an Israeli journalist, Ari Shavit (2000), who had said to him that he sounded 'very Jewish': 'Of course. I'm the last Jewish intellectual. You don't know anyone else. All your other Jewish intellectuals are now suburban squires. From Amos Oz to all these people here in America. So I'm the last one. The only true follower of Adorno. Let me put it this way: I'm a Jewish-Palestinian.' The context for this was a hard-hitting interview demanding Israelis face their responsibility for Palestinian suffering, so it should not be read as a generous offer of alliance, but rather as a criticism of all the other, failed 'Jewish intellectuals'. Nevertheless, it rescues something from the debris: the idea of the Jewish intellectual, the 'true follower of Adorno'. Despite the irony that Adorno was not 'technically' Jewish (his mother was Catholic and his father had converted to Christianity), Said's assertion makes an important gesture towards a Jewish offering, one that is universalized here in the person of the Palestinian-American intellectual.

That is where the discomfort at the embarrassment comes in: Why should I be embarrassed at trying to resurrect this history, and not now even as a 'non-Jewish Jew' (Deutscher, 1968) but as someone committed to my Jewishness? After all, if both Fanon and Said have some time for Jewish identities, who am I to be apologetic – and at this time too, when so much seems to depend on asserting that antisemitism is a form of racism, and is not somehow exempt from the antiracist activist critique? Accordingly, building on this and on the issues raised in the previous two chapters, I will try to develop my project to offer something that makes these universalizing links, yet is also rooted in my particularism, as an attempt to construct a bridge between Jewishness and antiracist solidarity.

Mixed up in this is the issue of psychoanalysis, its Jewishness, its colonialism, its universalist claims, its specificities, its blind spots and its potential. If I want to assert an alliance between Jewish and decolonizing theory, a rendering of critical theory that is both 'Jewish' and decolonial, then psychoanalysis – after all, a profound influence on Adorno and Butler, if not so much (but not negligibly) on Walter Benjamin – should offer something. A place to begin, in any case, is with the notion of barbarism.

Barbaric Jews

One way of reading some of Freud's more compellingly unfortunate remarks, couched in the language of colonialism, is as part of an effort to position Black Africans and indigenous Australians in the place of the 'other' to white Europeans, a place previously largely occupied by Jews. As discussed in the next chapter and elsewhere (Frosh, 2013a), the main issue is the division proposed by Freud, especially in *Totem and Taboo*, between the world of the 'savage' and that of the 'civilized' – meaning, generally speaking, European men (Freud, 1913). That Freud should write in this way is not surprising, given the European colonial context of the late nineteenth and early twentieth century. As Said (2003) notes, the strangeness to Freud of the 'non-European' other was in some ways simply the converse of his immersion in the received history of European civilization, deriving from the Greeks and Romans as well as from the Bible (p.16). Yet, as Said also points out, Freud had an intriguing understanding of the 'semite', with whom he identified at least part of the time, as the opponent of the European – or at least of the Christian.

The famous instance where this visibly occurs is in the passage in *The Interpretation of Dreams* where Freud (1900) is recollecting his father's 'unheroic conduct' in the face of a Christian antisemite who knocks his expensive (Jewish) fur hat into the gutter (p.197). Freud links this event with his identification with the 'Carthaginian general' Hannibal, who had been made by his father to swear revenge on the Romans; and then traces further back into childhood his liking for Napoleon's 'Jewish' marshals. Said (2003) comments, 'Reading *Moses and Monotheism*, one is struck by Freud's almost casual assumption (which also applies to Hannibal) that Semites were most certainly not European [...] and, at the same time, were somehow assimilable to its culture as former outsiders' (pp.15–16). This last point is an important indicator of a kind of wished-for shift in Jewish identity *towards* Europeanism, but Freud's association of semites with non-Europeans is a significant one not only for Said, but for Freud himself. Sander Gilman (1993) has perhaps made most of this, arguing that Freud was largely responding to the widespread antisemitic tropes of his time that feminized Jews as 'castrated' as a consequence of circumcision and associated them with blackness and primitivity. It should be recalled here that many of these tropes linked Jews and 'savages', perhaps most especially – *pace* Fanon – cannibals. Marita Vyrgioti (2018), studying the place of cannibalism in psychoanalysis, comments on the currency of this at that time, and its very material effects on the lives of European Jews in the form of public 'ritual murder' trials. She concludes that 'the cannibal fantasies projected on Jewish communities exposed financial, cultural, social, and religious anxieties and informed the anti-Semitic imagery of a people which *live among us, eat our flesh, and suck our (Christian) blood*' (p.45). Responding insouciantly to this imagery, Freud (1939) explains in *Moses and Monotheism* how the invention of the monotheistic God by the Jews is a step forward for civilization because it requires an act of intellect and an escape from sensuality. Christianity is then a regression to the more material practices that require visible icons, whilst Christians are at times barely disguised barbarians. 'We must not forget,' Freud writes, 'that all those peoples who excel to-day in their hatred of Jews became Christians only in late historic times, often driven to it by bloody coercion. It might be said that they are all "mis-baptized". They have been left, under a thin veneer of Christianity, what their ancestors were, who worshipped a barbarous polytheism' (p.91).

The work that is done in this material is certainly a kind of colonizing, as Brickman (2003) amongst others points out, in which the Jewish other is made European and civilized at the expense of the 'primitive' other of colonialism, a point to which we will return. Yet there is also something else at stake here, which takes off from the reference to the 'barbarous' in the previous quotation. The effort that Freud puts into repositioning Jewishness as civilized and European is necessary precisely because of the haunting of the European vision of Jewish identity by its opposite, namely by the fantasy of 'barbarism' that is core to antisemitic discourse – as opposed to the real barbarism demonstrated by antisemites in Freud's day and especially just after his death in 1939. Freud objected to the association of Jewishness with barbarism, despite his liking for Hannibal: for him, Jewish identity offered a high ethical ideal, a point he made several times, for example in his letter to the Vienna B'nai B'rith (Freud, 1926). But not only is this objection coincident with a view of non-Jewish ('Christian') civilization as itself largely 'barbarous'; one might also argue that Freud's central perception, the existence of an unconscious life in all human subjects, however civilized they might claim to be, is testimony to the presence of barbarism everywhere – and not just as something to be overcome. To put this more delicately: Freud's rhetoric has some significant 'political' effects. First, it shifts the location of barbarism away from the Jew and into the colonized Black 'other', thus buying into the colonial mindset; but contrastingly, it places barbarism in non-Jewish (specifically Christian) Europe itself. However, it also offers scope for a revaluing of barbarism as resistive of conventional order and hence potentially liberating. This relies on the idea that the universal presence of a 'primitive' unconscious amongst humans makes the barbaric mobile and formative. What is taken to be the civilized norm – that of colonial rationality – is underpinned by the hugely potent, repressed yet disruptive forces that lie at its heart. If the Jews are linked to these forces, being supposedly barbaric, then Jewishness and 'savagery' are to be taken seriously as positions for conjoined opposition to the dominant colonial order.

In his exuberant study of 'decolonial Judaism', Santiago Slabodsky (2014) discusses various ways in which it might make sense to read Jewishness as 'barbaric'. His first move is to establish the historical association between Jewish barbarism and other 'barbarians' within the discourse of European identity and of whiteness in general.

> For most of the modern period, European discourses portrayed Jews as non-Westerners. While the descriptions varied depending on geopolitical context, normative descriptions of Jews often oscillated between assimilable primitivity and irremediable barbarity. The specific narrative of Jewish barbarism proved particularly persistent across time, space, and ideological persuasion. Even champions of liberal values [...] considered Jews a threat to civilization and permanently interrelated them to other barbarians of the Mediterranean and Atlantic including Muslims, Subsaharan Africans and Amerindians. These discourses regularly posited Jewish masterminding of and participation in plots to destroy European civilization, whether defined as Christendom or capitalist imperialism.

(p.4)

Slabodsky notes how much this perception has shifted since the end of the Second World War (although the antisemitic claim that Jews sponsor the Muslim 'invasion' of the West is still current), in light of both the Shoah and the foundation and increasing normalization of the State of Israel. Lentin (2020, p.133) adds to this the observation that 'Many Jews have also been willing participants in this integration into civilization, which meant giving up what we had in common with other racialized peoples; our shared "barbarism".' Nowadays, it is much harder to think of Jews as aligned with the subordinated other, yet this history is a profound one. It is even true in Europe *after* Emancipation, which we should recall came late and only tentatively. For instance, in Austria, access to citizenship for Jews was only made official in 1867, during Freud's childhood, beginning a process of dissolution of Jewish community life that nevertheless refused Jews full entry to the society into which they were supposedly assimilating. Enzo Traverso (2016, p.9) comments that '[t]his is the source of the mixture of particularism and cosmopolitanism that characterizes Jewish modernity' – a creatively fertile mix, it is true, but always an uncomfortable one verging on the edge of exclusion. It did not in any case take long for their rights to be rescinded in the most dramatic and thoroughgoing way, in the treatment of Jews not just as barbarians, but as beasts and vermin. Amongst the important issues here is that with the rise in 'racial' antisemitism, Jewish barbarism became incorrigible; that is, conversion to Christianity would no longer solve the Jewish problem since Jews remained Jews whatever their formal religious status. This shift was not unheralded: after all, one point of the Inquisition was to chase after 'New Christians' who remained Jewish in their beliefs and secret practices even after supposed conversion. Nevertheless, it was radically different in scale and severity – there was now nothing that a Jew could do to become civilized. The more that Jews might try to do so, the more pernicious they appeared: a secret conspiracy to undermine European civilization on behalf of the barbarian hordes lurking at the gate.

The idea of barbarism as developed by Slabodsky is binary and in some ways categorical, opposing the barbaric to the civilized rather than, for instance, working with the notions of hybridity that have been more characteristic of postcolonial and diasporic studies. This binarism has its difficulties, not least that Jewish 'cosmopolitanism' has always been linked with absorption of the influences of surrounding cultures and has often included incorporation of Western classicism as well as Jewish texts and traditions. Nevertheless, Slabodsky's ideas are productive in pressing for barbarism as an *oppositional* response to the coercive power of Western colonialism, incorporating Jews along with other colonized subjects. Distinguishing 'border thinking', a notion developed by Walter Mignolo (2000), from hybridity and playing on the image of the *marrano* – originally a term of abuse for 'New Christians' or *conversos* deliberately mobilized here as antagonistic to the colonial (and Christian) norm – Slabodsky (2014) asserts the resistive power of the colonized other as something to be sought out and catalysed. 'The *Marrano*,' he writes (p.34), 'does not prevail over the dualism like a hybrid but reacts creatively to this imperially-imposed identity'. Whereas the hybrid 'attempts to undermine colonial dualism by dissolving identities', the border thinker 'creatively develops identities, even if these identities turn upside down the reified imperial constructions' (p.35). In practice, this means taking the elements written off by the colonial empire as barbaric and empowering them, disrupting the colonial project. Jews are potentially as much part of this as any other colonized group because colonialism has made them the same. The European Enlightenment 'othered' Jews by presenting them as the outmoded barbarians of reason – a direct inheritance of the supersessionism of the Church, in which Christianity is taken to have displaced Judaism, leaving the unconverted Jews as primitive relics. There is also another historical link, arising as much from the colonized South as from Europe itself, but feeding the colonial imagination in a way that is not much attended to. Slabodsky notes how from the sixteenth-century Amerindians were identified as Jews, with the emergence of writings 'detailing the commonalities between Natives and Jews. In particular, the accusations focus on cannibalism, sexual perversion, lust, and, most importantly, anarchical and seditious political behaviour' (p.60). More generally, '[f]rom the dawn of modernity in the seventeenth century until the Holocaust in the twentieth century, the narrative of barbarism made Jews and Blacks political co-conspirators using political and sexual perversion to subvert coloniality's structures of domination' (p.62).

There are various ways in which this narrative of barbarism might be utilized for oppositional practice. Slabodsky's main structural division is between those Jewish writers and thinkers who regard barbarism as a 'negative' but displace it from Jews and the colonized 'barbarians' onto European civilization (i.e. it is Europe that is barbaric); and, alternatively, those who take ownership of barbarism as a positive alternative to the so-called civilization of the West. The former tendency is the stronger one amongst European Jewish intellectuals and has an unexpected association with Theodor Herzl, the founder of modern Zionism.

Jacqueline Rose (2011) notes his reference in 'A Solution of the Jewish Question', published in *The Jewish Chronicle* in 1896, to 'the profound barbarism of our day', by which, he explains, 'I mean anti-Semitism.' Rose comments, '[l]ong before the horrors of the Second World War will offer its deadly confirmation to his insight, Herzl has more or less stated that barbarism – like partition, we can say – originates in the West' (p.73). Herzl's solution was Zionism; in other cases, Jewish texts are drawn on and presented as the genuinely civilized alternative to European barbarism. In this, we might see a move away from a view of Jewish critical fervour as arising mainly as a response to antisemitism. Instead, Jewishness is seen to have its own dynamic of critical engagement with the social order, with its social practices, traditions and texts being mined for insights into how to build a good society. Arguably, this is precisely the task that the rabbis of the Talmudic period set themselves as they discussed the meaning of biblical texts and developed commentaries that offered spiritual, legal and practical guidance for Jewish communities. It might also be seen as part of the 'Jewish' project of some more contemporary writers, for example Judith Butler – though this is also made more complex by Butler's astute awareness of how making universalizing claims for a Jewish ethics can itself reproduce the colonial impulse. Presenting Jewish thought as linked with 'alterity', a theme discussed previously in Chapter 1, Butler (2012) begins her book on Jewish ethics discussing the move away from 'ontology' and towards 'relationality' that posits the other as central to formations of the human subject, and asking 'Is this Jewish?' 'It establishes the relation to alterity as constitutive of identity, which is to say that the relation to alterity *interrupts* identity, and this interruption is the condition of ethical relationality. Is this a Jewish notion? Yes and no' (p.5).

'Yes and no' is already a Jewish answer to a question like this! Butler's claim here is not put in terms of barbarism, yet it has some echoes of it: the closed mind of (the) European (ontology) is displaced by the more transgressive and open possibilities of the 'Jewish' emphasis on the interruptive presence of the other. Butler begins this passage with an exclamatory moral statement: 'Relationality displaces ontology, and it is a good thing too' (p.5). In this tradition, then, the supposedly barbaric Jew draws on Jewish philosophy to offer a critique of the supposedly civilized West, turning the tables just as other barbarisms do – the famous but unfortunately probably apocryphal Gandhi quip (Journalist: 'What do you think of Western civilisation?' Gandhi: 'I think it would be a good idea') standing in for more developed postcolonial argumentation.

The second strand of barbaric thinking that Slabodsky (2014) outlines is one that retains the name-tag of barbarism for the colonized and for the Jew, but reads it positively. Here he draws on postcolonial thinkers such as Albert Memmi, a quote from whom begins Slabodsky's book: 'I am an incurable barbarian' (p.1). I return to some aspects of Memmi's thought in a later chapter, so will just note here that he held to a position that rejected assimilation and emphasized the contribution of Jews to the broader decolonial movement in the name of his own Jewish specificity, however hybrid this might be; and that he argued that an important step along the way would be to reframe Jewish self-understanding outside antisemitism and instead in conjunction with the emerging Africanist movement of the time. Dislocation nevertheless remains an important element in this self-understanding; that is, Jews have something to offer specifically because of their deracinated position, a position usually seen as antagonistic to the rootedness of the civilized subject. Cheyette quotes Memmi as follows: 'I was a sort of half-breed of colonization, understanding everyone because I belonged completely to no one' (p.51). For Slabodsky (2014, p.128), what matters is the triple alienation of Memmi: 'a native in a colonial country, a Jew in an anti-Semitic universe [and] an African in a world dominated by Europe,' which itself is a quotation from Memmi's (1953) autobiographical novel, *The Pillar of Salt* (p.96). Note here the resonance with the famous complaint attributed by Alma Mahler (1946) to her husband Gustav, half a century earlier: 'I am thrice homeless, as a native of Bohemia in Austria, as an Austrian among Germans, and as a Jew throughout the world. Everywhere an intruder, never welcomed' (p.109). The nomadic and othered Jew appears here as an affiliate of all homeless or oppressed people, having to find their way without ever gaining acceptance. Freud, too, speaking in 1926, had a similar tripartite framing of the impact of the excluded Jew, though couched characteristically in a combative way: 'My language is German. My culture, my attainments are German. I considered myself German intellectually, until I noticed the growth of antisemitic prejudice in Germany and German Austria. Since that time, I prefer to call myself a Jew' (Gay, 1988, p.448). Mahler, of course, converted to Christianity – a move that Freud always refused to countenance – in order to take up the position of Director of the Vienna Opera; but one might argue that the recurrence of Jewish themes in Mahler's music (an example being the appearance of a chaotic Klezmer band in the funeral march in the First Symphony) is not only nostalgic, but also a way of reminding his cultivated audiences that the barbaric Jewish disruption was still around.

Otherwise to colonization

We should recall the way Hannah Arendt (1944), prefiguring the
'barbarism' argument, valorizes the status of the Jew as 'pariah'. She
distinguishes this from Jewish 'parvenus', who identify themselves
with their oppressors through assimilation and self-enrichment (a
characterization that laid Arendt open to charges of antisemitism) and
in this way betray the historical consciousness of the Jews as outsiders.
The claim is that their pariah status may not be loved by Jews, but it
gives them critical leverage that should not be discarded; moreover,
Jews must be willing to self-address as Jews if their Jewishness is to
be materialized in this progressive form. Being on the outside as a
pariah gives some kind of authority to the Jew and makes it possible
to contribute to the wider struggles in the world even though, Arendt
cannot resist adding, the status of these radical Jews 'among their own
brethren' – the parvenus – is low (p.276). There is a lot one could say
about this (see Stonebridge, 2019), but the issue I want to hold onto here
is how pariahs, whatever their exclusion from the Jewish 'mainstream',
nevertheless register as *Jewish* in the struggle against oppression. In one
of her most powerful short pieces of writing, the visceral *We Refugees*,
Arendt (1943) lambasts the way in which 'we' do not want to be Jews.
Assimilation does not work, as the fate of non-Jewish Jews shows,
pushed from one country to the next, each time trying to be perfectly
German or French, 'willing to become loyal Hottentots, only to hide
the fact that we are Jews' (pp.271–2). It has never worked, even for the
conversos, unless they take up cudgels as *marranos* and barbarians.
Arendt's version of this, articulated through a number of exemplary
figures, is to emphasize the radical situation of the Jewish pariah, indeed
to claim everything ethical in Jewish culture and behaviour as being due
to that state, a claim that might resonate with Said's assertion of himself,
quoted earlier, as 'the last Jewish intellectual'. Concluding *We Refugees*,
just before her famous statement that at last it had become clear that
the fate of the nations is tied up with the fate of the Jews (this is 1943),
Arendt makes this bid for the soul of Jewishness:

> It is the tradition of a minority of Jews who have not wanted to
> become upstarts, who preferred the status of 'conscious pariah'.
> All vaunted Jewish qualities – the 'Jewish heart', humanity,
> humor, disinterested intelligence – are pariah qualities. All
> Jewish shortcomings – tactlessness, political stupidity, inferiority
> complexes, and money-grubbing – are characteristics of upstarts.

> There have always been Jews who did not think it worthwhile to
> change their humane attitude and their natural insight into reality for
> the narrowness of caste spirit or the essential unreality of financial
> transactions.
>
> (p.274)

The disconcerting reproduction of classical antisemitic tropes in this
passage is close to the surface, but so is an assertion of Jewish radicalness
as a kind of universalist message of alliance with others. Arendt's
bitterness is understandable: the 'we' in *We Refugees* was central to her
situation. The question is, to quote Butler (2012, p.5) again, 'Is this a
Jewish notion? Yes and no.'

Emmanuel Levinas, whose thinking I draw on considerably in
this book and who appears nowadays in most accounts of 'Jewish'
philosophy, definitely thinks the notion of relational responsibility is
Jewish. As noted in the previous chapters, in terms of Butler's (2012)
ontology-relationality division, Levinas (1991) is on the side of
relationality; indeed, the West's obsession with ontology is what rules
it out of an engagement with a truly human ethics that acknowledges
the place of the other and thus moves away from narcissistic self-
promotion. The profundity of the claim that Levinas makes lies in
the way it undermines assumptions of autonomous subjecthood and
instead makes otherness foundational to the subject, an otherness that
is both abstract and universal and immediate and personal. Levinasian
ethics means we have to respond to what he calls 'the Face of the Other'
(Levinas, 1991, p.104) as the primary demand upon us; and this Face is
both the immediate other person and the principle that we are not the
origin of ourselves and therefore are subject to the requirement that
we respect the differences produced by the heterogeneity of human
subjects. So far so good, then, but the difficulty is that in some of
Levinas's writing it is not clear that the philosophical requirement that
the other comes first is followed through politically, particularly when
it comes to the other who stands outside the Eurocentric norm. Here
is a famous problematic formulation, linked with Levinas's resolute
support for the State of Israel as both an ethical and a political entity,
from his paper 'Jewish Thought Today,' first published in 1961 (Levinas,
1963, p.164). He has just remarked that 'Jewish universalism has always
revealed itself in particularism. But for the first time in its history,
Israeli Judaism gauges its task only by its own teachings.' Immediately,
however, comes the sting.

Surely the rise of the countless masses of Asiatic and under-developed peoples threatens this new-found authenticity? On to the world stage come peoples and civilizations who no longer refer to our Sacred History, for whom Abraham, Isaac and Jacob no longer mean anything. As at the beginning of Exodus, a new king arises who does not know Joseph.

(p.165)

It is hard to find excuses for this, or indeed for other places where the Palestinians are positioned as Israel's other yet excluded from the kind of other that makes demands on the subject – that is, refused any Face. The reference to the new king (Pharaoh) just makes things worse: the Egyptians should have been grateful to the descendants of Joseph, who had saved them from famine, but instead turned on them, with disastrous results for themselves. Howard Caygill (2002) quotes Levinas in an interview just after the Sabra and Shatila atrocities of 1982:

[I]f you're for the other, you're for the neighbour. But if your neighbour attacks another neighbour or treats him unjustly, then what can you do? Then alterity takes on another character, in alterity we can find an enemy, or at least then we are faced with the problem of knowing who is right and who is wrong, who is just and who is unjust. There are people who are wrong.

(p.192)

For Caygill, this opens up a 'wound' in Levinas's whole system of thought; for Butler, it produces a 'quandary': 'The fact that the Palestinians remain faceless for him (or that they are the paradigm for the faceless) produces a rather stark quandary, since Levinas gives us so many reasons to extrapolate politically on the prohibition against killing' (Butler, 2012, p.39).

It is worth noting one complication in Levinas's (1963/1990) 'countless masses of Asiatic and under-developed peoples' passage. This is not to reduce its culpability: the phraseology itself, plus the subsequent reference to 'the greedy eyes of these countless hordes who wish to hope and live' (p.165) and the danger that 'Jews and Christians are pushed to the margins of history' (p.165) is evidence of Levinas's unwillingness to extend his system of ethics to everyone. Yet there is also an acknowledgement that the demands of these 'masses' are fuelled by something *necessary*. 'We hear in it', he writes (p.165), 'the cry of frustrated humanity, and while one certainly has the right to denounce one's own hunger as materialist, one never has the right to denounce the hunger of others'. This seems to restore the other, the one in need ('frustrated humanity') as an agency with which the subject ('one') might identify. Slabodsky (2014) makes an additional claim, which is that Levinas's views changed between the earlier work in which the barbarism of the West would be opposed only by Judaism, with the 'Asiatic and under-developed peoples' dropping off the map of ethical responsibility, and his writings from the 1970s onwards which were influenced by his engagement with Southern cone thinkers, some but not all of them Jewish.

> Following encounters in the early 1970s, Levinas was challenged by a group of South American intellectuals. He then expanded his critique of the West, mobilized the positive conception of barbarism from his new conversation partners, and recognized that the future of humanity resided in the barbaric margins of the West. He rubricated his turn by employing Talmudic texts to explain the need to form a large community of barbarians. This new community would be instrumental in challenging criminal imperial formations represented symbolically by Rome and contextualized in Europe and the United States.
>
> (p.94)

This supposed shift away from seeing non-European others as a threat and towards locating them in the context of an alliance against the West is not without its problems, of course: the continuing exceptionalist support for Israel makes the decolonial link unstable, though it is worth noting (as in Chapter 2) that there are moments in Levinas's work where the ethical critique of Israel is at least strongly implied. Levinas is perhaps trying to balance the argument for the special position of the Jew as repository of ethics, along with a political and personal commitment to the preservation of the State of Israel, against a universalist philosophy in which one has the most responsibility for the other with whom one has no particular connection, or even to whom one is opposed. This is a hard act, complicating any clear evaluation. Levinas struggled with recognizing the 'countless masses', but if Slabodsky is correct, he also indicated how this struggle could be resolved in a relational rendering of otherness that allies all those who are oppressed along with the Jews, in opposition to that 'same hatred of the other man, the same anti-semitism' (Levinas, 1978, dedication).

Jewish barbarism is the ethically superior position not only because it is relational rather than narcissistic, but because it affiliates itself with all the other barbarisms that seek expression, recompense and justice.

Back to psychoanalysis

This chapter started with Fanon and then Levinas and added psychoanalysis to the mix in constructing a Jewish barbarism that is decolonizing in its impulse and effects. Without going over this ground in detail – the Freudian assumption of a bifurcation between 'primitive' and 'civilized' that is subverted by the presence of 'primitivity' in the unconscious of all 'civilized' people, and by a barbarism that hides behind the supposedly advanced culture of Europe and is easily roused – as this will be discussed in the next chapter, let us think through the possibility that the 'Jewishness' of psychoanalysis might have something important to contribute to this resistive movement. For one thing, what is this 'Jewishness'? As described earlier, it is in part a historical and sociological statement about psychoanalysis. Almost all the originators of psychoanalysis were Jewish and for a large part of its history it was dominated by Jews, and this had substantial effects both in contributing a critical vision and in generating antisemitic attacks on psychoanalysis (Frosh, 2005a). The historical record is strong on this, but is that enough to claim a psychoanalytic link with the Jewish 'barbarism' argued for in this chapter? Psychoanalysis has had an uncertain history in relation to politics, as in many other things, with a strong institutional tendency towards conservatism (e.g. Damousi and Plotkin, 2012) as well as a tradition of radical thought and uses of psychoanalytic theory to fill out understandings of resistance and ideology and in some cases to offer models of critical mental health practice (Frosh, 2018). Obviously, I am siding with the radical element in psychoanalysis, its capacity to remain at odds with the normatively oppressive values of colonialism. Here, the leverage that psychoanalysis has given on analyses of racism is relevant, visible in Fanon's (1952) use of Lacan and Freud, but also in a wide range of more contemporary commentaries drawing especially on Kleinian, relational and Lacanian traditions (Frosh, 2013a). In addition, the recent applications of psychoanalysis in postcolonial theory have been highly creative, albeit at times fraught with contradictions (Greedharry, 2008). Does this represent the wresting away of psychoanalysis from the limitations of its Jewishness to find a more decolonizing setting, or is it a culmination of its Jewish elements that makes it a promising ground

for decolonial practice? As Jews become more normalized, at least for
the time being, should psychoanalysis become *less* 'Jewish' in order to
maintain its radical political edge?

This seems to me an irresolvable and uncomfortable dilemma,
another 'yes and no'. Nevertheless, I am advocating a reappropriation of
the Jewishness of psychoanalysis in the context of a 'barbaric' response
to the living legacy of colonialism and the broader effects of social
oppression on human lives. For example, Arendt's (1943) 'Jewish pariah'
qualities of 'humanity, humor, [and] disinterested intelligence' are very
close to psychoanalysis's 'Jewish' ideals – at least of the Freudian kind
(p.274). Ludwig Braun's speech to the Vienna Bnai Brith honouring
Freud's seventieth birthday has already been quoted in Chapter 1,
portraying psychoanalysis as 'genuinely Jewish' in being comprised of
'an independence of spirit, the willingness to do battle with an unjust
society, and a vision of the whole of nature and humanity' (Diller, 1991,
p.170). This is a universalizing Jewishness with which Freud felt at
home – as noted, his return letter quotes his 'respect for the so-called
"ethical" demands of human civilization' (Freud, 1926, p.367) – but
it also links with the disruptive elements of the revalued barbaric in
comparison with the 'unjustness' of the surrounding society. The
deracinated element in this is also important, not just for Freud himself,
but for later psychoanalysts who – largely because of their Jewishness,
but also at times in opposition to authoritarian regimes – have found
themselves highly mobile and unsettled, traversing boundaries and
working across re-forged and reimagined identities. Whilst the impact
of this on psychoanalytic theory has been mixed, it is arguable that the
general stance has been one that is open to relationality and otherness in
a way that echoes (albeit at a distance) Levinasian concerns. Something
comes at us from the other and demands not just recognition, but an
openness to being psychically challenged and changed. This is precisely
the 'yes and no' of 'interruption' as 'the condition of ethical relationality'
to which Butler (2012, p.5) refers in her comments on Jewish thought.

I have emphasized reasonably contemporary Jewish writings in
this chapter, but before closing it is worth noting that there is a huge
'classical' back catalogue of Jewish thought that is relevant to the
question of how to maintain a critical stance towards the social order
whilst also holding onto what might be termed a psychoanalytic
ethic. In some ways, these writings can be seen as more 'Jewishly
traditional' in that the practice of Jewish scholarship is to take biblical
texts and their commentaries, usually centuries or even millennia
old, and rethink them for contemporary concerns. Examples here

include Avivah Zornberg's incisive re-readings of the Bible through psychoanalytic lenses, producing new versions of moral engagement (Zornberg, 2009), as well as Levinas's (1990) brilliantly yet subtly subversive Talmudic readings from the 1960s, illustrated in Chapter 2. There is also *psychotherapeutic* relevance for some of this work. For instance, Philip Cushman (2007) claims that the Jewish tradition of study (the aspect of Jewish thought focusing on interpretation through questions and narratives) might inform contemporary relational psychoanalytic practice – indeed, that it often does so unawares, as '[i]n ways that we may not realize, Jewish therapists might be moved by deeply felt, embodied ways of being and thus moral commitments that have their origins in ideas and social practices hundreds or even thousands of years old and socially transmitted to us in ways implicit and constitutive' (p.82). The substance of this influence is to promote certain values ('engagement, historicity, interpersonal interaction, the dialectic of absence and presence, the prohibition against idolatry') and develop 'a process of study and authorial creation that seems structured to encourage learners to engage with and enact those values, which are among the most important concepts in Jewish thought' (p.53). Cushman's focus is on how these values are congruent with relational psychotherapy, and indeed this may be one way in which some of the issues raised here have psychotherapeutic relevance. The Butlerian claim that Jewish ethics promotes relationality and openness to alterity is in some respects well aligned with relational and intersubjectivist psychoanalysis, as Jessica Benjamin's (2018) rather different work on recognition and acknowledgement also suggests. Psychotherapy does not necessarily need to be overtly 'barbaric' to reflect these influences, though it is fair to say that the perspective I have adopted here suggests it should resist tendencies to be socially conformist and that it should also be actively engaged in anti-racist and decolonial practices.

Perhaps, however, there is an even more basic association. The most distinctive characteristic of the psychoanalytic formulation of the unconscious, whatever variations there are between schools, is its *negativity*, its opposition, that is, to the structures of rationality that characterize conscious mental life. Whatever we think we are doing to create order in the world – to colonize the barbarism of nature, both human and physical – is disrupted precisely by that barbarism; and this is not an accident or merely a problem to be solved. It is rather a recognition of *reality*; that is, the 'reality principle', which defers gratification and diverts pleasure in the name of what is possible, is ironically only part of the true reality of the human subject, in which identities are never fully formed or completely stable (Said's (2003) point) and in which something always works against the grain of settledness and control (this being a version of the Freudian death drive, but also a simple comment on the subversive nature of unconscious life). Politically, psychoanalysis, perhaps like barbarism, insists on the 'cruelty' of confrontation with reality as it is, however difficult that might be emotionally and philosophically. That is to say, the 'barbaric' elements in psychoanalysis and in politics have to do with resistance to those reconciliatory comforts that deny the actual suffering and oppression surrounding us – the barbarism of 'civilized' society itself. In this specific and quite precise sense, the unconscious of psychoanalysis is 'barbaric' and its Jewishness is part of that. Add sexuality and cannibalism, both concerns of psychoanalysis and fantasized attributes of the Jewish as well as the racialized 'other,' and what is created is the possibility of the 'community of barbarians' to which Slabodsky (2014, p.94) claims Levinas eventually aspired. Is this over-optimistic? No doubt, again, yes and no.

There is a tussle going on in Jewish communities worldwide, impacted upon equally by Israel's position as 'civilized' in the collusive sense that the new barbarianism frames, and by antisemitism as it (re-) emerges in Europe and elsewhere. Recovering the Southern tradition, as Slabodsky (2014) advocates, is a difficult task in this context; alliance-building between Jews and others is sought as an alternative to the assimilatory fantasy of recognition from the colonizing authorities, yet is also precarious. Still, here is a wager: the Jewish component of psychoanalysis has been central to its development and has fuelled its radical elements much more than its conservative ones, notwithstanding various setbacks and complications. This is because of the insistent and it seems never to be entirely overcome marginality of the Jews, through which they are at times absorbed into the body of the social, and at times expelled from it. It is also because there is a long history of Jewish 'barbarism' that mobilizes Jewish commitments to disciplines that subvert rather than confirm normalizing practices, as the case of the critical theorists attests, and hence that are set up to embrace other 'barbaric' practices, such as those of decolonialism. In this sense, psychoanalysis needs and can never escape its Jewish provocations; and in these can be found some of the energy with which it is possible for psychoanalysis to contribute to the ongoing struggle for a decolonized world.

Chapter 4

PRIMITIVITY AND VIOLENCE IN PSYCHOANALYSIS

Colonialism

The previous chapters have been concerned largely with the relationship between Jewish thought and psychoanalysis and with some strands in Jewish philosophy and history that push towards an ethical engagement with others and hence offer a way into thinking about a 'solidarity of the oppressed' linking opposition to antisemitism with antiracist activism. In this chapter, I want to do some more ground clearing, this time directed at some elements within psychoanalysis – the third term of my triad 'antisemitism, racism, psychoanalysis' – that hinder its resistance to antisemitism and racism. These elements are not so much the overt, concrete obstructions posed by the conservatism of much psychoanalytic practice, though these are of obvious importance: its institutionalization mainly in expensive privately funded clinical work, selection procedures for psychoanalytic candidates based on a process of personal judgement that risks a bias towards those who already seem to fit the picture of what a psychoanalyst should be, an individualistic orientation that underplays the role of the social environment in causing distress and so on. My interest here is rather in a set of implicit, 'unconscious' assumptions that have tied psychoanalysis to what might be termed a colonialist perspective and that need to be recognized and explicitly contested if they are not to block the development of a progressive antiracist approach.

The significance of this is not just in terms of the well-being of psychoanalysis or its practice in the clinic, but also in relation to the effect it might have on how people generally think of themselves. Jean Laplanche notes something about the 'reflexivity' of psychoanalysis that is important to recognize:

> Any epistemology or theory of psychoanalysis must take account
> of the very basic fact that the human subject is a theorizing being
> and a being which theorizes itself, by which I mean that it is a self-
> theorizing being or ... a self-symbolizing being.
>
> (Laplanche, 1989, p.10)

As psychoanalysis gained purchase in many societies (especially in
Europe and the Americas), it became a resource whereby people started
to understand themselves in its terms, producing effects that then are
understood from within psychoanalytic theory in a kind of positive
feedback loop. Psychoanalysis presents an important set of ideas about
human psychology; as these ideas become more culturally widespread,
people reflect upon themselves in relation to them; psychoanalysis
pursues these reflections, both in the clinical setting and in wider cultural
presentations (film, literature, education, political rhetoric, etc.); and these
in turn then demand further shifts in theory and practice, and so on. The
point here is that psychoanalysis does not merely *describe* the psychology
of human subjects; it also has an *impact* on this psychology – in important
respects, it *produces* the ways in which people think about themselves
and relate to others (it is productive of consciousness). This implies that
the assumptions of psychoanalysis infect people's modes of being outside
the clinical setting as well as within it.

This view that we are in a psychoanalytically 'saturated' world, in
which psychoanalysis both expresses and produces modes of subjectivity
that carry 'repressed' elements of the psychoanalytic unconscious with
them, is given some sharpness when we think about psychoanalysis as
a mechanism whereby apparently discarded elements of the social are
smuggled back in. What is meant here is that there are some important
social assumptions that are embedded in psychoanalysis and that are
therefore reproduced in the understanding it has of human subjects;
and that because this understanding affects how people see themselves
and others, the original assumptions continue to have valency in
current society. Amongst the most potent of these social 'discards' are
those that relate to colonialism and racism, which can serve here as
an example of how psychoanalysis can be inhibited in its contribution
to antiracism by its continued susceptibility to its own unconscious
assumptions and unrecognized, defensive 'goings-astray' (Laplanche,
1999, p.60), specifically in response to the challenge that comes from
those experienced as 'other'. Laplanche's idea is that just like individuals
might turn away from the impending awareness of something that
disturbs them, so psychoanalysis itself, starting with Freud, has ducked

a full encounter with 'otherness'. This 'domestication of the unconscious' (Laplanche, 1999, p.67) that places the unconscious in the control of the subject (i.e. that suggests that it is possible to master the unconscious) is always present in Freudian thought, in Laplanche's view, for a very specific reason: it reflects the tendency of the human subject – and hence of Freud too – to withdraw from insights that are too disturbing, in particular from recognition of the essentially alien nature of human subjectivity. In Laplanche's account, the key issues that are denied are the 'radical otherness of the unconscious and sexuality' (Fletcher, 1999, p.3), but we can perhaps extend this here to suggest that psychoanalysis has never quite been able to free itself from a distancing approach to 'otherness' and that this is because it has some of its own roots in a set of assumptions about the superiority of so-called 'civilized' society over what Freud (1913, p.1) calls the 'savage'.

Focusing on colonialism, the summary argument is that psychoanalysis carries with it colonial ideas that are to some degree hidden from sight, yet still influence its concepts and its constructions of the human subject. This does not mean that it is straightforwardly colonialist or racist; indeed, part of the point is that the ambiguities of postcolonial culture are reflected in ambiguities within psychoanalysis itself, which both holds onto some core colonialist tropes whilst also proving useful to the emergence of a decolonizing consciousness. Anderson, Jenson and Keller (2011), introducing their book on the postcolonial uses and critiques of psychoanalysis and ethnopsychiatry, comment on how psychoanalysis reflects (and implements) some central colonial *and* anticolonial impulses. Their view is that psychoanalysis was deployed in colonial settings to differentiate between 'civilized modern' and 'primitive native' subjects in terms of relative psychological sophistication, thus endorsing colonial views, but that it also offered a set of analytic tools for those who were critically evaluating colonialism and who were engaged in shaping postcolonial subjectivities.

> From the 1920s, psychoanalysis was a mobile technology of both the late colonial state and anti-imperialism. Insights from psychoanalysis shaped European and North American ideas about the colonial world, the character and potential of 'native' cultures, and the anxieties and alienation of displaced white colonizers and sojourners. Moreover, intense and intimate engagement with empire came to shape the apparently generic psychoanalytic subjectivities that emerged in the twentieth century – whether European or non-European.
>
> (Anderson, Jenson and Keller, 2011, pp.1–2)

Without tracing this dynamic in detail, the argument that psychoanalysis both embodies (some) colonialist assumptions and fuels the possibility of revealing and critiquing these, is an important one that is also borne out by the use of psychoanalysis by some significant postcolonial critics (e.g. Bhabha, 1991; Khanna, 2004). Nevertheless, psychoanalysis's analytic capacity to advance decolonizing thought is significantly inhibited by its continuing adherence to some unspoken colonialist allegiances, especially in its understanding of otherness. This applies particularly clearly in relation to an inveterate association between 'primitivity' and violence. In what follows, this association is explored as one primary instance (another one might be the versions of sexuality as 'impulse' or uncontrollable 'drive' that can be found in psychoanalytic theory) of the 'unconscious' repetition of patterns of colonialist thought. Deconstruction of 'primitivity' is vital to a decolonizing psychoanalysis as its presence as a core organizing concept is detrimental to the agenda of decolonization. This in turn has implications for psychoanalysis's understanding of Jewishness and of antisemitism, especially through the notion of 'barbarism', as well as its wider comprehension of anti-Black racism.

Freudian savagery

A lot of work has been done on the issue of Freud's use of the terms 'savage' and 'primitive', particularly in his 'anthropological' writings, and I have discussed this in detail elsewhere (Frosh, 2013a). Key to this is Freud's understanding of the source of violence in psychic life. In speculating on the historical foundation of 'civilization', Freud took up a position that violence lies at the core of social and personal formations, enacted in a revolt of the sons against the primeval father that marks the earliest dynamics of the 'primal horde'. The killing of this original father described in the Freudian 'just-so story' of the origins of society in *Totem and Taboo* (1913) and in the parallel tale of the killing of Moses in *Moses and Monotheism* (1939), his book on Judaism, shows up as Freud's attempt to explain the inheritance of a destructive element in social relations that derive from the earliest moment of species-experience. This is not a 'symbolic' statement, though it is often taken to be a psychoanalytic myth or metaphor. For Freud, there was a big and urgent question of atavism (Slavet, 2009), of how the recurrence of past events in the present might explain the intensity of violence in contemporary society that so often seems excessive to the situation.

This phenomenon, he believed, could only be understood through the lens of Lamarckianism, the 'inheritance of acquired characteristics' or more precisely here the transmission across generations of the legacy of trauma. We are still fighting the battles of the past; we are, in that sense, haunted by the ghosts of our ancestors and this explains why, for example, reactions to trauma or the 'behaviour of neurotic children towards their parents in the Oedipus and castration complex' can be so passionate – they are not only about what is experienced in the here-and-now, but are also connected to 'the experience of earlier generations' (Freud, 1939, p.99). In some respects this is an unexpected argument for Freud to make, in that the practice of psychoanalysis involves careful tracing out of the relationship between neurotic children and adults and their parents and immediate others, and one usually thinks of this as a process of gaining insight into behaviour by reference to the specifics of a person's biography and fantasy life, not through speculations about heritability. Laplanche (1989, p.34), for one, denies that Freud's appeal to the inheritance of acquired characteristics is even Lamarckian, in part because 'the phylogenetic heritage does not consist of characteristics or of improvements to an apparatus, but of scenarios which live on in a sort of *memory* ... primal fantasies may flesh out the individual's memory, and they are situated at the level of memory, not the level of function'.

Why does Freud need to appeal to prehistory and a kind of inherited traumatic memory in order to explain contemporary people's behaviour? Could he not, as Laplanche might advocate, focus instead on the actual experiences of infants, looking for the justification for children's intense responses in the reality of their social and interpersonal situation? In clinical practice and in his case histories, that is in fact largely how Freud worked, consequently avoiding any need to appeal to inheritance or his dubious mythology of the prehistoric world. Yet what Freud does here is not so much pursue what he regards as the inadequacy of explanation at the level of the individual's experience, but rather try to map the personal unconscious as full of traces of a founding communal violence that is irresolvable because it is *repeated* for everyone. In effect, we have a theory of collective trauma: the whole species (or in the case of the Jews in *Moses and Monotheism*, the people) encounters an overwhelming act of violence which marks it forever; we are not aware of this because it is held as a kind of unconscious knowledge; but as each of us catches a glimpse of the violence in our individual (Oedipal) relationships, so the shadowing enormity of the original violence returns. This is a model of traumatic inheritance built on 'après-coup' or 'afterwardsness', a temporality of repetition: something happens, we are never aware of it fully; but as we encounter the relatively small echoes of it in everyday life, we find ourselves responding excessively, unaware that it is the original formation that is in operation. For Freud at least, what happens takes the shape of a murder.

The idea that violence is implicated in the foundation of society is of course not unique to Freud but is also present in a wide range of theories that base their understanding of the social on an exclusionary process, one in which some people are allowed inside the boundary of the group and others are not (Palacios, 2013). In this sense, all social formations are violent in that they differentiate between those who can participate and those who are left outside; and these others then form an opposition that might be derogated or might become a threat and indeed might inflict actual or symbolic harm on the group. Psychoanalysis adds to this an account of how violence operates within the domain of the individual as well as the social: there is hardly any version of psychoanalytic theory that does not invoke violence and destructive aggression as a major element in the drive towards development. For Kleinians, for example, the intricacies of violence are very pronounced, as the death drive comes into the foreground and envy – seen as the pure 'representative' of the death drive – is made foundational to the functioning and organization of the mind. 'I consider that envy is an oral-sadistic and anal-sadistic expression of destructive impulses,' writes Klein (1957, p.176), 'operative from the beginning of life, and that it has a constitutional basis'. But even for Donald Winnicott – who is often seen as on the 'softer' side of object relational thinking and is highly influential in American intersubjectivist and relational psychoanalysis as well as in the British tradition – aggression and destructiveness are central to development, for example as a way of 'testing' the resilience of the maternal object in fantasy (Winnicott, 1969). What is at issue here is not the detail of one theory over another, but how psychoanalytic thinking about the foundations of the mind and hence of human subjectivity places so much emphasis on violence. That this vision of the human subject might be accurate is not quite the point, though it has to be said that the question of how to survive violence without responding violently is a core one for studies of human subjectivity and of ethics (Butler, 2009). What is more relevant here is how psychoanalysis drew from its social surroundings in making violence so central, and how this embedded in it assumptions about otherness and 'primitivity' that continue to resonate. Specifically, it worked with a set of equations that made violence foundational to society and the foundations of society equivalent to the supposedly savage and primitive *contemporary* cultures that were identified as such in the colonial imagination of the early twentieth century. Freud's well-known opening of *Totem and Taboo* is worth repeating in this context:

> There are men still living who, as we believe, stand very near to primitive man, far nearer than we do, and whom we therefore regard as his direct heirs and representatives. Such is our view of those whom we describe as savages or half-savages; and their mental life must have a peculiar interest for us if we are right in seeing in it a well-preserved picture of an early stage of our own development.
>
> (Freud, 1913, p.1)

According to Freud, this applies to many aspects of 'our own development', but especially to the relationship with violence.

Primitive remains

To return to the main argument, psychoanalysis warrants consideration as a theory that is infected by colonialist assumptions about violence yet positions itself as a project of enlightenment. In this context, psychoanalysis's theorizing of violence is underpinned by certain assumptions that 'unconsciously' reproduce the terms of a colonial imagination. For Freud, psychoanalysis was an emancipatory practice that would bring illumination and reveal the infantilism at the source of so much individual and social behaviour. The insight thus obtained would be a way of taming the unconscious and using its energy in the pursuit of a more creative, more 'civilized' world. This has barely happened, of course, and in Freud's lifetime it became clear that the European world was slipping into barbarism – with Freud himself caught up amongst the victims. The traces of this in psychoanalytic theory are very pronounced, and none of it should really have been a surprise. Indeed, they are theorized premonitorily in *Civilisation and its Discontents* (Freud, 1930): society is hypocritical, the unconscious is at loggerheads with it; there is little likelihood of dramatic change; violence is the source and origin of the social; death comes to dominate us all. If barbarism breaks down the 'garrison' of civilization, it can hardly come as a shock to those who devote their intellectual and professional energy to tracing the impossibility of coming to terms with the unconscious. But let us go a little further, too, in thinking through Freud's and psychoanalysis' positioning of the space of violence and savagery. For this word – 'savage' – is quite a key one in the formation of psychoanalysis.

As already noted, Freud's (1913) adoption of a binary differentiation between 'savage' and 'primitive' on the one side, and 'civilized' on the other, has been discussed extensively in many places, as has the way in which this 'colonial' discourse is disrupted by the Freudian assertion of the presence of 'primitivity' within every subject, however ostensibly 'civilized' they may be, in the form of an unconscious that does not obey the dictates of rationality (Frosh, 2013a). What emerges even from a preliminary examination of Freud's work on the 'primitive' is how closely aligned this idea is to that of the unconscious and hence how weak can be the division between the savage and the civilized. The unconscious runs through all of us – this is indeed one of the ways in which the apparent boundaries between and within subjects dissolve. Akshi Singh (2018, p.52) comments on this that:

> The "primitive" may occasionally be the fall guy in Freud's attempt to hold on to a progressivist view of civilisation, but he cannot be done away with so easily. Psychoanalysis, Freud writes, dealing as it does with the unconscious, with problems of death and mourning "has itself become uncanny to many people". In saying this, he suggests an intimacy between the primitive and psychoanalysis: it is as though the primitive is the double of psychoanalysis: they come to occupy the same uncanny place.

Psychoanalysis uncannily evokes primitivity, meshing the colonial and racist associations of the 'primitive' with its own critical commentary on psychosocial reality. In this way, psychoanalysis deploys the notion of the 'primitive' as a means of demarcating the contrasting state of 'civilization', yet it also carries primitivity into the heart of that very civilization, portraying 'civilized' subjects in the same terms as it describes the so-called 'savage'.

Freud (1921, p.123) extends this when discussing group psychology, where he again aligns the fundamental dynamics of modern subjects with those of the primal horde. For Freud, just as modern individuals repeat in the unconscious the battles of the past, so the groups we see today dramatize the same passions as the groups of prehistory, once again revealing how frail is the distinction between 'primitive' and 'civilized'.

[I]n so far as men are habitually under the sway of group formation we recognize in it the survival of the primal horde. We must conclude that the psychology of groups is the oldest human psychology; what we have isolated as individual psychology, by neglecting all traces of the group, has only since come into prominence out of the old group psychology, by a gradual process which may still, perhaps, be described as incomplete.

Groups come before individuals, and the groups we know today are in important respects a recapitulation of the 'primal horde' of the primitive past. Freud goes on immediately to qualify this by arguing that the leader of the primal horde was a genuine individual, not bound up in the libidinal ties and identifications that link each member of the group with one another in a 'horizontal' fashion but living outside the rule of the group. Yet whilst the leader is an individual, group psychology remains primary, and as Freud (1921, p.69) says elsewhere, 'from the very first individual psychology ... is at the same time social psychology as well.' The leader is the individualized exception who makes the group possible. 'Even to-day,' Freud writes (1921, p.69), 'the members of a group stand in need of the illusion that they are equally and justly loved by their leader; but the leader himself need love no one else, he may be of a masterful nature, absolutely narcissistic, self-confident and independent.' But the point is a more general one: contemporary group and individual psychology is structured along lines inherited from the primal horde, breaking down the division between what was 'then' and what is 'now' and in so doing undermining firm divisions between 'advanced' and 'primitive' societies. The unconscious runs through groups and individuals, patterning identifications and combining ego ideals in both 'vertical' (parental) and 'horizontal' (sibling) relationships, making libidinal bonds the source of group alliances. It is not regressive loss of boundaries that creates groups out of individuals, but the structuring of relationships in certain ways – ways in which people bind together in love for each other and for a leader and maximize these bonds through their exclusion of others. This is a primordial phenomenon, 'the survival of the primal horde'. The 'oldest human psychology' haunts people today as a remainder from 'savage' times and a reminder that our connections with and against others is deeply buried in our psychic structure.

Freud's account of the primal horde and its relevance for contemporary society has these contradictory elements in it: on the one hand, utilization of the classic colonial binary of civilized-primitive; on the other subverting this binary by arguing that all individual and group phenomena show 'survival of the primal horde'. The colonial side of this is evident in the way in which this imagery of savagery and primitivism is reproduced in accounts of violence, with the effect of running together the ideas of the primitive 'other' of colonialism and the violent elements in all human subjects. That is to say, where destructiveness is observed, it is commonly interpreted as a reflection of 'primitive' elements of the subject and accretes around it associations and fantasies of the 'uncivilized' other to which the colonial mentality is well attuned. Thus, the opposition between 'civilization' and 'the individual's dangerous desire for aggression' as expressed in *Civilization and Its Discontents* is a foundational one (Freud, 1930, p.124), as is the notion of the death drive as something that *returns* as a primordial situation, associated with fantasies about dissolution. Hence Freud's (1919, pp.241–2) gloss on death: 'Since almost all of us still think as savages do on this topic, it is no matter for surprise that the primitive fear of the dead is still so strong within us and always ready to come to the surface on any provocation.' This 'regressive' framework, assuming a kind of descent into savagery, is present too in the Kleinian fascination with destructiveness, which is made consequent upon an inbuilt death drive that produces envy as a 'primitive' affect linked with attacks on the maternal object. (Notably, Klein deploys the notion of 'primitive' freely to describe early, passionate affects and desires; but she also uses it in the same way as does Freud, as in opposition to 'civilized'. For example, she writes: 'Another question applies to the effect of late weaning, as is customary with primitive peoples and also in certain sections of civilized communities' – Klein, 1952, p.119.) The 'positive' move in Kleinian developmental theory through the depressive position and into reparation retains a sense of needing to overcome impulsivity through managing more complex (one might call them 'civilized') thought patterns that tolerate uncertainty and ambivalence in a way assumed to be difficult for children to manage. Under the conditions that prevailed in these great moments of formation of seminal psychoanalytic theories – and that still exert significant influence today – the idea of 'primitive' thinking and emotion slips easily into the figure of *the* 'primitive', who by virtue of precisely this 'primitivity' (irrationality, impulsivity, etc.) becomes the antagonist to the civilized. Only certain colonized individuals – 'elite natives' with complex and conflicted psyches that could be subjected to psychoanalysis – are potential citizens; the others are infantilized in their childlike consciousness, justifying European dominance in everyone's interests.

There are many ways to defend psychoanalysis against the charge of simple colonialism, which I have been doing in insisting on the breakdown of the distinction between 'civilized' and 'primitive' forced by the assumption of the universality of the unconscious in human psychic life, however 'advanced' the culture is supposed to be. As mentioned above, the leverage on colonial assumptions provided by psychoanalysis is testified to by the adoption of psychoanalysis by many postcolonial thinkers (Khanna, 2004; 2011; Frosh, 2013a). Nevertheless, something disturbing recurs here. Andersen, Jenson and Keller (2011), whose edited book is an eloquent testimony to ways in which psychoanalysis has been used as part of the decolonizing movement, also show how it sustains an understanding of 'primitivity' that faces both ways, carrying forward what is effectively a racist account of the colonized but also revealing how the genuine 'heart of darkness' lies on the side of the colonizer. Tracing the complex manner in which this happens, Andersen et al note how psychoanalysis expresses some of the patterns of post-First World War destructiveness in terms familiar from colonialism.

> If a central project of psychoanalysis was to demonstrate the universality of its central tenets, then finding vestigial traces of such 'primitive' characteristics as the incest taboo, filial ambivalence, fetishism, and the tension between the indulgence and repression of the drives in modern Westerners provided an explanatory logic for the evolution of the 'family of man'. The irruption of savagery among the civilized was less pathology than it was atavism ...
>
> (Andersen et al, 2011, p.11)

Even though 'psychoanalysis, as practiced and elaborated in colonial settings and, particularly, as adopted and adapted in the emergent postcolony, became reconfigured as a powerful critique of colonialism' (Andersen et al, 2011, p.11), it only did this by carrying forward the previous vision of otherness in terms of the primitive and savage – which has to do with the norms of a colonial society in which Black and brown others were seen as undeveloped and infantile. In an associated way the unconscious was understood as passionate, wishful, uncontained and immature, and violence as a form of 'atavism' was linked with primitive remains. Whilst other psychoanalytic schools (for example, intersubjectivists and possibly Lacanians) show less dependence on the primitive-civilized binary, the point is that psychoanalysis carries over the traces of this binary as it moves forward into the postcolonial era. In relation to the spread of psychoanalysis beyond its original European and North American heartlands, the continuing pull of colonial assumptions can also be found.

For example, in one of the most densely psychoanalytic cultures in the world, urban Brazil, there is a clear history of psychoanalysis as a 'civilizing' force that reinforces colonialism as well as providing tools for resistance, in much the way that Andersen et al. (2011) describe in the quotation immediately above. As will be discussed again in Chapter 5, early Brazilian psychoanalysis was embedded in a vision of nation-building that tackled questions of racial mix and sexuality as primary concerns of a society emerging from slavery and supposed primitivism (Russo, 2012a). This history of Brazilian psychoanalysis was reshaped through encounters with authoritarianism and social control during the twentieth century, resulting in a set of theoretical and practical concerns that were characteristically split between a conservative, 'conforming' psychoanalysis tied to normalizing visions of 'race' and sexuality (that is, psychoanalysis as a tool for social control) and a more critical psychoanalysis offering support for resistance to authoritarian dictatorship. One consequence was a tension that arose during the Brazilian dictatorship of 1964–85 between the official institutions of psychoanalysis and much of its clientele. Russo (2012b, p.174), for example, noting the contrast between the psychoanalytic promise of individual 'liberation' and the conformism of the psychoanalytic societies, comments: 'The silence or even the connivance of the "official" societies with regard to the military dictatorship was a hallmark of psychoanalysis in Brazil ... "official" psychoanalysis ... became a symbol of political conservatism at a time when psychoanalysis – at its height – was regarded as an instrument of liberation by a good number of its clients.' This history will be returned to, but whilst it is specific it is not unique. Similar tensions occurred, for example, in Argentina (Plotkin, 2012), although the story there showed different colonialist dynamics, as psychoanalysis was deployed to reinforce the idea of a 'European' dominant class. The ambiguities of psychoanalysis are revealed again in this material: on the one hand, adopting the vision of a 'savage' racialized society in which passions run high and need to be channelled and controlled; on the other, asserting the psychoanalytic vision of the reduction of repression and emancipation of desire as a universal prescription for greater human well-being.

Colonial and emancipatory dilemmas

The idea that psychoanalysis has its own 'unconscious' in which social assumptions are embedded is no more and no less metaphorical than the idea that any individual person has an unconscious. We cannot see this thing, the unconscious, in any way; we know, in fact, that it does not actually exist as a physical entity. Instead, it is evident from what people say and do, in their guarded as well as their unguarded moments, that stuff happens, it seeps through and the process of understanding it is always retrospective. The claim here is that we can see such 'seeping through' in the theory of psychoanalysis, and no doubt elsewhere too (for example, in institutional practices and clinical work) if we take the time to look for it. This seeping through has a number of forms, but the one emphasized here is the link psychoanalysis makes between violence and primitivity, a link that has its origins in Freud's thought and in the social forces of his day but is reproduced in later psychoanalysis and continues to freight contemporary discussions.

I suggested at the start of this chapter that whilst unconscious forces operate in all disciplinary formations, psychoanalysis's attempt to articulate and control them might particularly provoke them into action. Freud's apparent reluctance to acknowledge the unconscious ('we have been *obliged* to assume,' he wrote (Freud, 1923, p.14, my italic), 'that very powerful mental processes or ideas exist … which can produce all the effects in mental life that ordinary ideas do … though they themselves do not become conscious'), whether rhetorical or real, might entail a recognition of how the theory of the unconscious is a provocation. Psychoanalysis presents itself as a discipline of tentative mastery, but what is evident is that it has its own blind spots. Other work (feminist and queer) has shown how these include gender and sexuality, two dimensions that are central to psychoanalytic thought and yet have also proved to be hothouses for contestation. In this chapter I have concentrated on another such blind spot, that of colonialism. Directly and indirectly, it keeps looming into sight. I have argued that the colonial elements of psychoanalysis's heritage are visible in its conceptualization of violence, and specifically in thinking of violence as an 'atavistic' reproduction of a foundational savagery that, in its imagery and in its substance, is caught up with divisions between civilized and barbaric with very particular sociohistorical resonances. I have also tried to hold close to the idea that psychoanalysis can offer ways of thinking about violence that can aid the postcolonial project, which I take to be an emancipatory one. Specifically, the resistance shown in psychoanalysis to what Laplanche (1999) refers to as the 'Copernican' vision of the subject as necessarily permeated by the other is a resistance that can be analysed and understood – as he tries to do – in relation to the disruption the other causes to the ego's search for control. Building a psychoanalysis that is alert to the functions of otherness is not only a clinical task, reflected in contemporary work across a variety of psychoanalytic 'schools' that emphasize relationality and intersubjectivity (e.g. Benjamin, 2018); it is also a social and political task. It asks questions of psychoanalysis about how its original assumptions about the 'primitive' other are maintained in its ongoing conceptualization of the human subject; it particularly focuses attention on what these assumptions produce in relation to how violence is understood; and it suggests ways in which these 'unconscious' assumptions might be unpicked to enable psychoanalysis to offer more cogent accounts of violence in society.

Examining psychoanalysis's core assumptions about the human subject is a necessary step in opening it out as a means towards embracing encounters with those who previously have been othered by it. This has numerous ramifications for discussions not only of colonialism, but also of wider forms of racism. The unaddressed legacies of the assumptions prevalent in the culture out of which psychoanalysis arose still circulate, haunting psychoanalysis and blocking its potential for emancipatory antiracist practice. The 'primitive' or 'savage' is probably the most important of such legacies in the context of racism, applying mostly to anti-Black racism. In the case of antisemitism, the parallel tropes are those of insularity, scheming and sexual licentiousness, carried over into psychoanalysis through images such as the 'miser' (Frosh, 2011) as well as applied *to* psychoanalysis as a 'Jewish science' (Frosh, 2005a). This dynamic is certainly different in that Jews have historically been seen as appropriate subjects for psychoanalysis whereas, through the assumption of primitivity, Black people on the whole have not (though see the discussion of black psychoanalysis in Chapter 5). As already argued, there is a significant Jewish influence on the history and values of psychoanalysis; in this regard, psychoanalysis's colonial fantasies have been more damaging than its more occasional derogation of Jews and Judaism. This presents a challenge to psychoanalysis to confront its hidden colonialist values, something that the kinds of 'Jewish' ethics discussed earlier in this book can help it to do. It requires appreciation of, and resistance to, antisemitism as well as other forms of racism, or the potential for a positive encounter between Jews and others will be lost. This is the direction in which my argument goes now, but just to reiterate before moving on: psychoanalysis is grounded in a colonial outlook as well as in an emancipatory one, and the former needs to be recognized and combatted if the latter is to be facilitated. As we will see in the next chapter, the Jewishness of psychoanalysis is also to some extent bound up in this, at times contributing to the colonial move, at others offering grounds from which to dismantle it. If this can be kept at the frame, and in particular if the parallel histories of oppression, with all their important differences, can be understood, then the possibility of solidarity is raised both within and through psychoanalysis.

Chapter 5

RACIALIZED EXCLUSIONS, OR 'PSYCHOANALYSIS EXPLAINS'

Excluding Jews

Exclusions take place across many domains – sexuality, gender, class, nationality – and in many circumstances. All these need to be observed and documented, but it is probably fair to say that the racialization of exclusion is paramount. With regard to psychoanalysis, the exclusion, or at least the marginality, produced by antisemitism was a crucial context for its development and has also haunted psychoanalysis throughout its history. Antisemitism shares some of the characteristics of all racisms (stereotyping, paranoid fantasies of contamination and corruption, violent imaginings and practices, and so on) yet also has its own specific dynamics. Slavery does not really feature (despite the founding biblical myth of the Exodus), but the exclusion of Jews from the realm of the human did not begin with the Nazis. If the dehumanization of the Black subject was a foundation for colonialism, the pursuit of Jews into colonial areas was one of the features of the same historical period: the main target of the Inquisition in Latin America as well as in Spain and Portugal were the so-called crypto-Jews whose existence, both real and imagined, threatened to corrupt the self-proclaimed truth of the Christian church. As noted in earlier chapters, this linkage of anti-Black racism and antisemitism (both of these terms being anachronistic to this original context) continues into the current era, despite the immense shifts in the position especially of many Western Jewish communities in terms of affluence and security and the complications for anti-oppressive political alliances created by the policies of the State of Israel. For white racists, who might support Israel as part of their anti-Black, anti-Muslim and anti-Palestinian agenda, Jews are still the arch-enemy, for example the force behind so-called white replacement and the imagined 'flooding' of the West by migrants ('You will not replace us' merging with 'the Jews will not replace us' in the alt-right demonstrations of Trump-era America). Because the antisemitic and anti-Black stereotypes involve

Jews being clever and manipulative and Black people being 'primitive' and manipulable, the sources of racial unease and threat are assumed to be Jewish, flowing from an international conspiracy to rule the world, with one powerful Jewish tactic being undermining of the 'white race' through destructive immigration. The complexity of the question of how Jews feature as non-white in this phantasmagoria, but as white in most anti-racist discourse, is marked (see Chapter 6); the point here, however, is that the Jewish-Black 'alliance' in terms of being the excluded other is both historical and contemporary.

This is not to deny the differences, of course: anti-Judaism was a precursor of antisemitism that relied primarily on *religious* discrimination with especially strong Christian forms (Muslim anti-Judaism was more variable and was marked by more pronounced periods of inactivity and relative tolerance of Jews (Nirenberg, 2013)). Nancy (2020, p.49) comments,

> For centuries, then, in the best-case scenario, the Jews will be thought of as the poor wretches who have been led away from the true God; and, in the worst-case scenario, they will be seen as schemers determined to fight against him. At best, Christians will wish for them to convert – the very best minds desired this over and over again; and, at worst, they will wish for their disappearance.

Whilst this also applied to colonial forced conversion and genocide of indigenous peoples – who as we have seen were sometimes understood as 'Jewish' (Slabodsky, 2014) – Christian supersessionism, which is discussed further in Chapter 6, ensured that the attitude towards Jews was to regard them as excluded, or having somehow excluded themselves, from the community of the saved, and therefore that they were abhorrent living ghosts, relics of a pre-salvific time that by their very existence denied theological truth. Conversion could help remedy Jewish obscurantism, but as the Inquisition demonstrated, not securely or convincingly. Christianity re-read Judaism through its own eyes, a fact that amongst other things shows how the term 'Judeo-Christian' when applied to 'Western civilization' is at best a misnomer, at worst a way of reinforcing the obliteration of a specifically Jewish history and consequently a form of antisemitism in itself. For some, such as Lentin (2020), the use of the term 'Judeo-Christian' is a way of obscuring 'Christianity's antisemitism and rewrit[ing] the history of Europe to exclude Islam and Muslims' (p.148); more parochially, it denies the ongoing vibrancy and particularity of Judaism and Jewish life.

The division between white Christian and Jew was arguably the primary racialized division in Europe until the mid-twentieth century, however significant anti-Black racism built on slavery also was, yet this is often overlooked in the contemporary positioning of at least Ashkenazi (European) Jews as 'white', an issue discussed in the next chapter. In contrast, as Brickman (2003) notes, there is plenty of evidence of the association between Blackness and Jews, at least until the Holocaust. She comments (p.15), 'The rhetorics of colonialism and antisemitism converged: in Freud's Vienna, the language of racial inferiority was used not only for dark-skinned peoples in such places as Africa, Australia, and the Americas but also for the Jews of Europe, who were variously described as "Oriental," "primitive," "barbarian," "white Negroes," "mulatto," and "a mongrel race."' Sander Gilman (1991) has documented this most thoroughly, arguing that in the popular antisemitic mindset in Europe from the mid-nineteenth century onwards, 'being black, being Jewish, being diseased, and being "ugly" come to be inexorably linked' (p.173). As we shall see, the absorption of Jews into whiteness has its own motivations and effects; the point here is to recall that this is a relatively recent phenomenon, and a precarious one at that. Blackness and Jewishness have a history of encounter that includes seeing Jews as Black.

Freud and 'race'

In a recent volume dedicated to the relationship between psychoanalysis and liberation psychology, which amongst other things demonstrates how strong an influence the former was on the latter, Daniel José Gaztambide (2019) sympathetically discusses Freud's own appreciation of American Black struggles with racism, documenting Freud's awareness in this field to offset other demonstrations of his rootedness in colonial modes of thought.

> Freud's conception of his Jewish identity within his immediate historical context, was one of belonging to a people who sustained constant marginalization due to European society's imaginary and mythical equation of Jewishness and Blackness, a relationship Freud in his own myth-making saw the Jewish people repressed time and again in their collective memory, yet which returned time and again without end.
>
> (p.82)

The association of Jewishness with Blackness, which Gaztambide proposes is often 'repressed' by Jews themselves, is usually understood as I have done here, as a relation mediated by antisemitism. Within psychoanalysis, the argument runs that the 'Jewish science', because of its origins in the marginalized and minoritized history of the Jews in Europe, can be both sympathetic to and inspirational of Black struggle. There is a good deal of truth in this claim; Gaztambide again comments: 'When read through the lens of liberation psychology, Freud's Jewishness and that of the first generations of psychoanalysis provides a fascinating entry point to understanding the relationship between psychoanalysis and social justice' (p.5).

Yet Gaztambide pushes this parallel more strongly than just seeing Freud's and psychoanalysis' immersion in antisemitism as a prompt for its analysis of anti-Black racism and its siding with the oppressed, by suggesting that Freud's identification with Blackness was substantive in its own right. 'The relationship between Blackness and Jewishness,' he claims (p.25), 'occupied Freud's mind, and it would seem, that of the early psychoanalysts as well.' There is some evidence for this. Gaztambide draws, for example, on a clinical note by Lawrence Ginsburg (1999) that describes 'Fragments from the analyses of two American psychiatrists (whose formative years were centered in the post-Civil War South).' This suggests that 'Although the European anti-Semitism faced by Sigmund Freud was particularly relevant to his personal and professional identities, he was not unmindful of conflictual "race, creed and color" paradigms peculiar to the "New World"' (Ginzburg, 1999, p.243). Ginzburg describes two racialized encounters in the analyses of these two Americans, Clarence P. Oberndorf and Smiley Blanton. In Obendorf's case, the focus was a dream in which, as he reported,

> I was on the driver's seat of an old-fashioned country wagon drawn
> by a white horse and a black horse. From this Freud made the
> inference that my life had unconsciously been under the influence
> of two fathers, a white father Joe, and a black father Joe, our Negro
> coachman who had been a slave but who taught me many things
> besides currying a horse and riding bareback.
>
> (Ginzburg, 1999, p.244)

It seems that Obendorf resisted this racialized interpretation of his dream for some time before Freud got fed up with him and discontinued the analysis. In Blanton's case, the encounter seems to have been more whimsical, reflecting Freud's own concerns. Ginzburg (p.245) reports that 'After his ninth session with Freud on 9 September 1929, Blanton recorded the following exchange: At one point during the hour, Freud asked me if Jews were not put in the same category as Negroes. I said I had not met with this comparison. Freud said, "I often have!"' Ginzburg's interpretation of this is as follows:

> The colloquy excerpted from Blanton's *Diary of My Analysis with Sigmund Freud* seems to concern itself more with Freud's own ethnological dilemma (How white is one's Jewish skin according to the rules of American racism?) than Blanton's emotional universe. Blanton's observation that 'Jews were not (i.e., according to his American experiences) put in the same category as Negroes' (parenthesized clause inserted for clarity) did not leaven Freud's later theorizing in *Moses and Monotheism* about the Pharonic origins of the Jewish faith.
>
> (p.247)

Gaztambide (2019, p.27), expanding this, suggests that 'Putting together Blanton's and Oberndorf's vignettes we can see that Freud (1) was cognizant of the association between Jewishness and Blackness in his European cultural milieu, and (2) was able to think clinically about how a Jewish patient struggled with the libidinal cathexis of a racially grounded ambivalence between Blackness and Whiteness.' More generally,

> In his own discussion of his 'Moorishness,' the associations between Jewishness and Blackness, and discussions with colleagues over anti-Semitism and anti-Black racism, Freud evidenced his identification with Blackness as a Jew. In his clinical work, we can see his ability to interpret the triangulated relationship between a Jew and his struggle with an ambivalent conflict between Whiteness and Blackness structured by America's racial imaginary.
>
> (Gaztambide, 2019, p.29)

Again, there is something to be said in favour of this reading, even if it is founded on the relatively tenuous evidence of these two examples and may over-rate the significance of America for Freud. However, Gaztambide's reading of Freud's identification with Blackness as relatively sympathetic is challenged by alternative renderings of Freud as participating in a rewriting of racialization through which the opprobrium placed on Jews is displaced onto the Black subject. Not surprisingly, given the linguistic conventions of his time, Freud's own uses of the word 'black' in his writings do not refer to Black people – they mostly concern black hair or beards or clothes. His deployment of the more common term of his time, 'Negro', is also restricted, mainly to a racist joke that I will discuss shortly. Apart from this and some use of the term in *Totem and Taboo*, in which Black Africans and indigenous Australians are the topic, there is relatively little to distinguish Freud's attitudes from that of other liberal Europeans, although one early comment to his fiancée Martha about John Stuart Mill is interestingly ambiguous:

> In all his writings it never appears that the woman is different from the man, which is not to say she is something less, if anything the opposite. For example, he finds an analogy for the oppression of women in that of the Negro. Any girl, even without a vote and legal rights, whose hand is kissed by a man willing to risk his all for her love, could have put him right on this.
>
> (Freud, 1883, p.76)

Women have power over men, it seems; what this shows, at least, is that however familiarly sexist he might have been in his comments on women, which suggest that he did not see them as subjugated (he was clearly no feminist), Freud did at least appreciate the reality of the oppression of American Black people.

That said, a more compelling association comes from Freud's last great work, *Moses and Monotheism* (1939). This has been much discussed (e.g. Said, 2003; Frosh, 2005a) but for present purposes it is the famous claim by Freud that the biblical Moses was an Egyptian that is the key point. This is read by many, most notably Edward Said, as an indication of Freud's willingness to embrace a view of identity, including religious or ethnic identity – that is, in his case, Jewish identity – as given from outside, in the sense of being formed not as an intrinsic property of a person or group, but as a kind of intrusion, or at least an externally applied grid. As Said (2003, p.53) notes, this fractures any possible claims to an essential national or racial identity; it represents 'Freud's profound exemplification of the insight that even for the most definable, the most identifiable, the most stubborn communal identity – for him, this was the Jewish identity – there are inherent limits that prevent it from being fully incorporated into one, and only one, Identity.' This very convincing reading can be supplemented by an additional point, recognizable in Said's account but here articulated by Gaztambide (2019, p.79):

> Freud's positioning of Moses as a non-White, non-European, non-Jewish Other who constitutes Jewishness as such is also an attempt to reconcile a theme ... – the equation of Jewishness with Blackness, of being 'White-but-not-quite' ... Given how Egypt itself was *the geographical tissue that connected Africa, the Mediterranean, and Europe*, I argue that this reflects Freud's ambivalent attempt to rework his own relationship to Blackness, and the association embedded in his racist European culture between Blackness and Jewishness ... In this, his final text, Freud wrestles with a wound upon history which will not be forgotten, and which, in his eyes, impacted the Jewish people – the wound of anti-Blackness, anti-Semitism, and the quandary of the non-White.

The *Africanness* of Moses is a crucial point here, not to oppose one essential identity against another, but rather to disrupt the assumption that identity is something formed and solidified from within an already-established national or racialized group. Recall that Freud (1913) opposes the 'civilized' European to the 'savage' indigenous Australian or Black African; yet here we have this same 'savage' creating the monotheistic religion of Judaism, which for Freud was a high form of civilization, its prototype and most ethically sound manifestation. Psychoanalysis itself is identified with Judaism in Freud's last thoughts, as he draws parallels between the flight from Nazism and the Jews' exile after the destruction of the Temple in Jerusalem and their survival through study of their sacred texts (in his last speech to the Vienna Psychoanalytic Society, on 13 March 1938, he said, 'After the destruction of the Temple in Jerusalem by Titus, Rabbi Yochanan ben Zakkai asked for permission to open a school at Yavneh for the study of Torah. We are going to do the same' (Diller, 1991, p.206)). Thus, Africanness – Blackness – is the supposedly 'uncivilized' force that in actuality opposes fascism and Nazism and can be traced back to the origins of civilization itself, as the source of one of its highest achievements, and can even be seen as eventuating in psychoanalysis. The Jews are Black not just as an antisemitic trope of disparagement and exclusion from the European norm, but also as a culture that opposes the barbarism to which European society has reverted. In *Moses and Monotheism*, Freud posits that the demands of the Egyptian Moses on his people were too great for them to sustain, resulting in their assassination of him with subsequent regret and guilt and repression of the memory of the murderous act. Yet eventually, in Freud's own writings, the debt to this Moses comes back into focus and the Black source of Judaism is honoured. Gaztambide's (2019, p.82) summary focuses on this idea in an instructive way, even if its rendering of Freud's psychology is speculative. Freud, he writes, 'wrestles with his existential reality as a Jew by reconfiguring his relationship to Blackness as both cause of his depression (e.g. the association between anti-Jewishness and anti-Blackness), as well as a source of survival and liberation'.

Maybe; but even if this is not completely convincing as an analysis of Freud's 'own myth-making', or indeed of the argument that Freud was promoting an 'African' vision of Jewishness (consider, for instance, the dominant European artistic representation of Moses as white, albeit often with horns), it pounces on something that is productive in the theorizing of anti-oppressive relationships. This is the observation that the link between Jews and Black people is and has been one of overlapping identifications in the context of histories that certainly have their vital specificities (anti-Judaism, Black slavery), yet also have their productive and indissoluble alliances.

Joking aside

The argument that Freud embraced an alliance between his Jewishness and Blackness stumbles, however, on his ambivalences around 'race'. As noted, the primitive-civilized binary is one problem; another is the broader colonial position that he takes of 'othering' the Black African or indigenous Australian to make room for Jews as Europeans, that is, to put them in the place of Jews as the white Christian's 'other'. If the Jewish psychoanalyst and writer can position the 'savage' in Africa, then the Jew is no longer that savage and antisemitism – in fantasy, of course, not in reality – might fade away. This argument is powerfully articulated by Celia Brickman (2003), but her book was narrowly preceded by a seminal article by Claudia Tate (1996), concerned with a racist 'joke' by Freud. The joke is a crude one that Freud seems to have enjoyed, as he repeated it and heard it passed on by some of his followers. In a letter to Karl Abraham, Freud (1924, p.507) wrote, 'It was very opportune for me that you produced such appreciative words for Waldhaus Flims [a hotel Freud stayed at]. We booked there yesterday and want to arrive on 8 July. This time I am also taking with me a well-capitalized negro who will certainly not bother me more than that one hour in the day." This 'negro' was a white American; the reference, an editorial footnote quoting Ernest Jones explains, is to a colonial fantasy: when Freud began to practice, '[t]he consultation hour was at noon, and for some time patients were referred to as "negroes." This strange appellation came from a cartoon in the *Fliegende Blätter* depicting a yawning lion muttering "Twelve o'clock and no negro". On the surface, this 'joke' refers simply to the obvious truism that analysts rely on having patients for their income; but the racist framing demonstrates a specific social context and an underlying hostility, both to patients and to Black people. Tate (1996, p.54) traces the effect of this 'joke' as consolidation of racism within psychoanalysis:

> The first thing we notice is that by identifying himself with the lion and his patient as a "negro" whose purpose is to satisfy the lion's appetite, Freud has established (however unconsciously) an equation between the analyst/patient relationship and the most brutal form of the master/slave relationship, in which the slave is only a piece of meat to satisfy the master's ravenous appetite (for power, money, sex, aggression, or whatever).

The patient is a slave; the slave is at the mercy of the master; the patient is therefore at the mercy of the psychoanalyst, and the power dynamics of colonialism are reproduced in the consulting room. 'It is not difficult,' writes Tate (1996, p.54), 'to see why people who are still in many ways trying to escape the fate of slaves would be reluctant to embrace a practice that incorporates such a position at its very center.' Whilst psychoanalysis has of course mutated and developed, implementing professional regulations to protect patients from being 'eaten' and more recently widely adopting commitments to antiracism, albeit unevenly implemented (Malamed, 2022), the 'joke' lies at the heart of a foundational moment in psychoanalysis – the moment of Freud's articulation of psychoanalytic technique – and the attitudes lying behind it have had lasting effects.

Working psychoanalytically, in the sense of seeing a joke as symptomatic of an unconscious wish, Tate offers a detailed explanation of what it achieved for Freud, one that is in line with the argument that Freud was trying to distance himself and psychoanalysis from the derogated position of Jews in Europe.

> In addition to revealing the master/slave dimensions of psychoanalytic treatment, Freud's joke also reveals Freud's own racial anxiety, an

anxiety that, as others have pointed out, played a significant role in the way Freud and other Jewish analysts tried to position themselves and their practice in relation to Gentile society. Freud's own racism, in fact – and the master/slave aspects of psychoanalytic treatment that his racism invested in – can be seen as partly a defense against his anxiety about his own Jewish identity.

(Tate, 1996, p.54)

The position of Freud and fellow Jews as the abjected other of European antisemitism is well established; Tate's argument is that this fuels the project of psychoanalysis as a 'whitening' enterprise, which develops from Freud's personal Jewish anxiety and becomes especially marked once psychoanalysis reaches America. Initially, 'the joke's ironic performance of blackness allows Freud to stage his own white masculinity in the guise of the colonial master' (Tate, 1996, p.55). The repetition of the joke suggests that this does not work completely, that Freud's 'social anxiety' was not allayed by psychoanalysis – indeed, one might suggest, that it was made all the more prominent as psychoanalysis itself came under antisemitic attack. Once psychoanalysis migrated to America, a place of potent racial politics where the legacy of slavery makes the social dynamics of 'race' central to the experience of citizenship, the 'whitening' of 'Jewish' psychoanalysis created a distance between its adherents and the stain of Blackness with which it was born. In America, argues Tate,

> Freud's joke reconstitutes the polarized economy of power between Jewish therapy and ailment by transforming this relationship into a tripartite one of relative social privilege among whites, Jews, and Negroes before collapsing the triangular formulation into the simple polarity of white and black. This reconstitution has the effect of whitening the metaphorical blackness of Jewishness in direct proportion to the prominence of actual black bodies. Such prominence erases the Semitic blackness presumed by Aryans because Jews under these circumstances become absorbed into the category of whiteness. No doubt, such an exchange would seem like scapegoating to African Americans.

(p.57)

In this account, the racial anxiety of Freud as a Jew, revealed in his 'joke', produces a scapegoating process in which, in the American context, African Americans find themselves abjured as allies so that whiteness can be claimed. Tate moves on to connect this to the repudiation of femininity in Freud's work – the famous alignment of feminine sexuality with the 'dark continent' (Freud, 1925, p.244) – which again serves to redress an antisemitic slur, that the male Jew is feminized through castration (circumcision). 'Imaginary blackness masks Jewishness,' she writes (p.59), 'while the phallic deficiency of the female body not only affirms male plenitude but also confirms the masculinity of the Jewish male, as one who, in fact, possesses both the penis and the phallus.' Psychoanalysis is thus presented as a system through which a separation is induced between the racialized identification of Jewishness and Blackness, with the Black 'other' abandoned to be eaten by lions.

Tate's reading out from Freud's 'joke' to the dynamics of race is a provocative one that claims a legitimate basis for Black hostility towards psychoanalysis even as it consciously employs psychoanalytic methods in its analysis. It also treads on very sensitive ground, effectively making Jewishness – or at least Freud's response to his Jewishness – a contributor to anti-Black racism. How far this in itself is an antisemitic trope can be debated, as the idea is a very familiar one that Jews scheme in order to secure what advances they can. On a more positive note, the demonstration of the way in which psychoanalysis might be both part of the problem and part of the solution exemplifies the postcolonial as well as antiracist response to psychoanalysis, which provides tools for the deconstruction of the same colonial and racialized positions that it takes up. This can be seen in some of the responses to Tate's paper, for instance Daniel Gaztambide's (2022) reworking of some of its ideas in relation to his own Puerto Rican heritage. However, despite ending his piece with an evocation of the complexity of racialized identity and identifications, Gaztambide reads Tate as part of the 'Afropessimist' strand of thought, in which the desire for alliances between different oppressed groups is seen as disregarding the actual centrality of anti-Blackness to Western (notably American) society. The lesson Gaztambide takes from Tate's analysis of Freud's 'joke' is that:

> It is sometimes assumed that being a member of an oppressed group within a racial hierarchy would spur a natural desire to dismantle that hierarchy. The opposite would seem to be the norm. Put bluntly, while anti-Blackness serves as a central vehicle of oppression for non-Black colonial subjects – whether in Puerto Rico or Vienna – it does not necessarily lead to solidarity. Rather, the association with Blackness presents an injury, a symbolic castration that, in an attempt

at self-repair, reconstructs a desire for whiteness with anti-Blackness serving precisely as the vehicle for psychic and material uplift.

(Gaztambide, 2022, p.14)

This pits different oppressed groups against one another in what Jessica Benjamin (2016) calls 'only one can live' competitive victimhood and about which she notes (p.7), 'Our identification with the suffering of others can be interfered with by the identity of victimhood, in which a dissociated fear of forfeiting recognition plays a great role.' In this instance, it is anti-Black racism that is imagined at the 'top' of the pile of injustices and that is seen as being fuelled by the actions of all other groups, even those which might be expected to oppose it. 'Only one can live' is an all-against-all state of mind that inhibits popular front forms of social action.

From my point of view, seeking alliances, this is a depressing conclusion, envisaging psychoanalysis as a method to establish racial acceptance for Jews. This is at odds with the reading of Freud both as sympathetic to the Black-Jewish connection and combative in his frequent reiteration of his Jewish identity in the face of whatever antisemitic forces were ranged against him. Can the historical association between Jewishness and Blackness and the immersion of psychoanalysis in a Jewish ethics of inclusion rather than of racialized separatism enhance alliances between these groups, subjected to different forms of racism? Or is it actually the case that as psychoanalysis becomes absorbed into Western culture it also intentionally – if in important ways possibly 'unconsciously' and automatically – buys into a rhetoric of anti-Blackness? This latter position would indeed be congruent with the argument promoted by Afropessimism, that Black life is premised on anti-Black racism and is excluded from 'civilization' by the ubiquity and perennial nature of racism, which constructs Blacks as effectively not human. Here is Frank B. Wilderson III, one of the primary figures in Afropessimist thought:

> The Afro-pessimists are theorists of Black positionality who share Fanon's insistence that, though Blacks are ... sentient beings, the structure of the entire world's semantic field ... is sutured by anti-Black solidarity.
>
> (Wilderson, 2010, p.58)

The power of this claim about anti-Blackness is the way it articulates the impossibility of living outside the structures of racism. Slavery was the institutionalized origin of this, constructed by and feeding into the discourse of black non-humanity; in Paul Gilroy's (1993, p.63) words, slavery was and is 'the natal core of modern society'. The abolition of slavery did not change this – indeed, slavery has been perpetuated in the form of racial discrimination against Black people everywhere that colonialism operated. To use the trope activated by Christina Sharpe (2016) and discussed more fully in Chapter 8, we all live 'in the wake' of slavery, a wake that widens with time. Yet, pushing this further, those who are most in the wake – the descendants of slaves and the inheritors of the mantle of slavery – are still confined by it, so that they are distinct from those outside the wake, who are nevertheless impacted upon by its flow and force. Expressed more simply, let us just say that in this view, the lives of Black people are radically differentiated from the lives of white people; and the barrier between them, which is anti-Black racism, structures this differentiation as subjugation and exclusion.

Can we say that this really is the way the world is divided up? Some psychoanalytically inclined theorists, notably from the Lacanian school, have argued that there are parallels between Afropessimism and psychoanalysis. Thus, Karen Malone and Tiara Jackson (2022, p.205) open their complex and spirited comparison of the two with the assertion that:

Each field aims toward what cannot be spoken, residing in exile within the heart of subjective structuration. … The aim of both fields is to find the embodied residue subtending the social link, the residue from which that link parasitically feeds at an unconscious level; this is what binds the two fields. Afropessimism and psychoanalysis trace subjectivity up to and through the limits of its (non)creation.

The purport of this complicated statement is that both Lacanian psychoanalysis and Afropessimism are engaged in a ruthless act of interrogation in which the absence of the subject is confronted, that which is exiled or repudiated is named and brought into awareness, untamed. The argument, which focuses on parallels between the two approaches as a way of claiming their compatibility with one another, revolves around the idea that both Afropessimism and Lacanianism are alert to the insistent negation that is at the heart of subjectivity and of society as well. For Lacanians, there is a space outside language and the 'symbolic order', termed the Real, that is indefinable and unsymbolizable and yet marks the extremity of the human subject, that which is negated in order to make symbolic exchange possible.

Afropessimism, they argue, has the same structure, in that it posits that anti-Black racism is the central force in the construction of western culture and society, so that Black subjects are the excluded term, kept out from being symbolized or, perhaps more accurately, the negation against which the positivity of the western 'human subject' is measured. 'Antiblackness,' they write (ibid.), 'is, radically, the negation found at the emergence of the Symbolic's possibility.' Just as the symbolic order of language is built on the repression of the Real that would disrupt it, so the symbolic order of culture and society is built on the repression of Blackness. This both challenges psychoanalysis to confront the negativity embodied in blackness through the structuring produced by slavery and racism, and it offers Afropessimism an anchor in a theory that embraces this negativity in its conceptualization of the void at the heart of subjectivity. It also presents Blackness as the absolute other to society and deletes the prospect of an association with non-Black oppressed and racialized groups, all of whom share in some way in this exclusion. Gaztambide (2022, p.4), reflecting psychoanalytically on this, notes that 'For Afropessimists, ontological anti-Blackness renders non-Black people the beneficiaries of anti-Blackness and thus always already antagonists to Black people, making allyship and solidarity aporetic, asterisked propositions.' By 'ontological anti-Blackness' he references an Afropessimist claim of anti-Black racism as foundational and therefore of a different order to other racisms; the contrast is with 'ontological Blackness as the process by which oppressed people recognize their common humanity in the struggle against white supremacy' (p.2) – the stance that allows alliances to be formed.

Despite the claims of some antiracist psychoanalysts and psychoanalytic scholars such as Malone and Jackson that Afropessimism is congruent with their views, others have objected to the Afropessimist focus on negation. For instance, David McIvor (2020, p.44) summarizes some basic principles of Afropessimism and then comments that they 'seem fundamentally incommensurable with both the therapeutic ethic undergirding psychoanalysis and a democratic praxis of mourning'. McIvor draws on a Kleinian framework that emphasizes the importance of finding ways to integrate different aspects of the personality in the so-called 'depressive position' in order to deal with destructiveness, suffering and loss. Whilst offering the caveat that 'It is far too tempting to map Afropessimism using Klein's concept of "positions," to see the exaggerated and unceasing wakefulness as resting on paranoid-schizoid assumptions about social life and others,' McIvor goes on to wonder (ibid.), 'Yet it is the fantasy of annihilating the order of anti-Blackness – bringing about the end of the world – that animates the core of Afropessimism as articulated by Wilderson and others. Isn't a reparative politics of the depressive position inherently preferable to the sheer antagonism and cleansing violence of the paranoid-schizoid position?' To be fair, McIvor (p.45) immediately qualifies this apparently moralistic judgement by recognizing critically how it feeds into a pathologizing stance that 'deploys the authority of the (white) analyst to discipline and categorize a resistant analysand, and to interpret their resistances – towards mediation, commensuration, agency or compromise – as symptoms of an illness'. Afropessimism as the Black 'patient' patronized by the white analyst is the model here. Nevertheless, the stance McIvor takes is one in which the antagonisms articulated by Afropessimism would be better treated as a stage towards a necessary move towards mourning, attesting 'to the historical and enduring injuries of white supremacy while it directs hatred towards domination and loving repair towards the spaces and practices of self-government' (McIvor, 2020, p.46). It is mourning rather than rejectionism that mobilizes emancipation, in this view, something which will be returned to in Chapter 8 in the context of the 'wake'.

It is not for me to make a judgement on Afropessimism, though it is noteworthy that commentators from within Black Studies are not all convinced by it. Fred Moten (2013), for example, positioning himself as a sympathetic critic 'in apposition to Afro-pessimism' (p.739), clarifies and expands the Afropessimist notion that the Black subject is 'nothing' to demand that that 'nothing' is examined in its own terms for what it consists of – not, therefore, an absent nothing but a *present* one, with its own life and its own possibilities. He asks (p.778), 'What if blackness is the name that has been given to the social field and social life of an illicit alternative capacity to desire? Basically, that is precisely what I think blackness is.' The complexity of this writing is intimidating as it strives to articulate a different mode of being that is not defined solely by its negativity or excluded status (though *negation* is another thing, if by that we can indicate an oppositional stance towards the world as it is). There are hints about what this alternative might be: for Moten (p.742) 'Celebration is the essence of black thought, the animation of black operations, which are, in the first instance, our undercommon, underground, submarine sociality.' For Sharpe (2016), awakening (wakefulness) is partly to recognize the persistence of thinking and care in maintaining Black lives in the wake of slavery. Sheldon George (2018) in a similar way re-reads the syncretic incorporation of Christianity alongside African religions into the lives of black slaves and their descendants as a means of group-formation offering routes to self-affirmation in the face of racist oppression. Clearly, these are modes of resistance that arise from the perception of the ubiquity of anti-Black racism but fill out the space of Black lives as *lives*, not just as social or actual deaths. That said, the shared perspective remains: the power of racism is such as to structure the world into those who have a place in it (are grievable, in Butler's (2020) terminology) and those who do not.

Post-Freud, both the differences and the alliances have been visible. As some recent histories of psychoanalysis have emphasized (Zaretsky, 2015; Gaztambide, 2019), there has been more connection between psychoanalysis and Black communities than has often been recognized. In America, this had one mid-twentieth-century high point in the 'Harlem Renaissance', the flowering of Black life that was marked both by exoticism (pulling in white 'voyeurs') and intensely creative consciousness-raising. Zaretsky (2015, p.40) sets the scene for this by noting,

> What makes the encounter between African American intellectuals and psychoanalysis so salient to the theme of political Freud is that it did not occur through the development of a profession or of an isolated academic tendency, but rather through the engagement of Black intellectuals with an entire people. As a result, psychoanalysis took on a political dimension that was greater than usual.

As well as drawing attention to the role of some Black intellectuals in promoting psychoanalysis, Zaretsky's point here is in part that the practical nature of psychoanalytic interventions into Black communities and the porousness of the social and personal worlds of those communities – the obvious way in which the hardships of the social environment impact on psychological well-being and suffering – means that Black psychoanalysis can never be excised from social and political concerns. Zaretsky tracks the origins of the engagement with psychoanalysis through W.E.B. Du Bois's notion of 'double consciousness', the splitting of the Black psyche between self-awareness and construction through the gaze of the other (Du Bois, 1902), emerging ideas of a 'racial' unconscious (which can also be found in Fanon (1952)) and in particular the influence of the writings of the novelist Richard Wright.

Drawing on the work of Badia Sahar Ahad (2010), Gaztambide also discusses the contribution of psychoanalysis to the African-American culture of New York in mid-century, and specifically to the 'Black counter-discourse to American racialist ideology', as reflected in at least one significant publication, the New York City periodical *The Messenger*.

> In its pages, the *Messenger* articulated a 'coloured psychoanalysis' seeking to reconcile psychoanalytic, African-American, and socialist thinking. 'For a community of people who were bound by the politics of the exterior,' Ahad writes, 'psychoanalysis served the desire of many African American writers and scholars who sought to promote the psychological depth of the black subject' (p.16). Ahad is cognizant of how psychoanalysis contributed to discourses of primitivity, yet draws attention to how 'black subjects used psychoanalysis as a counterdiscursive method to assert a psychologically superior subjectivity' (p.16).
>
> (Gaztambide, 2019, p.91)

The two-sidedness of psychoanalysis in relation to 'race' and racism is evident here: without denying its contribution to the derogation of Black subjects through the adoption of the colonial primitive-civilized divide, psychoanalysis is also seen as offering tools for the articulation of Black psychic depth and hence Black consciousness. This political mission was also practical in relation to the mental health needs of Black communities, as reflected for instance in 1946 by the formation by Wright and the novelist Ralph Ellison along with Frederic Wertham, a Jewish psychoanalyst, of the Harlem Lafargue Mental Hygiene Clinic, which operated in the basement of a Harlem church until 1958. Although this was not a specifically psychoanalytic clinic but offered a range of services and referral routes to Black patients, it was a significant intervention in highlighting the paucity of non-racist, psychoanalytically informed psychotherapeutic interventions and seems also to have had an important role to play in offering data on discrimination that affected later court rulings on the Jim Crow laws. Zaretsky's (2015, p.62) summary of this aspect of the Lafargue Clinic's legacy states, 'the experience of the clinic, linked as it was to the Supreme Court integration decision [in *Brown vs. the Board of Education*, the 1954 ruling declaring racial segregation in schools to violate the American Constitution], provides an indelible moment situating Freudianism in African American memory as it exists today'.

Zarestky (2015) and Gaztambide (2019) both use the history of the Harlem engagement with psychoanalysis to explore the relationship between psychoanalysis and decolonial practice, deploying Fanon and (in Gaztambide's case) liberation psychology to that end. This is important and informative work, demonstrating amongst other things just how much accounts of the history of psychoanalysis have been narrowed to omit these progressive developments, or concentrated into discussions of Fanon as the sole voice of liberational psychoanalysis. Neglect of the Black history of psychoanalysis is itself part of an exclusionary process which sees psychoanalysis as only applying to Europeans or those 'civilized' to European standards. As noted briefly in the Introduction, the situation has been changing over the past thirty years as significant numbers of Black and other antiracist scholars and psychoanalysts have debated the promise and the limits of psychoanalysis, often building on the enormously influential writings of Fanon, especially his 1952 book, *Black Skins White Masks*, which shows a deep engagement with psychoanalysis as well as with Sartrean existentialism. This has now been written about extensively (for a recent collection see Laubscher, Hook and Desai, 2022), including in my own work (Frosh, 2013a). Perhaps the key point here is that Fanon addresses himself to a psychoanalysis that makes universalizing claims but can be reoriented with the specifics of black experience in mind. For example, the famous 'Look, a Negro!' episode reported by Fanon (1952, pp.111–12), in which he describes himself as positioned by the gaze and exclamation of the white child and its mother, is presented in part by Fanon in the terms given by the Lacanian mirror phase. In its 'pure' form, the mirror phase explains the ego-formation of the human subject as an aspirational appropriation of the image it sees of itself – one in which bodily and psychic integrity are promised to it, and its sense of self is promoted. For the Black subject, however, something else enters in: the reflection is not of the image as seen by the subject and directed by the gaze of the mother; it is a reflection of the *white*, colonizer's gaze. Fanon, writes Kelly Oliver (2004, p.21), 'describes the effects of the white mirror as undermining any sense of unification and control, and returning the black body and psyche to a state of fragmentation and lack of control'. Fanon goes on to explore in visceral detail the effects of this, including in relation to what is called 'epidermalization', the projection of the modalities of racism onto the Black body. But the simple point here is that his utilization of psychoanalysis has opened the way for other authors to deploy it in understanding the dynamics of racism, the racialization of the psyche in general, Black experience in particular, and the requirements and possibilities of a non- or antiracist psychoanalysis that is socially and culturally specific and historically conscious. This can be seen in much post-Fanonian work, one example of which will be given below. This work looks in several directions: towards a critique of psychoanalysis for its ethnocentrism and at times its racism (e.g. Evans Holmes, 2016), through compelling explorations of clinical issues that arise for Black and other 'minority ethnic' patients and analysts (Eng and Han, 2000; White, 2002; Davids, 2011), to the application of psychoanalysis for understanding and contesting racism itself (Hook, 2022). It also continues to raise the question that I have been concerned with in this chapter: is the fact that psychoanalysis emerged from a particular cultural context that was structured around antisemitism a *constraining* influence on its capacity to address anti-Black racism, or does this origin fuel the prospect of reaching out across what could be construed as a divide? Before worrying away at this once more with a detailed example of a particularly powerful analysis that rests on the borders of Afropessimist rejection of alliance yet still offers some ways forward, here is a short diversion into another aspect of the colonial inheritance of psychoanalysis, showing it is not just 'black' and 'white'.

Psychoanalysis explains ...

In relation to the decolonization of psychoanalysis, the gradual recovery of the history of psychoanalysis in Latin America and in India is of importance (Hartnack, 2011; Mandelbaum, Frosh and Lima, 2021). The papers in Warwick Anderson and colleagues' (2011) *Unconscious Dominions: Psychoanalysis, Colonial Trauma, and Global Sovereignties* collectively demonstrate how the enterprise of psychoanalysis contributed to the perpetration of colonial power in the twentieth century, nominating certain subject populations as potentially analysable and hence 'civilized', which means convertible into Europeans or at least 'suitably modern subjects' (p.8), and others as 'native' or indigenous, and hence on the subjugated, 'primitive' side of things. The regulatory or disciplinary functions of this are quite apparent: 'Psychoanalytic knowledge assisted in establishing a baseline for the native's personality, a critical dictum for the framing of colonial educational, judicial, and administrative policies in specific locales' (Anderson et al, 2011, p.8). In one instance of the ambiguity of psychoanalysis in colonial contexts, the founder of the Indian Psychoanalytic Society (incidentally, a very early Society, begun in 1922), Girindrasekhar Bose, who dominated Indian psychoanalysis for most of his life, was clearly a highly educated, privileged colonial subject who made his living from the analysis of members of 'the British-educated urban elite whose professional life was interwoven with the interests of the colonial rulers' (Hartnack, 2011, p.102). Nevertheless, he resisted much of Freud's ethnocentric thinking and associated himself strongly with the anticolonial movement; indeed, Christiane Hartnack notes (p.109), 'His pronounced anticolonial attitudes were conformist within the circles to which he belonged.' More significantly perhaps, his psychoanalytic work from the time of his doctoral thesis onwards was hybrid and critical in its use of Hindu ideas and its sensitivity to the specifics of his sociocultural milieu.

> Bose's creative efforts to integrate elements from European and Bengali Hindu psychological and psychoanalytic thought and practice were unprecedented in the field of academic psychology and psychiatry in colonial times and thus were groundbreaking. Instead of the binary concept of black skin – white mask that Fanon adhered to, Bose opted for interfaces (in the very sense of the word). His work was not limited by dichotomies but rather strove to establish connections.
>
> (Hartnack, 2011, p.109)

Hartnack may be being unfair to Fanon in this quotation because Fanon's supposedly 'binary' black-white conceptualization of the colonial world contains within it a nuanced understanding of the multiple influences on the construction of black and white subjectivities and can be read as a polemical device to uncover the psychopolitical workings of racism that are harder to unpick through notions of hybridity. Nevertheless, noticing that the colonized users of psychoanalysis have not necessarily been anthropophagous, simply absorbing the European 'truth' – and indeed that when they have been so it has sometimes been in a spirit of irony – is an important step towards realizing the potential of psychoanalysis itself for decolonizing practice and, as Hartnack phrases it, for establishing 'connections'.

Resonances of this can be seen in different colonial environments in Latin America, where psychoanalysis has had a huge impact (Plotkin, 2021). For example, in Brazil psychoanalysis played a role as a mode of socialization of a polity imagined to be uncontrollable in its forms of racial and sexual excess. As my Brazilian colleagues and I have described elsewhere (Rubin et al, 2016; Mandelbaum et al, 2021), the importation of psychoanalysis to Brazil happened early and was always ambiguously related to repressive policies (for instance, during the dictatorship of the late twentieth century) and to modernization processes that were both emancipatory and controlling. Psychoanalysis became embroiled with the Brazilian League of Mental Hygiene, which was founded in 1923 as part of the project of sanitization and hygienization of the Brazilian population, based on eugenic theory and aligned with the tendency to biologize 'madness', race and cultural aspects of society. Even though some early psychiatrists in the League developed projects that went beyond the initial eugenic framework, the country's racial mixture was seen as a problem and as a cause of Brazilian 'backwardness' that had to be overcome (Russo, 2012a). In this context, the psychiatrist Julio Porto-Carrero, who collaborated in the creation of the psychoanalytic clinic of the League, is an instructive figure. As Jane Russo (2012a) shows, his 'educational' intervention was based on two main aims arising from the psychoanalytic theory of sexuality, both of which can be read as normalizing and racialized, albeit partly in tension with one another. One aim was to remove the taboo that surrounded sex, working towards a non-repressive morality; the second was to control and sublimate the sexual instincts towards more 'civilized' ends. Russo proposes that although psychoanalytic practice first developed within the domain of hygiene projects, physicians like Porto-Carrero saw in its non-moralistic attitude a way to humanize the psychiatric movement. As such, it might be claimed to have had a *decolonizing* effect in relation to psychiatry, whilst still being part of a project of *normalization* based around colonial fantasies of race and 'miscegenation'. This contradictory use and impact of psychoanalysis is very characteristic of it, once again instantiating the way it can and has been deployed for colonizing and decolonizing ends. Cultural appropriations of psychoanalysis are also relevant here. For example, psychoanalysis had a notable presence in the art world and in debates surrounding the Week of Modern Art, held in São Paulo in 1922. Not only did several writers and painters enter into dialogue with psychoanalysis in their works, but the main document of modernism in the period, the *Manifesto Antropofagico*, written by Oswald de Andrade (1928), mentions Freud in the context of defending an original Brazilian identity free from repression and social restrictions. The social and cultural elites of the period also absorbed psychoanalysis in their search for modernity along European lines. On the other hand again, see-sawing between the different uses of psychoanalysis, the self-identity of Brazil as 'anthropophagous' explicitly relates to the idea of the colonized society as only developing through the materials it can ingest from the colonizer. Psychoanalysis is then one of those materials; and in being cannibalized in this way it is not destroyed, but rather consolidates from the inside a pattern of deference and control through identification and a kind of deathly possession. Anthropophagy itself, as a theme, is directly related to racist notions of cannibalism that have infected psychoanalysis throughout its history (Vyrgioti, 2022).

Perhaps the denial of race and racism in psychoanalysis can be seen in a small vignette concerning one of the originators of psychoanalysis in Brazil, Virginia Bicudo, who before becoming a psychoanalyst was a sociologist and professor at the Free School of Sociology and Politics of São Paulo, where her Masters degree dissertation in 1945 was entitled *Estudo das atitudes raciais de pretos e mulatos em São Paulo* (*Study of racial attitudes of blacks and mulattos in São Paulo*). At this time, her work on racism in Brazil was pioneering; but once she left sociology to become a hygiene educator and after that a psychoanalyst, she abandoned her research on racial themes. Indeed, she seems to have hidden her own 'mixed' background. Psychoanalysts from the Memory Centre of the Brazilian Psychoanalytic Society of São Paulo who organized an exhibition in her honour in 2010, on the occasion of the centenary of her birth, told us that when they were examining her archives they found in her house a collection of hats that, according to them, served Bicudo as a way to hide her 'crispy' hair, evidence of her *mulata* condition. In other words, not only did Bicudo abandon her *studies* of racism but also, on entering the Psychoanalytic Society as one of its founders, she sought to hide her own ethnic identity. This may itself be a symptom of the limited Brazilian psychoanalytic work on racism, and indeed the relatively small number of Black analysts (though there are some in Rio de Janeiro) or, apparently, Black patients. There is another indication of this rightwards shift, which was part of a tendency within mainstream psychoanalysis: in 1964, Bicudo participated in the 'March of Families for God and Freedom' in the city of São Paulo in opposition to the left-wing government of João Goulart, which later that year was overthrown in the coup d'état that marked the beginning of the military regime.

Psychoanalysis thus has been entwined with issues of race, racialization and racism in various places around the world in many periods of its history. It has been used in different ways to 'explain' the characteristics of racialized and minoritized groups (even when, as in India, they were actually in the majority) as part of a colonial tendency to use psychoanalysis as a tool to attribute apparent irrationalities – which could mean practices of resistance to colonial rule and to racism – to psychological and psychopathological factors. 'Freud explains,' as was a common slogan among the middle and upper classes of the main cities in Brazil during the dictatorship of the 1960s and 1970s (Oliveira, 2003, p.63), invites the reduction of socially induced suffering to personal psychic conflicts theorized by psychoanalysis. Psychoanalytic concepts become in some ways 'weaponized' with the effect of obscuring the specificities of different cultural situations and – more to the point – the operation of oppressive power structures and the legitimacy of dissent. The recurrent issue here is that psychoanalysis becomes presented as a mode of *universal* knowledge that can be applied to different groups and different social contexts without much alteration; yet, in reality, it is a product of a specific time and place, carrying considerable cultural baggage with it. This does not mean it has no value when used outside that environment, as is shown by the enormous impact of psychoanalysis in Latin America, India and more recently Japan and China. This impact is not solely to do with colonialism and is not limited to a Europeanized elite, but also demonstrates how psychoanalysis can provide tools enabling reflection on lived experiences and cultural problematics in differing environments. However, in order to speak to and about different cultural settings and social experiences, psychoanalysis has to be sensitive to them – and especially to the ways in which racialization and racist oppression operate, given their pervasiveness as well as their imbrication in the origins and history of psychoanalysis itself. Psychoanalysis's sensitivity to the questions posed by 'blackness' is crucial here, whether in its absence or presence; we have seen already that psychoanalysis can be, and has been, used as part of anti-oppressive and antiracist practice, yet clearly this has not always been the case. 'Psychoanalysis explains ...' is never enough, not just because psychoanalysis needs to be supplemented by other forms of critical thought and practice (though this is the case), but also because it is thoroughly imbued with ideological and political assumptions that need always to be challenged.

Responding to a seeker

Hortense Spillers's (1996) remarkable essay, *All the things you could be by now if Sigmund Freud's wife was your mother*, is a powerful intervention into the discussion of 'psychoanalysis and race', which indeed is its subtitle. Whilst there have been several other important discussions of racism, Blackness and psychoanalysis since the essay was published, Spiller's piece retains its capacity to challenge universalist psychoanalytic assumptions (i.e. that psychoanalytic concepts apply to all social and cultural groups in the same or similar ways) without discounting psychoanalysis's prospects for offering something to the emancipation of Black people. It does not deal with the Jewish aspects of psychoanalysis, but in exploring these issues it again raises the question of how to make psychoanalysis a bridge between different groups – and the limits of such an aspiration.

All the things you could be by now if Sigmund Freud's wife was your mother ends with an evocation of what psychoanalysis might have to offer to American Black experience. Writing of the Charlie Mingus jazz piece from which the title of the essay is taken, which according to Mingus 'means nothing' – presaging the 'nothing' of Afropessimism and Moten's (2013) encouragement to explore what that 'nothing' might be – Spillers expounds on the significance of psychoanalysis as follows.

> We traditionally understand the psychoanalytic in a pathological register, and there must be a very real question as to whether or not it remains psychoanalysis without its principal features – a 'third ear', something like the 'fourth wall', or the speech that unfolds in the pristinely silent arena of two star witnesses – a patient and he or she 'who is supposed to know'. The scene of assumptions is completed in the privileged relations of client and doctor in the atmosphere of the confessional. But my interest in this ethical self-knowing wants to unhook the psychoanalytic hermeneutic from its rigorous curative framework and try to recover it in a free-floating realm of self-didactic possibility that might decentralize and disperse the knowing one.
>
> (Spillers, 1996, pp.733–4)

Like the essay as a whole, this paragraph is allusive and complex, aiming perhaps to disconcert as much as to elucidate. Nevertheless, again like the essay as a whole, it is powerfully expressive both of a demand for a kind of freedom and the sensitive injunction that psychoanalysis should find a line of connection with Black experience. Psychoanalysis, Spillers suggests, can be utilized outside the clinical situation, constrained or distorted as that is by relationships of power and secrecy (the 'privileged relations of client and doctor'). Drawing on it in this way, it could offer an emancipatory route towards self-knowledge ('a free-floating realm of self-didactic possibility') that escapes this *centralization* of power (focused on the one 'supposed to know', which is a reference to the Lacanian idea of how the analyst is positioned in therapy). Ethical self-knowledge then becomes available to all, or at least is 'dispersed' away from the expert psychoanalyst. Trying to parse this for my own position, the drift of Spillers's overall argument is important. In *All the things you could be by now*, Spillers seems to critique (as part of a critique of transcendentalism) the use of psychoanalysis, whether Western or African-centred, in a manner in which understanding is somehow pre-given. This could be because of assumptions about the Real or 'race' or even culture, as in African-centred accounts that rely on a notion of ancestry or spirituality or assume some disconnection between the life of the individual subject and the community. For Spillers, psychic states are emergent and so not reducible to cultural or racial categories, which would be a form of sociological reductionism that deprecates the prospect of the individual having agency; yet they are of course also not divisible from the social.

Spillers breaks down the supposed contrast between African (externalizing) and Western (internalizing, guilt) modalities in the case study she offers of an African boy ('Samba'), which is drawn from one of the texts she interrogates, Edmond and Marie-Cécile Ortigues' (1966) psychoanalytic study of Senegal, *l'Oedipe Africain*. It is worth noting that this book is an important source for postcolonial psychoanalysis, and whilst it has been subjected to contemporary critique and reassessment it remains a seminal text committed to applying psychoanalysis in ways that are attuned to the cultural concerns and practices of postcolonial contexts. Reassessing *l'Oedipe Africain* in 2005, Alice Bullard comments,

> The Ortigues' honest confrontation with the strains and difficulties of providing therapy in this post-colonial and transcultural situation – a situation in which language, social structure and race created obstacles to transparent therapist–client relationships – is one of the unexpectedly enduring parts of their book. The Ortigues were frank about their position as cultural-outsiders, writing openly about their lack of understanding of their patients and their difficulties creating a therapeutic environment that allowed mutual identification. Practitioners and students today could learn from this open grappling with their uncomfortable, although not uncommon, outsider position.
>
> (Bullard, 2005, p.175)

In particular, the Ortigues's emphasis on hearing the 'voice' of the patient without preconception, without imposing the assumptions of psychoanalysis, but instead being led by their patients' speech – which itself can be understood as a psychoanalytic method – is seen as a crucial riposte to psychoanalytic colonialism. The Ortigues's astute awareness of their position as white outsiders to the culture allowed them to examine how their patients might themselves be seeking something more than their own culture could offer them, an understanding that avoids reducing the Senegalese in this book to 'cultural dupes', fixed in place by their social positions, and also promotes a kind of psychoanalytic humility in which the white researcher-analysts are continually thrown off-balance by what they encounter. 'In the era of independence,' writes Bullard (2005, p.178), 'the Ortigues recognized religion, race and residual colonial domination as important factors, but they sought to overcome these obstacles, searching for a means to facilitate the voice of the client/patient. Because they refused to allow individuals to be silenced by racial stereotypes or to fade into an abstraction of "collective identity," they made significant advances in their project.' Dagmar Herzog (2017) makes similar points about other 'ethnopsychiatrists' of the period, noting their relative willingness to depart from traditional psychoanalytic thinking and to acknowledge 'extrapsychic considerations', privileging the capacity of the societies they were studying to 'shape selves at the most elemental levels' (p.192). Spillers (1996, p.715) adds sharpness to this in generalizing the argument about psychoanalysis and race to confront assumptions about what 'blackness' might be and disrupt attempts to understand it through any single analytic grid.

> It seems to me that all dogmatic pronouncement, before and despite 'what the subject says,' is precisely the way in which traditional analyses, of various schools of thought, have failed, including all brands of nationalist thinking, as well as more informed opinions that have evolved a template of values to which 'the black man' is supposed to conform, and including, moreover, 'the black man' as a formulation itself. This whole vital soul, imagined to be snoring beneath the wisdom of the ages, conveniently poised for the exact liberatory moment, or 'leader', is actually an unknown quantity in this very 'soul' we thought we knew.

That is to say, nothing is known in advance and generally about the 'subject', including the Black subject; psychoanalysis has to stay with the question of what that subject (patient, analysand) might be asking for.

L'Oedipe Africain is clearly a complex book, especially in relation to the Ortigues's defence of the Oedipus complex as a universal structure that nevertheless has specific cultural variations, in this case in relation to 'African' patterns of paternity and sibling relations. Picking up on this, Spillers (1996) looks at how there is a transcendent appeal in psychoanalysis towards universal structures of psychic functioning, as well as specific cultural connections. 'There is the society, doubtlessly so,' she writes (p.725), 'but what about Samba? Another way to ask this question is the impossible, What does he say he wants?' As with some other classic critiques of Freudian universalism (Hirst and Woolley, 1982), the need to recognize the cultural specificity of the form taken by the Oedipus complex is part of the argument. The essay includes a striking reading of *brothers* as the key site for 'rivalry-solidarity' (Spillers, 1996, p.729), in contrast to the Freudian tale of the primal father. This is seen as emerging from the structure of Senegalese society, though it is worth noting that Juliet Mitchell (2000), amongst others, has made a similar case for the overlooked centrality of sibling relations in the West. The Senegalese association of the father with ancestors, mediating between them and the living, means that the father cannot be Oedipally challenged in the Western way; instead, it is the peer group that becomes the domain for the management of desire and aggression: 'What one must confront instead is the right to claim one's place within the group, as castration here is based on the collective register of obedience to the law of the dead, the law of the ancestors' (Spillers, 1996, p.729). Consequently, 'by a detour off the customary path, the oedipal problematic travels in this instance through the peer group, snared in the coils of looking and being seen' (p.728). The versatility of psychoanalysis in describing psychosocial mechanisms comes across in this account: individuals have their own agency and particularity, with structures of feeling and patterns of repression and sublimation that have universal features; but these are formed and expressed in relation to the cultural apparatus that is available to them.

Spillers ends (almost) with a discussion of the slave trade – how it disrupted the continuity of the ancestral generations and produced a radical break in culture. 'The riddle of origin that the Oedipus is supposed to constitute, first, as a crisis, then as a resolution of order and degree, was essentially cancelled by the Atlantic trade, as the "crisis," for all intents and purposes, has continued on the other side, the vantage from which I am writing' (p.732). The disruption caused by slavery not only blocks any singular African Oedipality or psychic structure – and hence an African-centred psychoanalysis – but also deracinates Black American life, for instance through denying Black subjects full access to literacy and therefore to the discourses upon which psychoanalysis depends. 'Carrying out that line of thinking,' she writes (p.733), 'we might be able to see in an apposite psychoanalytic protocol for the subjects of "race," broken away from the point of origin, which rupture has left a hole that speech can only point to and circle around, an entirely new repertoire of inquiry into human relations.' Rupture, the hole; this is what psychoanalysis needs to recognize in the Black psyche – which is to say, an engagement with history, especially the history of slavery that produced so many unnameable ancestors and unknown genealogies. Doing so, Spillers implies, not only requires of psychoanalysis that it attends to its culturalist assumptions, but it also raises the prospect of new forms of analysis, an 'entirely new repertoire of inquiry into human relations'. Relating back to the brief discussion of Black Studies earlier in this chapter, perhaps this is a link with Moten's (2013, p.778) assertion of Black possibility, of its potential place as an 'illicit alternative capacity to desire'.

In the light of all this, let us return to the passage from Spillers with which this section began, concerning the conditions for a race-sensitive psychoanalysis (Spillers, 1996, pp.733–4). As noted, what Spillers seems to be arguing for here is a turn for psychoanalysis away from its apparently 'therapeutic' activity (its 'pathological register') and towards becoming a resource for 'self-didactic possibility', which perhaps means becoming an emancipatory rather than an administrative enterprise. She acknowledges that this removal of psychoanalysis from the scene of its clinical practice raises the question of whether it continues to be psychoanalysis under such circumstances – a key issue for all discussions of what is sometimes called 'applied psychoanalysis' but is maybe better coded more neutrally as 'psychoanalysis outside the clinic' (Frosh, 2010). Spillers however is attuned to the ethics of psychoanalysis as a way of being and knowing – indeed of 'ethical self-knowing' – and hence for the lessons it might have for us once it can be separated from this scene of expert practice, the 'patient and he or she "who is supposed to know"', to use the Lacanian scheme for transference that Spillers alludes to. The point, surely, is that no-one knows. Psychoanalysis applied in the domain of race is both part of the problem, because of its colonial representations of so-called 'otherness' as something to explain, and potentially part of the solution, because of its capacity not to know, but to ask – to follow the 'Discourse of the Analyst', with its emphasis on the impossibility of complete knowledge, rather than that of the 'Master' if, again, one is willing to adopt Lacanian terminology (Lacan, 1991/2007). Spillers looks to find the 'psychoanalytic hermeneutic' in 'a free-floating realm of self-didactic possibility that might decentralize and disperse the knowing one' – that is, to throw our racialized assumptions off balance and allow a freeing openness to find its way in. The penultimate sentence of Spillers's essay, before a final Mingusian flourish, is 'We might need help here, for sure, but the uncertainty of where we'd be headed virtually makes no guarantee of that' (p.734). Can psychoanalysis be so open?

Exclusions

This chapter has been concerned with how boundaries and exclusions are made and can be overcome. The early examination of how the 'Jewishness' of psychoanalysis might speak to the possibility of an alliance against both antisemitism and anti-Black racism has given way in the later sections to one account of what an engagement of psychoanalysis with Black experience might look like. There is much more to say about all of this, which will be pursued in Chapter 8, but it is worth reiterating here that we need to go further than simply restate the familiar psychoanalytic trope that racism is a product of projections of the internally hated elements of the subject into the socially sanctioned categories of the abjected other. This is not to say that such constructions are of no use; on the contrary, they have formed the basis of some creative and productive psychoanalytic thinking on racism for some time (Frosh, 2013a). Here, however, my focus has been on how certain elements of psychanalytic engagement with 'race' and racism have been excluded, with the consequence both that there has been denial of culpability in some areas and of productive possibilities in others. For Jews, psychoanalysis has been a kind of 'home' – familiar, sharing in certain assumptions and practices, but also marginal, subjected to prejudice and antisemitism and consequently not (exactly) 'white'. For Black communities, psychoanalysis has often been pathologizing and colonial, yet also at times liberating either as a practice of socially reformist mental health intervention or as a set of concepts that offer potential leverage for self-emancipation. Nothing is settled, oppositions are fierce, resistance and power continue to operate in tandem, pulling against each other most of the time.

Chapter 6

WHITENESS WITH JEWISHNESS

White Jews

In his polemical short book, *Jews Don't Count*, David Baddiel (2021) addresses the question of the 'whiteness' of Jews, tracing ways in which the notion of Jews as white merges into an antisemitic discourse – or more precisely for his book, is a reason for the failure of antiracists to address antisemitism (i.e. racism against Jews doesn't 'count' as racism, partly because Jews are assumed to be white). Baddiel introduces the notion, which he says is not his own, of 'the law of Shrödinger's Whites … in which Jews are white or non-white depending on the politics of the observer' (p.51). Noting that for white supremacists 'Jews aren't white', Baddiel comments (p.50), 'Problem is, progressives, in general, tend to think they are white and, therefore, not really deserving of the protections progressive movements offer to non-white people facing racism. In some cases, Jews and Jewishness are used to signify even greater whiteness than normal.' Baddiel's (p.47) riposte to this is to tell antiracists to 'listen more to the enemy … And the racists say: Jews are not white.' So for white supremacists Jews are definitely not white; for many antiracist and decolonial activists, Jews are. In both cases, the effect is exclusionary.

Baddiel's construction of the effects of the attribution of whiteness to Jews on the political and antiracist Left is well founded and opens up channels for considering how and why it operates in many related circles, including, for instance, in postcolonial studies (Cheyette, 2017), and also for thinking about what whiteness itself might figure. David Schraub (2019), writing in a more formally 'academic' style than Baddiel but seemingly with no less critical passion, also identifies the precarity of Jewish whiteness, the way it seems to be a desirable accomplishment for many Jews, yet is always subject to the threat of withdrawal. The whiteness granted to Jews is 'conditional whiteness', he observes. It brings, on the one hand, relief at seeming exempt from colour racism, on the other, exclusion when white people seek to protect their privilege. 'An American Jew whose grandparents immigrated from

Austria,' he writes (p.380), 'might unambiguously benefit from White privilege when passing a highway patrol car, but not enjoy it in any way whatsoever when White supremacists are looking for a target to harass.' This statement is consistent with a widespread understanding of whiteness as conferring privileges on all white people even if they suffer from other kinds of privation or prejudicial hostility, for example as gay or trans* or, for that matter, Jewish. The fact is that white people do not have to contend with colour racism, with the routine discrimination, oppression and state violence of various kinds that Black and other 'non-white' people are subjected to. Helen Morgan (2021, p.10) describes this from within a framework in which she is examining the whiteness of psychoanalysis:

> whatever our personal history, wherever we were born, into which class, however young or old we are, if we walk the world as 'white', we see ourselves reflected wherever we look. We may have to bear the discrimination due to our class or sexuality or gender or disability, but we do so without the added burden of racism. We do not fear the forces of law and order, doors are not closed to us because of our skin colour, and we have the choice to ignore or even deny racism in the world we inhabit.

This is undoubtedly right, and it marks out part of the privilege of whiteness and explains why this might be desired by those who can pass as white – including many Jews, who might be drawn to whiteness precisely because of the security and promise of advancement that it offers. Indeed, Lentin (2020, p.134) claims that 'Jews' participation in the whitening of Jewry weakens the line of defence against the coloniality that produced the notion of Jewish, and other, racial difference,' thus making the divisions in the anti-racist movement partly attributable to Jewish white-aspirationalism. But the question here is whether the protection achieved from whiteness is true of Jewish experience, or of *all* Jewish experience, as represented in the 'Jews are white' association. Morgan herself notes that 'A person of Irish, Southern European or Latin American descent, or those who are Jewish or from other minority religious groups, will have their own historic background of suffering and oppression. Indeed, there have been periods in times and places when each of these groups have been designated as "non-white" or "black"' (p.13). Lentin (2020, p.156), too, notes that the whitening of Jews does not block antisemitism, because Jews are never 'white enough'; their whiteness, that is, is always *provisional*.

The accommodation of Jewishness to whiteness obscures the actual complexity of Jewish identity and, at least implicitly but also in practice, the antisemitic effect of this accommodation. Schraub (2019, p.380) reminds his readers of the wide range of Jewish ethnicities that exist ('Jews whose ancestry is not European: Sephardic Jews from Turkey or Latin America, Mizrahi Jews from Iraq or Tunisia, Indian Jews, Ethiopian Jews, African American Jews, and others') and comments on the effect on them of the flattening out of these variations into one notion of 'Jewish', which is then appropriated as 'white'.

> The merger of Jewishness into Whiteness places non-White Jews in a double bind – 'split at the root', to use Adrienne Rich's evocative phrase. On the one hand, the discrete experiences, problems, or histories of non-White Jews will not be recognized as Jewish insofar as they are non-White (since Jewishness is understood as a White experience). And on the other, insofar as these experiences, problems, or histories are recognized as Jewish, then they will cease to be acknowledged as non-White (since, again, Jewishness is understood as a White experience).
>
> (Schraub, 2019, pp.380–1)

The bind here is obvious: one cannot be Jewish and not be white, though it has to be noted that there is a more recent trend to celebrate Sephardic and Mizrachi Jews as somehow more 'ethnic' and less Jewish than Ashkenazic Jews and to appropriate them into the realm of oppressed minorities, even though there is no particular evidence that they are more liberal, antiracist or politically radical than their Ashkenazi peers (and in the context of Israel have, arguably, been less so).

What Schraub argues here is that blindness to the many different historical, cultural and ethnic identities that constitute Jewishness is reflected in a failure to conceptualize Jews 'intersectionally' in the way scholars might think of Black experience. Being Jewish is an attribute of a person that qualifies their whiteness and interacts with other 'marked' characteristics around sexuality, gender, disability and so on. Yet in much of the discussion around whiteness, the relevance of Jewish identity is neglected – which also means that 'Jews don't count' in connection with suffering from racism. For a Black Jew, for example, it may be that anti-Black racism is a strong and negative feature of their lives; but that does not mean that antisemitism as a separate 'intersectional' force is not also in operation. For other Jews, being accepted into what might be called the 'fortress of whiteness' (Guilaine Kinouani, personal communication August 2022) may seem to offer protection, but this is both a precarious achievement, with the danger always looming of being excluded from whiteness when the situation calls for it, and a route to losing sight of the specificity of Jewish experience. The price of entry to whiteness, which has undoubtedly been prized by many Jews, is to forego or circumscribe their Jewishness – unless or until it is forced back upon them. This may also mean that the 'law of Shrödinger's Whites' applies *within* Jewish communities as well as outside: many Jews aspire to the privilege of whiteness whilst seeking to preserve their Jewish identities, and also at times distancing themselves from the kinds of white ethnic nationalism that promote antisemitism. The effect of this has been to heighten discrimination within Jewish communities, whereby Black Jews are neglected or subjected to anti-Black racism – a situation now even recognized 'officially' (Bush, 2021). Ambivalence about white belonging operates in this way both externally and internally.

The assumption of Jewish whiteness has another troubling aspect. Whiteness is both central to societies of the colonial North – including, of course, the United States – and somehow invisible. On the one hand it is equivalent to 'privilege plus power'. As Neil Altman (2006, p.55) puts it in an intervention on whiteness in psychoanalysis, 'Whiteness is … an omnipotent fantasy, a fantasy of mastery and fullness. There is nothing inherently pathological about the impulse for mastery; … What makes the fantasy of whiteness a pathological defense is the way it is paired with blackness as its disavowed double.' Sheldon George (2018) reads whiteness similarly, in his Lacanian take on the legacy of slavery, arguing that 'Slavery allowed the master to embody in the slave a condition of lack that seemed to be the slave's exclusive, differentiating characteristic' (p.274). What this means is that the constitutive 'lack' in the white 'master' is covered over by the construction of the Black slave as inferior, reassuring white subjects that they are in fact complete and whole, and rooting American 'white identity in its signal notions of freedom and independence' (p.276).

Whiteness thus only exists in relation to its imagined other, Blackness, which is derogated and made into the receptacle for the insecurities of white life. The consequence of this is that whilst Blackness has a great deal of imagined content, whiteness is not envisaged as anything but the norm – the taken-for-granted base from which the aberrant other departs, a view that is shared by many psychoanalytic commentators (Gregory, 2022). Whiteness is in general an 'unmarked' category which, in an important political move, antiracism and the new domain of 'critical whiteness studies' (CWS) draws attention to. This is increasingly taking place with awareness of the nuances of white identities, that is, with some consideration of intersectionality, but its essentially *critical* focus remains central. Pauli Badenhorst (2021, p.286), for instance, draws attention to how 'second-wave CWS' goal is the active dismantling of white supremacy, racism and anti-Blackness, as such are fuelled by both public and covert performances of Whiteness, rather than the mere passive acknowledgment or confession of White privilege.' The absence of this critical intersectionality in relation to whiteness and Jewishness, however, means that instead of ameliorating the assumption of white privilege in relation to Jews, there is an escalation of whiteness by virtue of it being attached to Jewishness as a *magnifier*. That is, whiteness plus Jewishness equals more whiteness, or perhaps even Jewishness as the epitome of whiteness – a formula that shades into antisemitism. The point here is that, as Schraub (2019) notes, adding whiteness to Jewishness in the way that it is usually done – which is to say, without attention to the specificity of different forms of oppression, but rather as seeing Jewishness as always bound up with whiteness, as a kind of 'subset' of whiteness – means that the assumed characteristics of Jewish identity that make it signify privilege (i.e. the essentially antisemitic characterization of Jews as a group as rich, powerful, influential, etc.) come to constitute the whole. White Jews are privileged not because of their whiteness but because of their Jewishness, or due to *both* these factors.

> Whiteness and Jewishness do not simply sit side by side as social categories. Rather, Whiteness seems to be doing something to Jewishness. 'White Jews' are not 'White' and then also 'Jews.' Jewish Whiteness seems to inflect, in serious and fundamental ways, the understanding of what it means to be Jewish – or what Jewish experience could possibly be. At the extreme, it subsumes Jewishness entirely – Jewishness cannot be understood but through the interpretive frames offered by Whiteness.
>
> (Schraub, 2019, p.389)

How does this relate to antisemitism? Schraub argues that whereas the main practice of the analysis of whiteness is to reveal how a dominant but 'unmarked' identity position – whiteness – perpetuates racism, when applied to Jews it acts to confirm antisemitic tropes concerning how Jews are powerful and privileged. In summary,

> The Whiteness frame looks at its subjects and asks that we see their power, their privilege, their enhanced societal standing. So far so

good – it is important to unpack all of these things. But stereotypes of
Jewishness sound many of the same notes: they too look at Jews and
point out their putative power, privilege, and domination of social
spaces.

(Schraub, 2019, pp.401–2)

The failure to analyse Jewishness in its own terms, as itself a complex
mix of culture, ethnicity, religion and 'peoplehood' with a history of
being subjected to racialized antisemitic opprobrium that at times has
been murderous, leads to an occlusion of the Jewishness of Jews and
their re-signification as exemplary whites. Added to the political view
of Israel as both the nation-state of the Jews and a white settler-colonial
entity oppressing the Palestinian people, this means that the exemplary
whiteness of Jews can come to apply to all Jews (those who do not fit
the label are not really Jews). As noted above, this results in Jewishness
being a magnifier of whiteness and, as a consequence, it mobilizes
widespread antisemitic discourses.

The idea that Jews, unlike people of colour or the generally
dispossessed, do not have a separate identity in relation to being made
vulnerable to racism (here, antisemitism) – indeed, at times, that
antisemitism is either not a form of racism or, conversely, does not
warrant distinguishing from racism in general (and hence is lost as a
concept) – is not a new one. As Bryan Cheyette has shown powerfully
in different places, it builds on a long history of 'supersessionism' that
characterizes the West's attitude towards Judaism and Jews, first and
foremost through Christianity but also in secular studies, in Cheyette's
view including postcolonial studies. 'Supersessionist thinking,'
explains Cheyette (2017, p.428), 'grows out of the foundational belief
that Christianity is the fulfilment of biblical Judaism (and is structured
in secular terms around the "new" transcending or replacing the "old";
hence the Christian concepts of the "new" and "old" testaments) or, in
theological terms, the "old" chosen people being fulfilled or replaced
by a "new" Christian church.' This is why, as mentioned in the previous
chapter, the idea of 'Judeo-Christian civilization', used loosely and as
if it is unproblematic by many radical critics of contemporary society,
is a misnomer. The 'Judeo' in it is a construction of *Christianity*, a
backwards reading of Judaism and Jewish history in the light of the
politics of the Christian mission, which is to replace or supersede
Judaism with its own 'good news'. Judaism lays the foundation for
Christianity in the sense that it precedes it, but the reinvention of
Judaism by Christianity – the replacement of the covenant aimed
specifically at the Jews, for instance, with the 'covenant of the heart' that

includes all people and does away with Jewish practices (Osserman, 2022) – transforms Judaism and divests it of its own particularities. What is the difference between 'Judeo-Christian' and 'Christian' in the resulting structure? The answer is – nothing at all. The incorporation of 'Judeo' into the Christian culture that has defined and structured the West is a way of silencing Judaism; and when the notion of 'Judeo-Christian civilization' is used as a synecdoche for an oppressive system that needs to be resisted or opposed with alternatives, it can be a channel for antisemitism as well.

Cheyette suggests that in a secular age, religious supersessionism has been inherited by secular thinkers, including those who have turned to Christianity to ground their thinking about political theology (e.g. Žižek, 2009). This also applies in academic work, as in the case of the relationship between postcolonial and diaspora studies on the one hand and Holocaust and genocide studies on the other. 'The celebratory version of diaspora,' Cheyette writes (2013, p.6), 'tends to foreground a transgressive imagination and precolonial histories made up of intertwined cultures (and is associated with Postcolonial and Diaspora Studies), whereas a victim-centred version tends to stress particular communities of exile with specific and unique histories of suffering (and is associated with Holocaust and Genocide Studies).' Jewish studies is mostly located within the latter group and is consequently relegated to the 'old' that needs to be superseded. Perhaps Cheyette's fullest statement of this is here:

> In the case of Jewish and postcolonial studies, we have the shift from a supposedly old established discipline, which can be falsely constructed to be part of a so-called Judeo-Christian Western tradition (that is Ashkenazic Jewish studies), and a newer discipline of postcolonial studies that is understandably deeply suspicious of this Western tradition and the narratives of victimhood as part of this tradition. Although it has long been recognized that, most prominently, Jews, slaves, the colonized, and women are victims of Western modernity, this has not led, with notable exceptions, to an intersectional critique of Western modernity from these different perspectives. In fact, it could be argued that such commonalities have not resulted in solidarity but have made it remarkably difficult, in its earliest institutional years, for postcolonial studies to identify too closely with Jewish studies. The very fact that these fields had so much in common meant that, paradoxically, the new had to be particularly differentiated from the old.
>
> (Cheyette, 2017, pp.428–9)

Differentiating postcolonial studies from Jewish studies starts to resonate with a general cultural tradition of disposing of Judaism, and of Jewishness too, as archaic, ancient, intransigent, retrogressive. One result of this is that the multifarious reality of ongoing Jewish life is overlooked, including its continuing exposure to antisemitism, whilst when Jewishness is acknowledged it is as a relic of something to be overcome (superseded). Hence the demonstrable fascination with ultra-orthodox Jews, reflected in popular culture (the television series *Shtisel* is one example) even or especially when portrayed as backward-looking and reactionary (Sheldon, 2019). Indeed, ultra-orthodox Jews are sometimes seen as the *only* representable or noticeable Jews, as Keith Kahn-Harris has noted in relation to the constant re-use of photographs of members of the ultra-orthodox community to illustrate news stories about Jews, even when the stories have nothing to do with them (Kahn-Harris and Stothard, 2022). This also applies to some extent to right-wing Israeli settlers, who in their own way also represent the backwardness of Jews: nationalist, fundamentalist, extremist. Other Jews do not really count as Jews, but become something else – liberal whites, for example, or conservatives, or representatives of the Establishment; but not, it seems, living a specific reality of their own, which mixes these various attributes with the particularity of Jewish identity. Supersessionism here does not just mean religious supersessionism, which is now mainly a historical relic (although Christian fundamentalism, especially in America, might be realistically called on to dispute this claim); it means the much broader tendency to see the Jewishness of Jews as mainly a vestigial irrelevance. In a different terminology, this could be called assimilationism; in the context here, the assimilation is not so much to Christianity as to a generic whiteness.

It is, therefore, not only Black and other 'non-white' Jews who disappear when the whiteness frame is used, but all Jews, with those who remain recognized serving only to confirm the prejudicial stereotypes that activate and are activated by antisemitism – insular, fanatical, misogynistic, vestigial, anti-modern; and then, manipulative, exploitative, secretive, cunning, as when the Jewishness of an individual in the public eye for some crime is emphasized. From a Jewish perspective, as one might imagine, something is missing here. It is as if Jewish identity once again has become hidden, as if we are all 'crypto-Jews' – like 'everyone else' (Christians, whites) on the outside, whilst behind closed doors continuing with our weird, exotic practices. Lighting candles in the cupboard might be one way to think about it, a practice that was widespread amongst the descendants of the real crypto-Jews originating in Portugal and Spain. And in becoming assimilated, Jews are also represented as 'ultra-white', in the old language 'especially observant', in order to hide the actuality of Jewishness, once again feeding into the standard antisemitic trope of the secrecy of Jews, their hidden hand, the cabal-like way in which they act behind the scenes to rule the world. This is standard fare for white supremacists and other right-wing overt antisemites; but it can also be found slipping through into the political mainstream, both on the right and the left (Gidley, McGeever and Feldman, 2020).

In a subtle exploration of what he terms the 'mental pain of minorities', Salman Akhtar (2014) describes the fluctuations between invisibility and hostility that face many minority groups. Referring to the American situation, he notes the following about Jews, which reflects on ambiguities in the notion of 'minority' itself.

Fascinatingly, Jews, who make up only 3% of the country's population, are hardly ever described as a 'minority' group; their success in academic and social realms accords them prominence, power and exemption from being called 'minority'. It is obvious that numbers do and do not mean much when it comes to recognizing the presence of a minority. And, here we note a clash between the subjective and objective perspectives; Jews might regard themselves as a minority but others, especially those from relatively disenfranchised minority groups, might not see them in this manner. In other words, one might be both present and absent as a minority.

(Akhtar, 2014, p.138)

In the context presented above, this presence-absence of the Jews as a minority group is not just to do with 'success in academic and social realms'. Indeed, the assumption that this applies to Jews as a group overlooks the fact that many Jews are not successful in this way, so it has its own dynamic of supporting the myth of Jewish power that slides into racial stereotyping. But Jewish presence-absence is also mobilized through racist thought, in some ways similarly to other immigrant groups into the United States who have been 'whitened' as part of the process of distinguishing them from the black population, the perpetual underclass of American society. To this degree, the Jewish presence-absence is part of the general ambivalence with which minorities are perceived. 'Almost everywhere one looks,' comments Akhtar (2014, p.139), 'one finds that at the conscious level, the society feels unease at the existence of minority groups within it and strives to deny their presence. At the unconscious level, it longs for a minority group since that can be used as a "container" for its own unmetabolized concerns.' The negativity of both sides of this equation is striking, reflecting the experience that many minorities have of their lose-lose position in the wider society, the sense that they are not wanted for themselves but only as a way to free the majority from some of their own dilemmas. Minorities are not recognized as having the same rights as others, are not 'taken into account' and where possible are not thought about; but they are also blamed for the troubles of the society as a whole (economic woes, housing and employment problems, violence, drugs and so on). Jews share in this: on the one hand, they are not noticed, not treated as recognizable for their cultural specificity (though politicians might celebrate their more obvious customs when campaigning for votes); on the other hand, when it is useful to do so, they are seen as the source of the poison that runs through society. This also bleeds into the precarious way in which Jews' whiteness is acknowledged. As soon as there is a trace of what on the political right is seen as 'white treachery' – which means critiques of whiteness by white people – the spectre of antisemitism looms large, as if the only possible explanation for such an autocritique can be that the people making it are not 'really' white at all. We have seen this recently, especially in the United States, with death threats directed at psychoanalysts understood to have been responsible for 'attacks' on whiteness (O'Loughlin and Voela, 2021; Zeavin, 2022) accompanied by the assumption that these analysts must be Jewish and so not properly white (Derek Hook, personal communication, July 2022), but it is neither a new nor an unfamiliar phenomenon. Jews are white until they are not white, which can be very soon indeed.

But further even than this, there is something specific about the fluctuating position of the Jews (which is not to suggest that there is nothing specific about the situation for other ethnic groups, only that Jews have their own situation to contend with and this is often overlooked). Freud's (1920) description of the fort-da game expresses this especially powerfully. The story is of his young grandson, observed playing a game of throwing his toy (a cotton reel) into his curtained cot so that it is out of sight ('ooh'/fort/away) and dragging it back out again so that it returns to the child ('ah'/da/here). Back and forth, gone and come, outside and in. Freud makes a great deal of this in a compelling and moving way, discussing how the child is trying to control the comings and goings of his mother, why he keeps replaying something so painful (separation) and how he responded to her actual disappearance through death a very few years later. The origins of the theory of the death drive are partly to be found here. But we can also see something else at work, something that was frequently on Freud's mind as it was of the other secular Jews of his period. This was that the surrounding 'civilization', in his case the Viennese 'fin de siècle', which had 'emancipated' its Jewish population in the late 1860s, both welcomed the Jews as citizens and excluded them as Jews. Emancipation was part of a civilizing process that was intended to lead, often through religious conversion (most frequently adopted for social and professional reasons), to the Jews becoming 'normal', which is to say, in the terms used here, white. Yet the recalcitrance of antisemitism and of Jews – the refusal of both to disappear – meant that emancipation was always tentative, teetering on the edge of renewed suppression, eventuating as we know in a genocidal return to violent abjection of all Jews, however 'civilized' they might have thought themselves to be. Fort-da is not a linear progression but a repetitive one, barely even cyclical as the 'da' follows the 'fort' so immediately for the child (separation followed by return); or for the Jews perhaps it runs the other way around – every 'da' undermined by its immediately consequent 'fort'. As Freud knew well, antisemitism was pervasive in Austrian society and institutionalized in its political networks; any promise of inclusion of Jews in the society was premised on their disaffiliation from Judaism itself ('fort'), and by the end of Freud's life was not possible at all (the 'da', one might say, became a command full of threat, not a hope; became another form of 'fort'). If 'whiteness' was a property of the dominant majority culture in Europe, signifying privilege and power, then the whiteness of Jews was a fluctuating presence that depended on the whims of this majority, and in the end was destroyed. Jews may not have technically been 'Black', but they were certainly never stably white.

If the Jews are not white, or not all Jews are white – the debate might linger here – then what are they in relation to whiteness? At times, for instance in the nineteenth century in Europe, they have been imagined as Black (Gilman, 1993). As previously mentioned, Slabodsky (2014) has also shown how much the 'barbaric' histories of Jews, Amerindians, black Africans and other colonized subjects have coincided. For the Tunisian Jew Albert Memmi, deeply engaged as he was with decolonial thought and activism, the Jews were a specific category who suffered from colonial oppression and so could have an alliance with others who shared that experience – yet often were, as he was himself, refused the opportunity to do so. Santiago Slabodsky notes,

Memmi insisted that as there is a global Black condition, there is a general Jewish condition shared by global Jewry ... For Memmi, the West had been portraying Jews as antithetical to its own self-understanding. This discourse made Jews share a common 'misfortune' with other members of the network such as Blacks, Muslims and others.

(Slabodsky, 2014, p.135)

This suggests that the positioning of Jews as antiracist is a function of the shared experience of being the recipient of racism – in this case, antisemitism. Not being white, one is of necessity aligned with Black, as whiteness is established only in relation to Blackness. The identification is incomplete, because the complexity of non-whiteness is enormous and even in the eyes of white supremacists all non-whites are not the same (for example, the 'alt-right' imagine that although the Jews inspire Muslims and African-Americans to take over America, they are not to be confused with these groups themselves). Yet if whiteness is central to the 'privilege plus power' nexus, and whiteness is also a fantasy based on the repudiation of blackness, then Jewishness is not whiteness. The fantasy is there ('da'), but reality ('fort') gets in the way all the time; the positioning of Jews as white is part of an antisemitic set of values that discards the reality of Jewish history, Jewish culture and Jewish lives.

Jewish values and whiteness

If Jews are not white, is their affiliation to antiracist struggles based only on a solidarity of the oppressed, that is to say, on the congruence of antisemitism and other forms of racism, or is something else viable? Despite the complication produced by the material reality of the State of Israel as a divisive entity both within the Jewish community and between Jews and putative antiracist allies, does it make sense to think in this way, as I have been trying to do in this book, and to suggest there might be a direct line that links Jewishness with opposition to discrimination and oppression and that is not dependent on antisemitism – which, however central it is to Jewish history and thence to Jewish identity, is not exactly a positive force for good? Without antisemitism, if such a state of affairs is imaginable, would Jews still align themselves with the oppressed, or would Jews genuinely become 'white'? I want to return to this question here with reference to psychoanalysis, noting again briefly the broader context of Jewish thought and adding the dimension of Jewish 'non-whiteness' to my discussion in earlier chapters.

The development of a Jewish ethical stance on racism – specifically, an assertion of racial equality as a fundamental principle – has a history that predates the potential articulation of antiracism in modern terms, and arguably lays the foundations for an inclusive psychoanalytic ethic. The conventional origin of this is the oft-repeated biblical injunction not to oppress a stranger 'for you know the heart of a stranger, seeing you were strangers in the land of Egypt' (Exodus 23, 9). This injunction is taken very seriously at least in theory as a model for Jewish attitudes towards outsiders, even if in practice, as discussed previously, it is often constrained by the insularity of many Jewish communities – fuelled largely by antisemitism but also by worries over assimilation and conversion and at times, it has to be said, a reading of the notion of being a 'chosen people' as implying superiority. When in the nineteenth century the Jewish enlightenment movement developed and secular Jewish identity became increasingly more viable, the universalistic ethics of Judaism could be promoted as a badge of pride without necessarily committing its wearer to religious observance. This was very much the case for Freud, who despite his lifelong and unequivocal atheism remained strongly identified with his Jewishness. As I have noted earlier in this book, the ethical side of this is central to Freud's identification with Jewishness, or at least to his understanding of it, and it was one of the attractions he felt towards the mission of the B'nai B'rith, the Jewish 'lodge' in Vienna, whose members saw in Judaism a source for humanitarian values that were universal in their application and hence superior to the bigotry of antisemites. Freud himself, in 1935 as well as in his letter to them of 1926, claimed that he had always felt linked to the Bnai Brith over this issue of ethical ideals, even though he had ceased to work actively with the organization decades before: 'The total agreement of our cultural and humanitarian ideals, as well as the same joyful acknowledgement of Jewish descent and Jewish existence, have vividly sustained this feeling' (Klein, 1985, p.86). The ideals of Jewish ethics as imagined by progressive secular Jews – a life of service, integrity and honesty, intellectual clarity and balanced respect for others, alongside a capacity for recognition of differences and of the competing capacities for construction and destructiveness endemic to the human condition – are so close to those of Freudian psychoanalysis as to make it apparent how the latter might have been born out of the former.

Yet the ambiguities inherent in this position are very marked, given the way Freud's thought was *also* embroiled in the colonial and racial assumptions of his time, as described in other chapters, and the work that he did to align Jewishness with Europeanness at the expense of the so-called 'savage', geographically positioned in Africa and Australia (Brickman, 2003). Nevertheless, this ethics is an important marker of psychoanalysis's attitude, in which the division between 'civilized' and 'savage' is broken down by the ubiquity of unconscious processes. This is what links it to a critique of whiteness and also to the set of Jewish identifications described above. If the colonial and racist hierarchical division White-Black is one that can only be sustained by the denial of the unconscious as it runs through all subjects, disrupting the boundaries that seem to claim superiority for one group over another, then the approach of psychoanalysis to racism is to seek to understand and disturb the way in which this imagined division is nevertheless held onto, sustained over time affectively as well as through the social and economic structures that aim to perpetuate it. More simply, psychoanalysis asks what it is about whiteness that is so precious that it has to be defended so violently. Of course, a large part of the answer to this is political in the sense of relating to power and interests; but the affective dimension seems to go further, intruding violently into the world of fantasy and often into core aspects of personal identity. My suggestion here is that Jewish non-whiteness adds to this psychoanalytic imperative towards antiracism by disorienting the White-Black division in an additionally complex way. Psychoanalysis, born in large part out of the Jewish experience of the dynamic of outsider-insider in the late nineteenth century (fort-da), contains within itself this ambiguous whiteness that both draws it into colonial and sometimes racist modes of thought and opposes that thought at the same time. Moreover, Jewish non-whiteness helps push forward a more complex picture for antiracism by virtue of disorienting simplistic divisions. It unsettles Manichean White-Black categorizations (containing ambiguous whiteness), something which makes it ever more troubling to the racist consciousness.

Antisemitism is yet again a route into this. According to Ernst Simmel (1946), in a classic study of psychoanalysis and antisemitism, hatred of Jews is 'the process of civilization itself,' suggesting that antisemitism is not something grafted *onto* modernity as an external force that disturbs what would otherwise be 'a culture of law, order and reason' but is expressive of the irrationality that lies *within* modernity and is generated by it. Writing in the volume of essays that he edited out of a symposium on antisemitism organized by the San Francisco

Psychoanalytic Society in 1944, Simmel makes the connection between modernity ('civilization') and the worm that destroys it.

> Applying our method of psychoanalytic-dialectic thinking, we must infer not that antisemitism annihilates the achievements of civilization, but that the process of civilization itself *produces* antisemitism as a pathological symptom-formation, which in turn tends to destroy the soil from which it has grown. Antisemitism is a malignant growth on the body of civilization.
>
> (Simmel, 1946, p.34)

The idea of a 'symptom-formation' is used by Simmel here to express the destructiveness of antisemitism as something that exudes from, and returns as a malignant growth to, the body-politic. But it also suggests, psychoanalytically, behaviour that has a function in dealing with a conflict – the symptom as a kind of compromise formation between expression and repression of a disturbing unconscious idea. Perhaps this might be better expressed here by the Lacanian notion of the *sinthome* as something that binds together the subject, a kind of solution to the problem of how to stay whole in the face of fissiparous tendencies in psychic and social life. In any case, this suggests that antisemitism – and by extension, racism – can be understood as solving a problem for the dominant society; or in the language of this chapter, it proposes that whiteness is a screen defending against the problematics of unconscious desire. This theme can also be found in some of Slavoj Žižek's writings, with unreason thought of not as a fundamental psychic structure, but one that is socially overdetermined.

> Is capitalism's hatred of the Jew not the hatred of its own innermost, essential feature? For this reason, it is not sufficient to point out how the racist's Other presents a threat to our own identity. We should rather invert this proposition: the fascinating image of the Other gives a body to our own innermost split, to what is 'in us more than ourselves' and thus prevents us achieving full identity with ourselves.
>
> (Žižek, 1993, p.206)

Against the implication that it is the inner state of the subject that is primary in seeking out an external cause, Žižek (1997, p.76) also gives us a more elaborated version of antisemitism in which it is produced by the structure of capitalism itself: 'social antagonism comes first, and the "Jew" merely gives body to this obstacle.' Culture's investment in this figure of the 'Jew' produces it as an element in the unconscious, and with it arises the widespreadness of antisemitism itself.

Some of the implications of this position can be seen in the small number of psychoanalytic investigations of whiteness that have emerged in recent years especially from American psychoanalysts (some of them Jewish), even though these rarely address antisemitism. Neil Altman (2006, p.55), for instance, sees 'the fantasy of whiteness' as 'a way in which whites seek to ward off feelings of lack or of ordinariness, i.e., a lack of specialness or privilege and a sense of unfreedom or constraint.' Furthermore,

> White people, like all people, wish to rid themselves of certain psychic qualities, often sexual and aggressive ones, which are in fact inherent in all human beings. This is another explanation for the choice of the words white and black to characterize people whose skin color tends to vary somewhere along the pink-brown continuum. With black and white, the twain never meet, and psychological similarity is denied. Having parts of oneself projected into others creates an unstable situation. The disavowed position is always there, haunting the self, requiring continual warding off.
>
> (Altman, 2006, p.61)

Jamie Steele (2021, p.396), examining the idea of white supremacy as fear of Blackness, similarly notes the actual fragility of the white armour (as opposed to 'white fragility', which is a way of avoiding confronting racism by specious claims to being oppressed as white): 'If interrogating one's whiteness involves interrogating one's emptiness, rather than merely projecting this identification upon others' blackness, it must involve facing a profoundly painful process. No wonder it is so heavily defended against by whiteness, both psychically and socially.' Steele goes on,

> Because white identity exists as a default which asserts itself as the normative body against which non-white (i.e, inferior, not-normal) bodies are defined, the act of interrogating whiteness – of rendering it visible – serves to disrupt the core of white identity. It is through this newly stirred-up disorganization – from the safety of invisibility to the horror of abject erasure – that sadistic defenses are formulated as a balance against the masochistic self-hatred of the internalized sense of meaninglessness or chaos. White supremacist activism can be conceptualized in this frame as an externally organizing defense

to manage the internal chaos by putting people of color 'back in their place' - which is to say, where they can no longer 'interrogate' or illuminate the whiteness of the subject at hand.

(2021, p.396)

Joshua Gregory (2022, p.7), from a Lacanian standpoint and following Kalpana Seshadri-Crooks' (2000) analysis, notes similarly the way in which whiteness covers up a lack in the subject, obscuring it with an imaginary wholeness reliant on disparagement of the Black other:

> For whiteness to assume the position of master signifier, then, is to deny this lack - which is not actually to resolve the lack, of course - and, in so doing, to substitute an illusion (or delusion) of wholeness which insists, in spite of itself, on preserving the fiction of a white subject who does not lack; who, in effect, takes the imaginary as their real and their demands as able to be satisfied in the same way as needs.

And Adrienne Harris (2012, p.207) argues,

> It may be that there is in 'whiteness' a 'psychose blanche' ... Deeper than depression, deeper than rage, there is a blankness, a place where there is not sufficient structure for mourning, where the psyche gives way. Perhaps this is what 'whiteness' is: the disruption or erasure of mourning, a gap in the psyche, which through 'whiteness' functions like an imploding star, refusing signification. It is not trauma solely that is whitened out but also destructiveness and memory.

These quotations are indicative of a trend to examine whiteness as a failure to tolerate emptiness, lack and ambivalence. The argument is that what is unbearable in the white psyche is projected into the other, namely the Black subject who is automatically implicated in whiteness as both its other and its constitutive force. What this means is that whiteness only exists in opposition to something defined as Blackness, whether this be the relatively narrow differentiation of the African-originated Black or a more general Blackness as 'non-whiteness', to include Asians, Amerindians, Romanies, Indigenous peoples - and Jews. The 'problem' for whiteness then becomes at least twofold. On the one hand, much that is core to liveliness and hence to a sense of subjective being - but that is also troubling - is projected outwards towards the other: 'White people, like all people, wish to rid themselves of certain psychic qualities, often sexual and aggressive ones, which are in fact inherent in all human beings,' as Altman claims in the quotation above. This creates a sense of emptiness that means the identity of the white subject can only be sustained through a form of character armour that blocks the encounter with this empty self; in Steele's words, 'the act of interrogating whiteness – of rendering it visible – serves to disrupt the core of white identity.' Whiteness is then preserved through a process of renunciation, but one that is not mourned because it cannot be recognized, as, for example, described in the passage from Harris (2012) above. This argument is also resonant of Judith Butler's (1997) long-standing account of gender melancholy, which has also been deployed by others (notably Eng and Han, 2000) in the context of racial melancholia: the 'deadness' of whiteness is because its enlivening desires are *foreclosed* in the sense of being prevented from ever reaching consciousness and therefore from being mourned; the additional stage here is a projection of these disowned aspects of the self into the other, who is then hated for possessing them. On the other hand (that is, the second part of the problem), the non-white subject also becomes a threat both because that other is so much more real than the white subject and also because the way in which whiteness survives is by domination of the other so that it cannot manifest its own desire. If Black others come close, their very presence threatens whiteness not just with what it has discarded, but also with the guilty non-secret of its oppressiveness, the actions it constantly takes to maintain itself by keeping the other subjugated. Even the failure to mourn lost aspects of white subjectivity becomes weaponized: it creates guilt, which is repudiated and projected outwards, leading to a situation in which the Black other is seen as guilty for the trouble that whiteness causes.

There are various difficulties with this account, which shares in a generic psychoanalytic understanding of racism as involving the projecting of intolerable impulses into the socially derogated other (Frosh, 2006b). These mostly relate to the psychologizing of racism and the under-theorization of the social and political sources of racist structures, including those that make some groups 'socially derogated' in the first place. It also continues to root itself in an undifferentiated notion of 'otherness' that automatically relates it to Blackness and thereby tends to reproduce the White-Black, us-them assumptions of colonial thought in general. Still, when reflecting on whiteness and the continued impassioned adherence to white supremacy that feeds racism so profoundly, psychoanalysis provides important routes to conceptualization of the affective pull of racism and the 'service' it does to the white psyche. Perhaps the Lacanian concept of racist 'enjoyment', articulated through the notion of *jouissance*, usefully draws this together. *Jouissance* is, as ever for concepts in the Lacanian pantheon, a complex and often obscure idea, contradictory and vague, but it has been used in a surprisingly versatile and impressive way to help make sense of the impassioned dimensions of racism. This is because of the way it ties together unconscious dimensions of excess, enjoyment, pleasure and pain. *Jouissance*, according to Derek Hook (2018, p.251),

> results from the drive's relentless push for gratification; it is not as such an affect, a desire, or a mode of pleasure. It is, by contrast, a kind of suffering; it maintains a proximal relation to pain, to what is excessive, traumatic. More succinctly: *jouissance* is a type of painful arousal inflected with the death drive, by the erotic appeal of overstepping a boundary (of health, pleasure, moral or societal norms).

Applied to racism, *jouissance* refers both to the enjoyment involved in domination – the 'excess' of power that makes it more than simply access to resources, but instead creates a kind of embodied delight in subjugating others, including sexually, as the history of slavery demonstrates – and to the sense of dissatisfaction that results from the impossibility of ever having one's desires fully met. The consequence of this latter sensation is that it is assumed by the subject not that there is a constitutional lack that makes enjoyment impossible, but that the entitlement to enjoyment – the privilege of whiteness – has been *stolen* by the other. Black embodiment and sensuality; Jewish cleverness and social solidarity: these are examples of the assumed *jouissance* of the other, that the white envies and resents. Drawing extensively on Slavoj Žižek's articulation of this idea, Hook (2018, p.258) comments that racism

> is not most fundamentally about psychological rivalries, or about the need to displace onto the other what one disavows about one's self. Racism is instead to be understood as a response to the "real" of enjoyment – be it at an individual level (in respect of finding a way to relate to one's own "stolen" *jouissance*) or at the societal level (as an attempt to account for the multiple contingencies, conflicts, and deadlocks of a given society).

It is noteworthy that Hook here emphasizes the structural components of racism, that the operation of *jouissance* is not only at the level of the individual but is baked into the social order. Slavery is again the principal model for this, but all colonialism exemplifies it, and it can be found too in the social arrangements that promote anti-Black racism, belligerent ethnonationalism and systemic antisemitism.

In a later paper, Hook (2022) draws on material from the Lacanian analyst Eric Laurent, who writes that 'The malicious *jouissance* at stake in racist discourse … is the fundament of any social bond. The founding crime is not the murder of the father, but the will to murder he who embodies the *jouissance* that I reject' (Hook, 2022, p.25 [m/s]). The argument that Hook develops from this is again that a core element of racism is envy of the other's *jouissance*, and that racism is characterized by a perceived 'theft of enjoyment'. Moreover – and here we might be getting to the heart of whiteness – the hatred of the other for embodying the *jouissance* that the white subject feels they do not have is not simply a manifesto for dominance and obliteration of the subjugated non-white. It is also a mode of enjoyment in itself, a necessary way of remaining present and also of reinforcing belonging both in the conventional sense of alignment of groups (whiteness defined by the presence of blackness) and also of confirming that whiteness has real substance in itself. Hook again:

> In racist fantasy, I would rather believe that this libidinal treasure – the very feature which underlies my superiority – has been usurped by some foreign other, rather than concede that my initial projections of national/cultural/racial greatness may have been unfounded from the very outset. This means then – a paradoxical point, worth reiterating – that in many forms of racism, I willingly gravitate to the position of the victim, and experience myself as under attack.
>
> (Hook, 2022, p.31 [m/s])

Whiteness always feels itself to be under threat ('you/the Jews will not replace us') and it needs to do so in order to feel real. Privilege is precarious but this precarity is important to it, as defending it becomes a matter of self-worth. The privilege of whiteness is mythologized as due to superiority, but this myth can only be sustained if the actual experience of white insufficiency is attributed to the malevolent actions of racialized others. And those others who are enjoying themselves so much at whiteness' expense? They need to be attacked or they will take over the world.

This chapter has moved some way at the end from a specifically Jewish approach to a more generally psychoanalytic one. Yet there is something here that might be worth considering in relation to Jewishness, whiteness and this account of racism. The antisemitic imaginary of the Jew as scheming, conspiratorial, anti-nationalist and corrupting is core to racism even though it is by no means its sole element. This is because it embodies most transparently the scheme of envy of the other's enjoyment: in fantasy, the Jew has what the white subject wants. From the other side, Jewish expositions of the importance of approaching the other as having the same rights and standing as oneself ('you know the heart of a stranger, seeing you were strangers in the land of Egypt') fuels the drive to oppose racism from the position of being an outsider – in this context, from the non-white position. Absorbing Jews into whiteness denies this possibility and loses the specificity both of antisemitism and of Jewish antiracism; it also, perhaps just as significantly, obscures the dynamic of racism by denying the centrality of Jewish otherness. Historically, two major sources of racism are extractivist colonialism (including slavery) and religious supersessionism. These run together, of course, with Christianity, the prime vehicle for anti-Judaism, often offering legitimation for slavery (though also opposing it at times), demonstrating the intrinsic relationship between antisemitism and anti-Black racism. Jewish suffering and other forms of racialized oppression relate to one another; Jews receive projections and envious attacks just as obviously and destructively as do other groups subjected to racist abuse and genocidal assault. It is true that the status of Jews with regard to whiteness fluctuates and that there are consequences of this. In particular, the 'undecidability' of Jews as white or not is an element in the way they are experienced as dangerous by racists, who are precisely committed to placing everyone into a definite category. But this fluctuation is itself maintained by antisemitism as a specific feature of Jewish life and has marked Jewish precarity for much of recent history. Jews also have a tradition that opposes this, however fraught and contested it might be at times. Activating this opposition requires that Jews both own their white privilege where it is in operation and separate themselves from it; and it also needs other antiracists to recognize that Jewish solidarity with them has specifically Jewish roots that do not reduce to white guilt.

Chapter 7

BEING ILL AT EASE

Fort-Da again

The best known decolonial writer deploying psychoanalysis is Frantz Fanon, whose book *Black Skin, White Masks* (Fanon, 1952) has become a kind of foundational text of antiracism and postcolonialism. As described in Chapter 3, *Black Skin, White Masks* contains some ambiguous comments about Jews, in some places averring solidarity and in others introducing a version of Jewishness that sets the experience of antisemitism apart from that of anti-Black racism. Fanon's hegemony in the field of decolonial thought remains strong and is justifiable on the grounds of the force and acuity of his portrait of the colonial situation and of the impact of racism; but at times it seems that this hegemony also blocks other voices from being heard, with their own contributions to make from the position in which they found themselves. In this chapter, I want to attend to some writings by Albert Memmi, by no means a neglected figure in the history of decolonial and antiracist thought, but nevertheless a less prominent one than Fanon, and one writing from a very specific experience: that of the decolonial activist who also happens to be a Jew.

At the end of his autobiographical novel, *The Pillar of Salt* (1953), which was almost exactly contemporaneous with *Black Skin, White Masks*, Memmi uses his fictional avatar Alexandre Mordekhai Benillouche to sum up the dilemma that occupied him throughout his life, from his adolescent attempts to distance himself from the Jewish Tunisian culture of his family, through his engagement in the anti-colonial struggle, to his eventual – actually quite briskly post-independence – move away from Tunisia to the France which he had been fighting against (in the novel, Benillouche leaves Tunis for Argentina).

> I am ill at ease in my own land and I know of no other. My culture is borrowed and I speak my mother tongue haltingly. I have neither religious beliefs nor tradition, and am ashamed of whatever particle

of them has survived deep within me. To try to explain what I am, I would need an intelligent audience and much time: I am a Tunisian but of French culture ... I am Tunisian, but Jewish, which means that I am politically and socially an outcast. I speak the language of the country with a particular accent and emotionally I have nothing in common with Moslems. I am a Jew who has broken with the Jewish religion and the ghetto, is ignorant of Jewish culture and detest the middle class because it is phony. I am poor but desperately anxious not to be poor, and at the same time, I refuse to take the necessary steps to avoid poverty.

(Memmi, 1953, p.331)

There is more to this than a representation of psychological ambivalence and the perpetual deracination of Jews. First, it is worth noting the striking echo of Freud here, which is probably not deliberate but simply due to their shared experience of being secular Jews, enticed away from their Jewish identity towards the wider culture, yet also ineluctably drawn back in both because of antisemitism and for emotional reasons. Memmi writes, 'I am a Jew who has broken with the Jewish religion and the ghetto, is ignorant of Jewish culture.' Freud's (1930, p.xv) parallel comment in the preface to the Hebrew edition of *Totem and Taboo* has already been quoted in Chapter 1:

an author who is ignorant of the language of holy writ, who is completely estranged from the religion of his fathers – as well as from every other religion – and who cannot take a share in nationalist ideals, but who has yet never repudiated his people, who feels that he is in his essential nature a Jew and who has no desire to alter that nature.

For Memmi too, the attachment to Jewishness is irresistible despite his active rejection of it in his early life, but unlike Freud he has some clear explanations for it. In the novel, Benillouche has to reconsider this rejection when faced with the reality of the hostility of his compatriots, reflected in a 'pogrom' against the Jewish community by their Moslem neighbours and in the alacrity with which the colonizing French accede to Nazi demands once the Germans invade. But in Memmi's slightly later writing, now in his own voice, he also offers a defence of the appeal of Jewish religious practices as a medium for collective solidarity with deeply personal associations as well as important functions in supporting a precarious community.

In agreeing to sing the Haggadah at Passover or to celebrate Purim, I did not think that I was confirming the existence of God or the miracle of the Red Sea or of the fall of Haman. Simply, I was returning to my own people, to my father, my mother, my brothers and sisters, and to the ghetto, in a half-serious, half-childish collective game which either irritated or amused me according to my mood; an almost obligatory game, however, if I wanted to be one with them again or merely not to hurt them. The truth or the falsity of the traditional dogmas, the post-reasonings of apologists as to the presence of God or the rejection of God which by the very violence of my refusal would confirm it, and other theological jugglings, had truly nothing to do with it.

(Memmi, 1962, p.296)

This self-justification will be recognizable to many secular Jews, and probably to alienated adherents of other traditions as well (this is part of Memmi's point): whilst the core of religious belief has been stripped away, the regular practices of at least the communal and familial elements of Judaism continue as a means to acknowledge relational connectedness. In Memmi's politicized language, this is a mode of solidarity essential to the maintenance of a minoritized and oppressed community, an argument to which we will return. The broader point, however, is the familiar 'fort-da' one that Freud (1920) recognized in his grandson's play and that, as previously described, stands as an important analogue both of the psychoanalytic process and of the modern Jewish condition. 'Fort' – go out; 'da' – return. This describes both the attitude of the surrounding world to Jews (you are welcome until we expel you) and of emancipated Jews to their own communities and religious or communal practices (I am going away but keep coming back). Memmi is one of many writers and thinkers who have articulated this process, in his case as in some others with a kind of realistic bitterness that recognizes the justice of national liberation struggles but laments the anti-Jewishness that goes along with them. 'When the Tunisian Constitution appeared,' he writes (Memmi, 1962, p.7), 'it established the Moslem religion among its essential provisions. For a number of reasons that have nothing to do with my subject, I did not find that too shocking; but why would I, who had rebelled against my own religion, accept, under compulsion, the Moslem religion which was now official?' After the Suez crisis, in any case, there was little room for Memmi or his Jewish compatriots in Tunisia; and whilst Memmi remained attuned to the decolonial struggle, he moved gradually rightwards in his political orientation.

'Benillouche's' self-description as 'ill at ease in my own land' is an expansion of his introductory assessment of himself as 'a native in a colonial country, a Jew in an anti-Semitic universe, an African in a world dominated by Europe' (Memmi, 1953, p.96). That is, the fictional character's self-presentation is of someone automatically displaced by his multiple identities, thrice oppressed (colonized 'native', Jew, African) or at least what we might now call minoritized; and linguistically alienated. In the novel, he gives a speech to fellow prisoners in a Nazi labour camp and finds he needs the nuances of French, as his Arabic is not subtle enough. In relation to his own compatriots, he writes (p.289), 'I realized how much closer I would have been to them and how much more intimate had I spoken their own tongue.' The specificity of this is important: whatever the identification that Benillouche/Memmi might have with the anti-colonial struggle in Tunisia, and this identification is profound, his own position is a fraught one, at odds with some of the major nationalistic elements of that struggle and especially their foundation in Moslem identity. The question this immediately raises is whether Jews can engage with liberation struggles alongside other oppressed peoples, or whether everyone has to fight on their own. The later history of Memmi as a defender of the State of Israel against leftist criticism might be part of the database for considering this issue.

Memmi's family was rooted in Tunisia, long-standing members of the poorer elements of Jewish society there, albeit possibly with Italian as well as Berber ancestry (Shatz, 2020). They lived on the edge of the ghetto in Tunis, a position that gave them a vague sense of superiority but little protection either from the routine antisemitism of everyday French colonialism or the periodic violence against Jews that came from the surrounding Moslem population. Memmi himself was clear-eyed about both and understood them in the context of shared oppression. For him, antisemitism and anti-Moslem racism were part of the same general phenomenon, a pervasive racism that can be found everywhere. Even in his major book focused entirely on Jewishness, *Portrait of a Jew* (1962), he has space for the links between antisemitism and the racism that he sees as structuring colonialism and perhaps the world generally. He writes (p.53), 'When I hear the ritualistic phrase: "I am not a racist but …" I know that the racism-trolley has started, that the questioning has begun, that sooner or later, my life is in danger.' Compare this to Fanon's (1952, p.92) parallel comment quoted earlier, from the Black rather than the Jewish perspective, that 'It was my philosophy professor, a native of the Antilles, who recalled the fact to me one day: "Whenever you hear anyone abuse the Jews, pay attention, because he is talking about you'". Memmi is assertive about the responsibility that people suffering from different forms of racism might have towards one another, as well as the pressure towards division that colonialism and racism imposes. The following passage is Memmi's powerful response to what he describes as the common defence he hears against Jewish claims of being subjected to antisemitism: 'You think of yourself too much! Come now! You enjoy pitying yourselves! Have a little pity for others!' (Memmi, 1962, p.28).

> Far from thinking I am the only one in this situation, I believe, on the contrary, that racial discrimination is more widespread than anything else in the world. I note, with horror, that most individuals, most peoples, are basically inclined to xenophobia. Far from believing I am the sole victim in 'a world of peace and justice,' I think, unfortunately, that the statement should be reversed: the Jewish tragedy is part of a much broader human category – the category of oppression and misfortune. But, I repeat, I do not understand how the misfortune of others can be reassuring and comforting. All the misfortune in the world gives me no consolation at all for my own. It does not console me for anything. All the injustice in the world cannot make me accept the injustice I suffer. On the contrary, it feeds my anger, it whips up my fury against the shame and the outrage. Because I am a Jew, am I to console myself with the thought of anti-Negro racism or racial difficulties in the colonies? What my would-be comforters suggest to me is that since, after all, xenophobia does exist, it is up to me to suffer patiently the insult to the Jews! I understand perfectly. There are, in short, two attitudes: either one accepts all the suffering or one rejects it all. Well, I reject it in totum as I reject in detail each face of oppression.
>
> (Memmi, 1962, pp.29–30)

A clearer statement of Jewish-Black solidarity could hardly be made. There is no satisfaction in observing the 'misfortune' of others; 'xenophobia' is widespread, one form of racism leaks into another and with 'racial discrimination [being] more widespread than anything else in the world' it is necessary to reject it in all its forms ('in totum') as well as in each of its manifestations, for example as antisemitism.

Memmi here adopts a broad antiracist position that, whilst it does not explicitly theorize colonialism, views the racist mindset ('xenophobia') as all-pervasive. His opposition to antisemitism and exploration of anti-Jewish oppression is therefore primarily justifiable as part of the wider struggle against racism in all its forms. Indeed, in *The Portrait of a Jew*, Memmi seems to acknowledge a kind of stratification of oppression in which the Jew suffers from one of the *oldest* forms of racialized hatred but is not necessarily the *worst* affected. As a Jew, he writes (p.320), 'I am above all an oppressed person and the Jewish fate is essentially a condition of oppression.' In this respect, 'my figure resembles astonishingly that of many others: to be precise, of other oppressed peoples'. Uncertainty over whether Jews are oppressed like others is due to oppression having different features in different cases ('oppression does not always have the same appearance'). Oppression can be class oppression or colonial oppression; the oppression of the Jew 'stands midway between the two: it is within the same nation without being involved in the class struggle'. And broadening the range: 'the oppression of the American Negro is still more complex; it includes at the same time economic, cultural and political pressure. The oppression of woman is probably the most artful, being tempered and disguised by eroticism and maternity'. Still, there is something exceptional about the experience of Jews, due to the longevity of antisemitism, which isolates them even as it impels a collective response to racisms of all kinds. Memmi (1962, p.253) emits a discouraged feeling about the state of Jewry in reaction to what elsewhere has been called 'the longest hatred':

> Unlike the colonized, the Jew has been oppressed for so long that he no longer even believes strongly in his right to live among other men. In any case, to the inhabitants of the ghetto – and every Jew carries within him his own ghetto – for the Jewish masses, persecution seems vaguely to be a natural calamity. It seems to them to flow almost of necessity from their lives among non-Jews.

Such an attitude might promote paranoia and would certainly seem to justify an ethnocentric response on the part of Jews; and Memmi even shares their perception of the world as unremittingly antagonistic towards them: 'that popular belief is, I am convinced, fundamentally correct and historically justified: persecution is the paroxysm of social and historical discomfort; now malaise is consubstantial with the Jewish fate' (1962, p.253). Still, even in the face of this argument about the specificity and severity of the Jewish situation, Memmi maintains a position of solidarity with other oppressed peoples. His political struggle is universal, fuelled in part by his awareness of the ravages of colonialism arising from his own direct experiences in Tunisia; but also by his (perhaps increasing) sense of the centrality of antisemitism in a racist world. Or maybe all that is being said here is that Memmi is drawn by his own identity-position to feel the Jewish dimension most strongly and with most bitterness, whilst remaining aware of, and committed to, the need for a general antiracist and anti-colonialist politics. This is a standpoint with which many leftist Jews would identify, which is perhaps one reason why the periodic betrayals by the Left hurt so much.

The development of this account of both the specificity of antisemitism and the universality of racism, and hence the need for antiracist resistance that emphasizes solidarity between different groups, is a complex one that takes careful unpicking. On the one hand, it is a response to the fissiparous pressure of a racist world in which different minoritized groups are set against each other (the anti-Jewish 'pogrom' described in *The Pillar of Salt* is an example, as is the avidity with which Jews are rounded up once the Germans invade Tunis). On the other hand, Memmi's longer analysis stresses how antisemitism has its own particularities and demands intra-communal solidarity, which is why he understands the appeal of Islam to the decolonizing Arab states and can accept the exclusion of Jews from them, whilst also lamenting exactly this exclusion, which in many respects represents an active process of expulsion. The history here is fraught and has much to do with the emergence of the State of Israel, but for the purpose of this chapter I want to trace only how two of Memmi's major books, *The Colonizer and the Colonized* and *The Portrait of a Jew*, throw light on the question of solidarity around antisemitism and racism.

Colonizer and colonized

Albert Memmi's *The Colonizer and the Colonized* was published in 1957 and remains an articulate if polemical account of the colonial relationship, in some ways seeming increasingly relevant with its understanding of the place of religion and nationalism in decolonial liberation movements. Complementing Fanon (1952), who focuses his account of the colonial situation on racism and has become a key source for later interpreters of how racism infects the psychic life of both black and white subjects, Memmi directs his attention to the investment of the colonialist in the privileges of the colonial situation and the impact of this on the colonized subject's self-perception. For Memmi, all colonialists participate actively in oppression even when they seem to side with the oppressed; he does not even exempt himself from this, acknowledging that his position as a Jewish Tunisian marks him out as distinct from the Arab majority who are the truly colonized. This is what warrants his account of the colonizer: he can find traces of that person in himself, so in important ways he can identify with it. In his self-reflective *Preface* to the book in 1965, Memmi articulates this point at length, describing how complex his position was in Tunis (he left there for France in 1956) because whilst Jews were 'like all other Tunisians' treated as 'second-class' citizens, they were different from the Muslim population and identified differently in the decolonial struggle. 'They were undeniably "natives," as they were then called,' he writes (p.9), 'as near as possible to the Moslems in poverty, language, sensibilities, customs, taste in music, odors and cooking. However, unlike the Moslems, they passionately endeavored to identify themselves with the French.' This even stretched to bearing 'arms side by side with the French in the streets of Algiers' and meant that Memmi's own denunciation of colonialism and links with the decolonial movement placed him in a difficult position with his Jewish community. 'Because of this ambivalence,' he writes (p.10), 'I knew only too well the contradictory emotions which swayed their lives.' Memmi writes about this in a relatively dispassionate tone, but one has to wonder what the cost was to himself as he faced the tensions in his position, and how much painful disavowal was at work.

Amongst several notable points about Memmi's reflection on the ambiguous position of the Jew in a colonized society is the demonstration that even at this stage of his political development, he was positioning himself as Jewish and as such had no expectation that he would be fully included in the post-liberation polity. As a Jew, he had some privileges, however minor; or at least, Jews in Tunisia aspired to the situation of the colonizer, to French culture, and they felt they had something to lose. Someone like Memmi, a Jew who sided with the mass of the Tunisian people against the French, was something of an exception and found himself marginalized in both communities, a position from which he was never freed. On the one hand, Memmi was part of the oppressed mass, never at this stage accepted by the French (and even having to struggle for citizenship later, when he lived in France); on the other hand, he identified with French culture and spoke French as his main language. 'I was a sort of half-breed of colonization, understanding everyone because I belonged completely to no one,' he writes (p.12). The advantage of this estranged position is that he could reflect on both the colonized and the colonizing groups from the inside: even though not a colonizer himself – actually, far from being one – he had an inkling of what the colonial situation meant to the colonizer and of the fear of its dissolution. He could also write honestly about the colonized, in

this vein similarly to Fanon, without idealization and with awareness
that the postcolonial path was likely to be a rocky one. Most of all, he
could appreciate that whilst one group had privileges and the other only
burdens, one group were oppressors and the other oppressed, both were
constructed *by* colonialism itself. The attributes of the colonizer and
the attributes of the colonized, including the various assumptions of
'civilization' and 'primitivity', 'development' and 'backwardness' that
so permeate rhetorical justifications for colonialism, are *produced by*
the colonial situation and are not the reason for it. Writing about the
'fashionable notions of "dependency complex," "colonizability," etc.'
(p.132), notions that Fanon (1952) had ferociously deconstructed,
especially in his critique of Octave Mannoni's (1956) *Prospero and
Caliban*, Memmi agrees that there might be 'a particle of truth' in the
idea of 'a certain adherence of the colonized to colonization'. However,
he writes, 'this adherence is the result of colonization and not its cause.
It arises after and not before colonial occupation.' More generally
(p.100), 'The colonial situation manufactures colonialists, just as it
manufactures the colonized.' This manufacture has powerful economic
interests at its heart – Memmi rebutted criticism of his book that held
that it underplays the economic basis for colonialism, and certainly
there is plenty of textual evidence that he saw economic gain and
extractivism as key features of the colonial project. However, it also has
a psychological dimension: 'colonial privilege is not solely economic,'
he writes (p.8). 'To observe the life of the colonizer and the colonized
is to discover rapidly that the daily humiliation of the colonized, his
objective subjugation, are not merely economic. Even the poorest
colonizer thought himself to be – and actually was – superior to the
colonized. This too was part of colonial privilege.' Being able to think of
oneself as superior – the feeling that one *amounts to* something more
than could have been the case back in the 'mother country' – is a crucial
element of the investment in colonialism, especially for the relatively
low-level member of the colonial group for whom the small privileges
that colonialism brings are important props to self-esteem. This applies
too to the group of subjects who are neither colonized nor colonizers,
including Jews as 'candidates for assimilation' (p.57), and also to a range
of 'petty tyrants': 'What revenge and what pride for a noncolonized
small-time carpenter to walk side by side with an Arab laborer carrying
a board and a few nails on his head! All have at least this profound
satisfaction of being negatively better than the colonized: they are never
completely engulfed in the abasement into which colonialism drives
them' (p.61). The hierarchization of colonial society has benefits for

many and seduces them into being its adherents; the rejection of these other groups by the decolonizing forces becomes partly comprehensible as a result.

Memmi's book is split between an account of the colonizer and of the colonized, with if anything more energy devoted to the former. Much of this energy comes from his critique of the 'colonizer of good will' (p.11), the leftist who identifies with the struggle against colonialism from the position of his own privilege. Nadine Gordimer (2003) takes Memmi to task over this in her introductory comments to the 2003 edition of *The Colonized and the Colonizer*, in which she argues that the place of the Left in freedom struggles across Africa since the publication of Memmi's book demonstrates that he was mistaken. 'Memmi was wrong,' she writes (p.39), 'in that there was a minority of colonizers, mainly of the Left spectrum, who identified themselves with the position that colonialism was unjust, racist and anti-human, and were prepared, first, to act against it along with the great mass force of the colonized and, then, to live under that force's majority government.' Her criticisms are in some respects clearly well founded; for example, she points out that the situation of Jews in South Africa was very different to that of Jews in the Maghreb, and it may well be true that Memmi's experiences are too specific to his national location to justify the generalizations he makes. But this neglects Memmi's strength in writing so strongly from his particular place, from the inside of the outsider position. These 'impotent' leftists, as he describes them, were those people with whom he felt most comfortable, yet also observed with ironic detachment.

> I could but smile with my friends at their halting assurance that Andalusian music is the most beautiful in the world; or that Europeans are fundamentally bad (the proof being that they are too harsh with their children). Naturally the result was suspicion on the part of the colonized. And this in spite of the immense good will of this type of French colonizer and the fact that these Frenchmen were already despised by the rest of the French community. I understood only too well their difficulties, their inevitable ambiguity and the resulting isolation; more serious still, their inability to act. All this was a part of my own fate.
>
> (p.11)

Pace Gordimer, the argument Memmi actually presents here is that the leftist colonizer's opposition to colonization idealizes the colonized at the expense of true commitment, that when the situation becomes fraught and the colonized rise up against all their masters, their situation will become untenable. This relates not only to the violence of the decolonial movement, but also to the place of religion and nationalism within it; and specifically because the leftist 'discovers that there is no connection between the liberation of the colonized and the application of a left-wing program. And that, in fact, he is perhaps aiding the birth of a social order in which there is no room for a leftist as such, at least in the near future.' (Part of Gordimer's argument is that this has not turned out to be the case in South Africa, where many white anti-Apartheid activists have remained committed to the new nation state.) For Memmi, the point is not the aspiration of the leftist member of the colonial group to help create equality and justice under a decolonized regime; it is rather that group membership, or perhaps better-put the structure of power relations, determines the stance it is possible to take, and the position the subjects of colonialism – whichever side they are on – find themselves in. The leftist colonizer might have every good will but remains part of the colonizing group and will be seen as such by the liberating power: 'Colonial relations do not stem from individual good will or actions; they exist before his arrival or his birth, and whether he accepts or rejects them matters little. It is they, on the contrary which, like any institution, determine a priori his place and that of the colonized and, in the final analysis, their true relationship' (pp.82–3).

Memmi sees colonialism as founded in economic gain and categorizes it as akin to fascism: 'What is fascism, if not a regime of oppression for the benefit of a few? ... The human relationships have arisen from the severest exploitation, founded on inequality and contempt, guaranteed by police authoritarianism. There is no doubt in the minds of those who have lived through it that colonialism is one variety of fascism' (pp.106–7). But he is also well aware of its intimate relationship with racism, which he regards as a central element in the maintenance of the colonial state and the colonial relationship in general. Racist assumptions are used to justify economic exploitation and administrative as well as military and judicial discrimination and oppression. Without such severity, racism claims, the 'primitive' aggression of the colonized will break out and both the colonizer and the colonized need to be 'protected' from this. The standard justifications for colonialism find their way into the racist assumptions of everyday life: the colonized need to be governed, in their own interest, by more civilized and advanced groups; they cannot make use of education; they cannot be trusted in positions of power. They are, in important ways, dehumanized.

Racism appears then, not as an incidental detail, but as a
consubstantial part of colonialism. It is the highest expression of
the colonial system and one of the most significant features of the
colonialist. Not only does it establish a fundamental discrimination
between colonizer and colonized, a sine qua non of colonial life, but
it also lays the foundation for the immutability of this life. The racist
tone of each move of both the colonialist and the colonizer is the
source of the extraordinary spread of racism in the colonies.

(p.118)

Racism in the colonial setting thus has an economic base, but it
operates independently of this, confirming the colonizer in a 'madness
for destroying the colonized' (p.131) and also having an impact on the
self-perception of the colonized. Examination of the effects of this takes
up most of the second part of Memmi's book. Just as the colonizer is
constructed into the position of oppressor by the colonial situation,
so the colonized is made (p.133) 'into an oppressed creature, whose
development is broken and who compromises by his defeat'.

Memmi's examination of the racialized impact of colonization on the
colonized takes in the place of the family and religion and an aspiration
to assimilation that links Jewishness and Blackness in a startling way,
through the concept of self-hate.

This phenomenon is comparable to Negrophobia in a Negro, or anti-
Semitism in a Jew. Negro women try desperately to uncurl their hair,
which keeps curling back, and torture their skin to make it a little
whiter. Many Jews would, if they could, tear out their souls – that soul
which, they are told, is irremediably bad ... The point is that whether
Negro, Jew or colonized, one must resemble the white man, the non-
Jew, the colonizer. Just as many people avoid showing off their poor
relations, the colonized in the throes of assimilation hides his past,
his traditions, in fact all his origins which have become ignominious.

(p.166)

This, too, has echoes of Fanon's (1952) analysis of the impact of racism
on the colonized subject, the famous mirroring process in which the
Black subject is constructed in the alienating and disempowering
gaze of the white. But the end point of this is not so despairing; it is
rather that for both Fanon and Memmi there is only one way out of
the colonial situation, to revolt. For Memmi, the psychological and
political realization of this arises after it becomes clear that the attempt

by the colonized to assimilate, to become one with the colonizer's 'superior' image, will fail; at that point, it is evident that the only route to emancipation is to reject the colonial situation entirely. Failing to receive recognition from the colonizing other throws colonized subjects back on their own resources, fuelling a potentially revolutionary process in which they have no option but to refuse and resist colonialism itself.

> Attempts at imitating the colonizer required self-denial; the colonizer's rejection is the indispensable prelude to self-discovery. That accusing and annihilating image must be shaken off; oppression must be attacked boldly since it is impossible to go around it. After having been rejected for so long by the colonizer, the day has come when it is the colonized who must refuse the colonizer.
>
> (p.172)

Recovery of religious traditions, self-assertion in nationalistic identity, total opposition to all Europeans in the colonies whether or not they side with the colonial enterprise – these are trademarks of the decolonizing movement. They are not necessarily welcomed by Western liberals and leftists, because they often appeal to non-universalistic principles of national self-identity and even – as has become obvious in many places – authoritarianism and theocratic nationalism. Yet they are not to be written off as an aberration. Certainly, they derive from the damage done by colonialism, but they are also part of the story of its end.

As a partial aside that relates to Memmi's position, the national self-determination that characterizes the decolonial movement is understood by some as a legitimate Southern Cone response to colonialism, not to be judged through the continuing racist and colonialist mindset of the old European masters. According to Slabodsky (2014), Memmi's view was that 'mythical nativism' was a legitimate Africana development towards the reappropriation of cultural values for social and political use. New-old myths of national self-determination are needed, in this view, to fuel the journey of decolonial emancipation. This might also apply to Jews, in that adopting a Southern perspective one might see Zionism as 'a decolonial movement that responds to the condition of global Jewry. As a consequence, it should be interpreted as a movement of the "national Liberation of Jews on par with other liberation movements, in the Maghreb, in Africa and elsewhere in the world"' (Slabodsky, 2014, p.139) – a problematic and contentious stance, of course, though one shared at the time Memmi was writing by many critical thinkers, for example, Herbert Marcuse and Max Horkheimer (Jacobs, 2015).

Portrait of a Jew

Memmi's view of Jewish history and culture is not exactly optimistic.

> There is indeed optimism in the Jewish tradition, but an optimism
> beyond despair. It is the optimism of the psychiatrist after his patient's
> abortive suicide; since the bottom has been reached, now only better
> can come. This attitude has almost become a mental habit of the Jew.
> After each family catastrophe, my mother used to thank God in this
> way: 'Blessed be Thou, our eternal God, who hath preserved us from
> a greater misfortune.'
>
> (Memmi, 1962, p.18)

The old Jewish telegram joke comes to mind: 'start worrying, letter
to follow.' Memmi writes that he is tempted to say that there are no
happy Jews; or rather (p.21), 'There are Jews who, perhaps, are happy
in spite of their Judaism. But because of it, in relation to it – no!'
Indeed, the opening pages of *Portrait of a Jew* are so damning of the
social condition of Jews that it might even pass for self-hatred, if it
were not for the fact that Memmi is absolutely clear that this condition
of repeated, inescapable suffering and unhappiness is not due to the
nature of Jewry or Judaism, but to the force of the external world, that
is, to antisemitism. This comes home to every Jew, however separated
or assimilated they might be; at some point, the world intrudes on them
and makes them experience themselves as a Jew, and as hated for that.

> One way or another the day always comes when you discover that
> you are a Jew, just as you discover that you are mortal, not because of
> the collective and abstract promise of death, but because of your own
> individual condemnation.
>
> (p.25)

The consequence of this is that no Jew can be confident or satisfied; the
situation of exclusion or aggression is turned inwards into a kind of self-
consciousness that is forged in and by antisemitism, making the Jew into
an aggravated and confused subject: 'Ashamed or bragging, persecuted
or proud, Jewishness can never be anything but tormented' (p.28). And,
hilariously but to Jews recognizably (p.31): 'Very few among us that I
have seen, for example, were able to lie still in the sun, stretched out on
the grass or dreaming in a chair as I have seen, with envy, non-Jews do.'
This is a joke, discernible perhaps only to Jews, reminiscent of the one
glossed by Devorah Baum (2017, p.1):

There's a joke Jews sometimes like to tell about the moment when two non-Jews, Tom and Dick, bump into each other in the street.

TOM: How are you?

DICK: Fine, thanks.

Ha! Just imagine not being Jewish! 'Fine, thanks!' What a blast!

Lying still in the sun is not for Jews; the agitation produced by the history of calamity will not allow such unguardedness. 'Fine, thanks' – whoever heard of that? Given the situations of uprootedness and persecution that mark the Jewish past, and of course near-contemporary genocide, the whole character of the Jew has become one of restlessness. 'It would have been a miracle, incredible, utterly incomprehensible,' writes Memmi (1962, p.34), 'if such constant and prolonged insecurity, handed down from generation to generation, had not resulted in a complete inner restlessness.' Again, this is not because of anything intrinsic to Jews, but because circumstances have made them thus; constant threats leave their mark, create the anxious Jews we know. Their objective circumstances dictate their psychological and social behaviour.

For Memmi, antisemitism is an indisputable and widespread fact of life. 'I believe firmly,' he writes (p.47), 'that anti-Semitism is profoundly widespread and real; I fear we must start with this generalization, for it is among the half-truths of the nation in which I live.' Antisemitism simply 'breaks out' (p.48) in people, as if it lies in wait for any excuse and then acts independently of any intentional state, so we are not talking about conscious decisions to hate Jews, but simply the way the world works, with the discourses of antisemitism representing a foundational structure of society. It is 'a collective and world-wide phenomenon' (p.48) that colours all relationships between Jews and non-Jews and makes the life of every Jew 'unliveable as a Jew' (p.49). That is, in this view of things – as strong a denunciation of racism as can be found anywhere – antisemitism is so all-pervasive and so routine, so embedded in the fabric of the world, that the intentions or goodwill of any non-Jew will never suffice to contest it. There is an echo here of the pessimistic attitude Memmi takes in his earlier book towards the anti-colonial member of the colonizing group as well as parallels with Afropessimism. For Memmi (p.50), 'every non-Jew, directly or indirectly, shares the responsibility for the Jewish misfortune; every non-Jew, willingly or unwillingly, shares the responsibility for oppressing the Jew'. There is, therefore, nothing special about the antisemite; rather, even though it might be useful to think psychologically or sociologically about why one person holds more strongly than another to antisemitic discourses, antisemites are honest representatives of their society, which is intrinsically antisemitic. Antisemitism is a breeding pit for antisemites but thinking of individuals in this way is not the relevant point; 'there is nothing original about anti-Semitism, its curses, its accusations, its aggressions merely express the surprise, the rage and the will to murder of all non-Jewish society' (p.52).

Given the vehemence of Memmi's account of the force and ubiquity of antisemitism, it is perhaps not surprising that he sees it as having a damaging effect on the Jewish psyche. But in *Portrait of a Jew* he is insistent that the apparent differences that distinguish the Jew from the non-Jew are facets of racist thinking and are not actualities; or if they exist, they are the product of antisemitism rather than the justification for it. The force of antisemitic societies is a profound one, imposing itself constantly on any and every Jew. 'To be a Jew,' Memmi writes (p.57), 'is first and foremost to find oneself called to account, to feel oneself continuously accused, explicitly or implicitly, clearly or obscurely'. This 'accusation' leads Jews to recognize their difference from others – a set of differences imposed upon them that also become undeniable, even if some Jews (to Memmi's disdain) choose to pretend that there is no difference between Jew and non-Jew. Dismissing the idea of biological or 'racial' differences between Jew and non-Jew ('it is the idea people have of the Jew that suggests and imposes a certain idea of Jewish biology' – p.114), Memmi nevertheless thinks that, 'Like the colonized native, the proletarian, and most certainly in his own guise, he is a concrete negativity' (p.80). There is a 'Jewish fate' (p.81) that arises from the relationship between Jews and non-Jews; this includes the antisemitic association between Jews and money which positions all Jews as somehow implicated whenever economic issues are at stake. Memmi describes his own situation with evocative fluency: growing up in the poverty of the ghetto, noting that all the Jews he knew were poor, the claim that Jews are rich and financially exploitative is patently absurd. 'I had no doubt that the real Jew was the poor Jew, for I myself was the real Jew,' he writes (p.130). For Memmi the Marxist, the function of this economic charge against the Jews is clear:

> Jews are said to be essentially the propertied class, financiers, businessmen and middlemen; in short the great specialists of the

economy, its rulers and its profiteers. This is, at bottom, merely a poorly disguised variant of the traditional picture of the fat Jew (fat, this time), smirking on his mountain of gold, while the masses groan, crushed beneath the yoke of international Jewish plutocracy ... That scarcely rationalized proposition finally reveals its true nature: an abusive and grotesque generalization. It amuses the real specialists, the actual rulers of economy. They know well enough in whose hands economic power lies.

(p.140)

Antisemitism serves the needs of power. All the differences ascribed to the Jew – intelligence ('too intelligent'), economic segregation, religious difference – are in support of the idea of the evil of the Jew, society's scapegoat, inheritor of a history of religious intolerance (Memmi devotes attention to the ubiquitousness of Christianity's framing of the Jew as other) and its racialized modern forms. Memmi claims (p.173) that 'The Nazi accusations are only a secularization of this theological method of radical condemnation. Modern racism is merely employing a language more adapted to the present day.' Even other oppressed groups benefit from antisemitism: 'The Jew is the oppressed of all that society, including its other oppressed members, any one of whom, even the most underprivileged, feels in a position to despise and insult the Jew' (pp.175-6). Memmi's account makes all non-Jews complicit, whether or not they oppose antisemitism, because they benefit from the oppression of the Jew – an argument put forward in different contexts such as Afropessimism in relation to white privilege, so perhaps startling but nevertheless cogent to read here.

Memmi moves on to discuss the relationship of the Jews to the colonial situation, noting that even though the Jews of Tunisia identify with the French, the French do not identify reciprocally with them, any more than the local non-Jews do.

In North Africa the Jews far outnumber the French. Who has heard anything about them? What future has been foreseen for them? It will be said that their fate is the same as the fate of the Tunisians or the Moroccans and, tomorrow, of the Algerians. But everyone in North Africa knows perfectly well that this is a pious lie ... In short, each side pretended to believe that the Jews belonged to the other side, so that they would not have to bother about them.

(pp.207-8)

Jews have a special position as scapegoats of the world and the association of Jews with leftist, anti-oppressive politics will make little difference, as Memmi knows from his own experience: 'today I have been forced to admit that this instinctive solidarity with the downtrodden, which I do not deny and which I shall continue to proclaim, will not save me ... even if those downtrodden of yesterday were finally to take their revenge; for their cause is not exactly mine' (p.222). Socialism demands that Jews give up their Jewishness in order to participate in the struggle, even though, Memmi thinks, this would not actually work to make the Jew acceptable; in any case, there is an overriding need to act as a Jew, for all the reasons he has previously given. 'Why should I sometimes act as a Jew?' Memmi asks (p.227), 'Because the Jew exists! Because the Jew exists as a Jew, to himself and to others. He exists and at the same time he is never recognized politically except to be made use of, defeated and killed.' All people have to fight from their specific position against oppression. This is as true of Jews as of others – except that Jews are *particularly* oppressed, *especially* rejected, repudiated and separated out and then attacked for being separate. Memmi's despondency about this is very marked. Jews can join the national liberation struggle but will be excluded in the end, as he himself was. Jews must fight for their political rights alongside others, knowing there is no option to abstain; yet abstention would probably be the logical course, given that whatever happens will eventually exclude the Jews as an outsider. Take his own position in the Tunisian anti-colonial struggle:

> The independence of Tunisia and of Morocco, the Tunisian experience, was not directed against the Jews, but neither was it made with the Jews; it was made without them. It is in the very way in which new nations were born that differences became clear, were confirmed, showed us plainly that we were not part of it. It is in the way that Tunisia became a nation like other nations that we became, as we were everywhere else, a civic and national negativity.
>
> (p.246)

Moreover, in this specific historical situation (p.251): 'One of the first acts of the new governments was to tighten the bonds of solidarity with other Arab nations, an understandable and legitimate move. Now one of the foundations of that solidarity today happens to be a pronounced anti-Judaism.' The anti-colonial struggle leaves the Jew out, or rather, it actively opposes the Jew, maintaining the exclusion of Jews as a foundation stone for all contemporary social orders.

What possible response is there to all this negativity? For Memmi, as in *The Colonizer and the Colonized*, it lies in the form of a kind of national self-determination, the formation and maintenance of solidarity amongst those positioned in the same way as oneself. This is not just an issue for Jews, but rather a way in which Jewish solidarity parallels that of other groups. As in other places, Memmi here makes a direct connection between the Jewish and the Black experience (p.270): 'When the Negro asserts himself, he asserts himself as a Negro. The Jew, striving to survive, strives to live as a Jew.' In the face of the borderless transmission of antisemitism lies the boundaryless connection of all Jews, who have similar experiences to one another and therefore resonate with each other, creating a bond forged out of suffering. This appeal to a kind of automatic understanding of Jews for one another is, in fact, not a claim about Jewish specificity or religious chosenness or any other kind of essentialist ethnic identity that magically draws groups together, but a simple statement of the necessity for oppressed groups – however much they may make common cause – to attend to their own needs.

> I believe, in short, that every living group is interdependent. Jewish solidarity is in the first place one example of the vast solidarity of all oppressed persons, a defense reaction of a particularly vulnerable group … solidarity includes more than cases of stated oppressions. It is also the way all isolated peoples, all minorities, defend themselves against solitude and danger.
>
> (p.280)

Jewishness is a social fact; antisemitism is pervasive and inescapable; universalistic struggles towards emancipation are important but will leave out Jews in their specificity; communal solidarity is therefore both a product of oppression and an essential resistive response to it. This is celebrated warmly in Jewish culture and tradition, in family life and community support. It is even visible in Jewish religion and its practices that bring people together: 'The religion of the oppressed person is not only a religion: it is a cement and a dike, an opportunity and a powerful means of reunion' (p.300) – a point also made by George (2018) in relation to African-American Christianity. This is even though Judaism is marked by 'those restrictions, that formalism, that watchful and stifling intolerance … found in the institutions of many oppressed persons' (p.304), a price paid for their survival in a hostile world. Rigid religion, social mores and family life are interpreted by Memmi as protective mechanisms that are necessary for survival, even though they exact a high price from their adherents; they are part of the negativity forced on Jews by the negativity of the surrounding environment. But there is no satisfactory way out of this: solidarity amongst Jews perpetuates the differences but is also necessary for survival, solidarity (p.312) 'is an answer to threat and heterogeneity, but it confirms that heterogeneity and keeps alive that threat as much as it tends to mitigate it'.

Alliance

I have devoted considerable space in this chapter to describing and quoting from Memmi's writing and drawing attention to the parallels between his account of the colonial relation and that of Jewish identity forged in an antisemitic world. His emphasis on structure is notable: colonial society produces the colonizer and the colonized, with all their economic attributes and psychological complexity, so that even those who strive to resist it find themselves positioned on one side or another according to their social identity and not necessarily their chosen allegiance. The anti-colonial colonist is still on the side of the colonizers, benefitting from colonialism, unable to fully grasp its depredations, unwanted once the colonized rise up. Similarly, the deeply rooted structure of antisemitism, prevalent in all societies through the impact both of racialized scapegoating and Christian anti-Judaism, produces a world in which all non-Jews share in its benefits and in which there is no escape for the Jew other than in insular solidarity, which is both a necessary move and a source of continuing isolation. The decolonial Jew in the colony, which was Memmi's own situation, is especially caught in the pincers of the struggle. Not quite one with the fully oppressed, yet victims of a long hatred, partly identified with the colonizing power, yet unwanted by it, Jewish radicals are doomed to find themselves excluded from both groups. Accepting this as a historical necessity seems to have been important for Memmi, which means understanding that radical Jews are fighting for something (decolonization) that will result in their own eventual marginalization and exclusion.

The tension in Memmi's writing between a universalistic identification with the struggle of all oppressed people against racism and colonialism, on the one hand, and the vivid and even bitter response to universalized antisemitism on the other, is highly instructive. It reflects a familiar 'fort-da' dynamic in which Jews are called into engagement with others through historical connections and ethical principles – the mobilizing sources discussed previously in this book – yet are also figured as outsiders due to antisemitism and racialized discourses of difference (for instance, 'Jewish whiteness'). It leaves politically progressive Jews with a conundrum that has certainly lasted since the emergence of Zionism in the late nineteenth century, and is arguably endemic to the post-Enlightenment West, perhaps beginning around the time of Spinoza. This is at its extreme the disjunction between the pull towards insularity and self-protective isolation, of which national self-determination might be one instance, and the chance of emancipatory outward-lookingness, with its potential danger of the degradation of Jewish culture through assimilation and vulnerability to antisemitic assault. The consequence of this can feel like a series of rebuffs: as one reaches outwards, expressing solidarity with oppressed groups, so one also exposes oneself to rejection. The recent history of the construction of Jewish whiteness is part of this story as is the neglect of antisemitism as if it is a minor element in racism that does not bear much weight because it relates to a supposedly 'privileged' group (the 'Jews don't count' argument). It can seem that the only good Jews are those who deny any Jewish heritage, with the exception of some extreme religious Jewish sects who are prized on the antiracist left because of their anti-Zionism, neglecting their typically reactionary, racist and misogynistic practices and beliefs. Under these circumstances, it can take a considerable degree of self-effacement to fit comfortably with the decolonizing struggle; and those who make the choice to contest oppression and build affiliations across boundaries whilst retaining their Jewish identities have to accept the possibility of non-recognition, rebuff and even antisemitic hostility. Memmi seems to have had the insight and strength of character to do this, but his purported move rightwards in the postcolonial era (he died in 2020) may have been a sign of the cost.

Holding on to the tension in this is a psychoanalytic as well as a political issue. Memmi's portrait both of the colonial situation and of the Jewish one is an expression of the difficulty of maintaining alliances that intersect with deeply engrained racisms, including antisemitism. He seems to suggest that the resilience needed for this might be gleaned through intra-ethnic solidarity: Jews with Jews, Black people and people of colour with their own communities. Perhaps these solidarities supply both a physical home – a space of familiarity, mutual support and a relative haven from antagonism – and a psychological one, offering a gathering point for the inner resources needed in order to venture outwards not only against oppressors, but even to risk the unpredictable responses of those with whom we might imagine allegiance. Fort and da again: going out and coming back, this time as a tentative pattern of decolonizing oneself in the context of the prevalence of antisemitism not only in overtly racist circles, but in much of the world.

The famously 'light sleeper' that is antisemitism is a real presence and also an imaginary one, in that it infects the unconscious lives of Jews and non-Jews alike, interfering with the commitment to a broader antiracist alliance. This can create resistance of the psychoanalytic variety amongst Jews – that is, a wish to do away with the connection with others and instead to rely solely on solidarity only with other Jews, in the belief that no-one else can be trusted. What Memmi expresses, however, is a version of solidarity which recognizes the reality of antisemitism and hence the pull towards insularity yet remains firmly aligned with promoting the solidarity of all the oppressed, even if he is also pessimistic about where this will lead for himself personally and for his group. His writings suggest that antisemitism, like colonialism and racism generally, is rooted in the structure of society and so has to be opposed in a radical way, by the overturning of that society, something which is not solely a Jewish affair and also not something that Jews can absent themselves from. Struggling with this is an ethical and political act but also a psychosocial one, in that it requires both resistance to the social forces at work in sustaining antisemitism and racism, and overcoming inner obstacles to political resistance derived from (understandable) fears and disappointments and the bitterness that experiences of antisemitism bring. When those with whom one believes one is in alliance turn on one, it feels like betrayal – and in many ways it is. Yet refusing such alliances is both a strategic error (because it weakens the power of the oppressed) and an ethical failure, because linking with oppressed groups, making them neighbours rather than others, is a core ethical and psychoanalytic imperative – and a Jewish one too. Memmi's (1962, p.30) summary statement, quoted near the start of this chapter, is worth returning to: 'There are, in short, two attitudes: either one accepts all the suffering or one rejects it all. Well, I reject it in totum as I reject in detail each face of oppression.' Both are needed: the rejection of each specific oppression, including antisemitism, and the rejection of all oppression 'in totum'.

Chapter 8

PSYCHOANALYSIS IN THE WAKE

Psychoanalysis and racism

To anticipate my argument in this final chapter: if the world in which psychoanalysis acts is structured by and through racism, opposition to racism must become the ground of being of psychoanalysis itself.

This book has concerned itself with the implications of psychoanalysis, Jewishness, antisemitism and antiracism in and for one another. Much of my argument has been based on the idea that psychoanalysis is genuinely rooted in Jewish life and culture, whatever its many other sources may have been, and that despite the ambiguities notable in psychoanalysis's history in relation to colonial thought and political conservatism it has a commitment to emancipatory empowerment and hence to anti-oppressive practices. I have also claimed that there is an orientation towards relational ethics in Judaism and Jewish life and that this should translate into alliances around opposition to antisemitism and anti-Black racism, and I have explored some routes that might be taken in doing so. This still leaves open numerous questions, especially concerning ways in which psychoanalysis might be brought into this nexus of connections. In particular, what specific contemporary challenges does psychoanalysis face in opposing racism, and how can it best overcome them? There are many answers to this in relation to the structure of psychoanalytic practice and perhaps especially its training regimes, and there are examples from around the world of psychoanalytic societies grappling honestly with the question of racism and trying to establish routines for opposing it. But there is also a great deal of constraint, and if the amount of conscious resistance to antiracism is rapidly lessening (so it is unusual to now hear psychoanalysts state that opposing racism is outside the purview of psychoanalysis, especially in relation to clinical work), there is still a great deal of anxiety about taking up the issues and possibly some unconscious resistance to doing so as well. This leaves open the question of how psychoanalysis might respond to the challenge of racism as it appears in the contemporary field, which means taking seriously voices coming from the Black community as well as from what for psychoanalysis has been the historically more visible Jewish one.

I want to approach this question in a limited way, by looking at one especially powerful and influential account of anti-Black racism understood as the lived currency of slavery. This is Christina Sharpe's (2016) book *In the Wake: On Blackness and Being* (cited from here on as *Wake*). This is not a psychoanalytic text; indeed, psychoanalysis does not appear in the book's index and it looks mostly to be far from the author's mind (though she has engaged publicly with psychoanalysts). It is also only one of several texts that could be chosen. However, what distinguishes Sharpe's text and a number of others with which it is often paired that have found their way into mainstream awareness – books such as Claudia Rankine's (2015) *Citizen* and Saidiya Hartman's (2019) magnificent *Wayward Lives, Beautiful Experiments* – is its extraordinary literary power and accessibility, yet its uncompromising *necessity* as a visceral expression of the 'ongoing disaster' (*Wake*, p.5) of slavery. The book has made its way speaking to and of the Black experience, creating consciousness of the manner in which everyone lives 'in the wake' of slavery, something that still ripples outwards further and further, leaving no shoreline untouched. This is, according to Sharpe, a distinctive characteristic of trauma: that the wake spreads rather than narrows.

> A ship moving through water generates a particular pattern of waves; the bow wave is in front of the ship, and that wave then spreads out in the recognizable V pattern on either side of and then behind the ship. The size of the bow wave dictates how far out the wake starts. Waves that occur in the wake of the ship move at the same speed as the ship. From at least the sixteenth century onward, a major part of the ocean engineering of ships has been to minimize the bow wave and therefore to minimize the wake. But the effect of trauma is the opposite. It is to make maximal the wake.
>
> (*Wake*, p.40)

Slavery is the arch-trauma here; it maximizes, tarnishing everything, unsettling any complacencies, turning claims of comfort into manifestations of denial. My suggestion here is that *In the Wake* – to reiterate, taken as one of several expressions of the way in which slavery and anti-Blackness structures the world – is not just enormously powerful and challenging for everyone, but it also asks some questions that psychoanalysis ought to be able to address about the living legacies of supposedly past trauma, about intergenerationality and, very specifically, about how we understand the workings of 'race'. Again, to try to be clear, I am not looking for a psychoanalytic *interpretation* of these things; this is not difficult to construct and there are some useful psychoanalytic theories of racism already available (e.g. Rustin, 1991; Seshadri-Crooks, 1994; Kovel, 1995; Abel, 1997; Dalal, 2002; Davids, 2011; Frosh, 1989, 2013a; Hook, 2013). Instead, I see psychoanalysis as challenged by the wake, and want to try to articulate some of what that challenge might be.

Who can speak?

Before going further, the issue about speaking from a position outside the Black community needs to be addressed one more time, perhaps especially because *In the Wake* has become so popular amongst thinkers on the legacy of slavery and the Black experience that its critical challenge threatens to disappear under the weight of appropriation, however well-intentioned and honest this might be. To what extent can I, embodied as Jewish and white (with all the complexity of that association, as we have seen in previous chapters), ventriloquize the Black experience conjured in *In the Wake*, and in whose name do I speak of it? By what right can I, or anyone else for that matter, invoke an experience that I have not had? Is it enough to claim a specific form of solidarity through my Jewishness, as outlined throughout this book, not as an essential category (this would reinstate 'race' as real), but as a historical feature, a material reality that, through antisemitism as well as a certain cultural ethics, places Jews on the side of those who have to fight racism? This 'barbaric' antiracism needs to be reclaimed; Jews belong in this fight, as I have been arguing, and psychoanalysis, whether or not one can countenance thinking of it as a 'Jewish science', belongs there too.

But this is insufficient, especially given the centrality of certain forms of Jewishness in the historical formation of psychoanalysis itself. If psychoanalysis has not fully addressed anti-Black racism, then Jewish members of the psychoanalytic community are as responsible for this as anyone else. I think I have to let this question hover without full resolution while noting some important imperatives. One is that there is an ethics at issue here, that of taking responsibility for something when it is forced upon us. It is not always easy to do this, but what *In the Wake*, Black Lives Matter and the decolonizing movement all do, alongside evoking and expressing black lives, is demand acknowledgement of historical and contemporary injustices, of the damage done and being done by people in my position (white, academic, liberal), and of the reparation and action required to put it right. These expressions of Black life and aspiration may not be *of* white or Jewish communities, in the sense of arising from within them, but they certainly speak *to* them in requiring a response. A second ethic is that of imagining the position of the other. I cannot accept that all attempts at alliance are forms of cultural appropriation; this book is indeed premised on the possibility of linking across difference in a more general 'solidarity of the oppressed'. Speaking from one's own rendering of the experience presented by others is a necessary step for recognition of that experience and for action, even though it carries the risk of speaking in others' name rather than letting them speak for themselves. (But people can read Sharpe's book; they do not need me to explain it to them; my aim is different.) Most of all, however, there is the question of whiteness itself, of the benefit that comes to all white people through the subjugation of people of colour (the 'white premium'), but also of the losses, the violence that does violence to everyone, albeit not the same kind or degree of violence, but still the impoverishment and the generation of guilt and the need to do something about this. White people have to respond to what is being presented to us so powerfully and so utterly convincingly.

The simplest point is, then, to my mind the most compelling: whiteness, including a certain kind of Jewish whiteness, with all the caveats to it described in Chapter 6, has a privileged place in psychoanalysis, and this means that there is an ethical imperative placed on white scholars and practitioners of psychoanalysis to speak of and oppose the pervasiveness of racism and the damage that it does. In this context, interventions such as *In the Wake* can be understood to speak *from* the Black community *to* those who have historically forged the direction of psychoanalysis, demanding recognition and acknowledgment. Despite the potency of antisemitism, including its presence within the psychoanalytic community (Frosh, 2012), which gives a specific spin on things, this includes Jews.

The weather

In the Wake presents contemporary anti-Black oppression as a continuation of past oppression. Amongst its deliberations on, and evidencing of, these continuities are its repeated evocation of numerous present evils, all of which are understood as 'in the wake' of slavery. 'In the wake,' Sharpe writes,

> the semiotics of the slave ship continue: from the forced movements of the enslaved to the forced movements of the migrant and the refugee, to the regulation of Black people in North American streets and neighborhoods, to those ongoing crossings of and drownings in the Mediterranean Sea, to the brutal colonial reimaginings of the slave ship and the ark; to the reappearances of the slave ship in everyday life in the form of the prison, the camp, and the school.
>
> (*Wake*, p.21)

Those elements to which Sharpe gives especial prominence, returning to them again and again just as they keep returning to (but also slipping from) awareness (wakefulness), are the refugees crossing and drowning in small boats in the Mediterranean, the Haiti earthquake of 2010 and the deaths of Black people at the hands of police in the United States. The last of these was a powerful catalyst for the Black Lives Matter movement and a major trigger for its resurgence in 2020, four years after *In the Wake* was published. We could add to this the differential effects of the Covid pandemic, in which people of colour around the world have suffered significantly more than white people in a way that has made prominent the ongoingly vicious disparities in health care, poverty, education and policing that have been hidden in plain sight for ever. Moreover, the present tense of anti-Black violence and the constant expectation of death (a necropolitics of daily life, we might say) run right through the book from start to end.

The book opens with deaths in Sharpe's family and a dedication page to family members that includes 'For those who have died recently' and 'For those who died in the past that is not yet past'. Later, Sharpe offers a stunning presentation of the story of the *Zong*, the slave ship that became the centre of a celebrated legal case in the late eighteenth century when the owners sued for insurance payouts on cargo – that is, human beings – who had been thrown overboard supposedly to save the ship. In one of the most powerful weaves of the book, all these events are linked through the wake: they are understood not just to have their source in the history of slavery, but actually to *be* that history, which means, the situation continues. Laying out her intentions early on, Sharpe announces, 'I've been trying to articulate a method of encountering a past that is not past' (*Wake*, p.13). This is a political and historical statement, but it has psychoanalytic resonances and significance too in the idea that a past that is not resolved, that is not treated with justice, remains present, an idea to which I shall return.

This is the first, but pervasive, instance of what are, to my mind, some striking echoes of psychoanalytic ideas in *In the Wake*. These do not, however, necessarily open the text out for psychoanalytic exploration so much as challenge psychoanalysis to think about the rooting and relevance of some of its ideas in the context of 'race' and racism. Perhaps Sharpe's idea of '[t]he Weather', the title of the final chapter of her book, makes this clear. The weather is the climate of racism and slavery; it penetrates everything and is also the backdrop to everything; it determines how the ship will sail, but it is also what is not exactly noticed, what stands present as an often-unremarked context for lived lives. 'It is not the specifics of any one event or set of events that are endlessly repeatable and repeated,' writes Sharpe 'but the totality of the environments in which we struggle; the machines in which we live; what I am calling the weather' (*Wake*, p.111). For Sharpe, this is an expansion of Fanon's (1970) statement, 'We revolt simply because, for a variety of reasons, we can no longer breathe' (Fanon, 1970, p.50 in *Wake*, p.111). Fanon's evocation of breathing, in its disturbing prescience in relation to the cries of 'I can't breathe' that have been brought to the fore by the Black Lives Matter movement, shows how ubiquitous, permanent and recurrent – how repetitious – the wake is. The weather determines how well one can breathe: 'In my text, the weather is the totality of our environments; the weather is the total climate; and that climate is antiblack' (*Wake*, p.104). For Sharpe, the route to take here is through the notion of 'aspiration', both drawing breath and hoping for something, aspiring to breathe the air of freedom. 'Who can breathe free?' asks Sharpe (*Wake*, p.112), in a context in which breathing is denied ('I can't breathe') and the weather is continuously hostile? 'I've been thinking', she writes (*Wake*, p.109), 'aspiration in the complementary senses of the word: the withdrawal of fluid from the body and the taking in of foreign matter (usually fluid) into the lungs with the respiratory current, and as audible breath that accompanies or comprises a speech sound'. The damage done and the possible way out of this are indicated here. Can psychoanalysis attune itself to this weather and to this aspiration, finding ways to recognize and acknowledge the actual conditions of Black lives as well as seeking routes to fulfilling Black aspirations – that is, allowing and promoting articulation of the sounds of a body that is in need of free air, the air of freedom? The point here is that if it ignores the weather, psychoanalysis cannot reach out to the suffering subject who is buffeted by storms; or less obviously allegorically, without acknowledgement (that is recognition plus responsibility, to use Jessica Benjamin's (2018) framework), contemporary lives stay mired in the continuity of slavery. It also makes clear just how indivisible the social and personal dimensions of experience must be. Listing her losses at the beginning of the book, Sharpe makes the point of how they are not arbitrary, but rather socially contingent: 'The overriding engine of US racism cut through my family's ambitions and desires. It coursed through our social and public encounters and our living room' (*Wake*, p.3). Racism may not determine every element of all our lives, but there it is, cutting through them, a rupturing 'flow' that cannot be dammed or indeed, to change the metaphor, bracketed out. Psychoanalysis needs to notice this: how can we not speak of racism when, like the weather, it is always there, rupturing the best laid plans?

In the wake of the ship

The wake has some distinct meanings in *In the Wake*. The dominant one is the wake of the slave ship, and hence the wake of formal slavery; we still live in this wake. American racism has long outlived the abolition of slavery – indeed, slavery basically survived its own abolition during reconstruction after the Civil War – but it is not just in the United States that this applies, even if every racism has its own particularity. The revelations in recent years about the compensation paid by the British government to slave owners, but not to slaves, when slavery was abolished, and the extent to which the wealth of Britain was predicated on slavery, have firmly challenged the myth of British imperial largesse (Hall et al., 2016). In any case, the continuing institutional racism and anti-Black agitation at governmental and civic level (for instance, the British Home Office's 'hostile environment' towards migrants and refugees) is only one recent transparent manifestation of the continuities of colonial racism in the UK. Similarly, the outrageous death rate of young Black men at the hands of the police in Brazil, which was the last major country to abolish slavery, testifies to its continuity even amongst a nation that supposedly prides itself on its 'racial mix'. We are all in the wake, clearly in different positions, some drowning, some in boats: 'to be in the wake is to occupy and to be occupied by the continuous and changing present of slavery's as yet unresolved unfolding' (*Wake*, pp.13–14). We might call this the grammatical tense of the past continuous or the past progressive, except that the continuing act referred to has not as yet ever passed and it is not progressive, unless one takes that to mean 'progressively worse'.

Psychoanalysis should have a lot to say about this. It is a form of hauntology, in which what is left unresolved from the past continues to operate in the present, often as an unknown or unrecognized force that impacts upon, speaks to or through, disturbs and disrupts any attempts to settle comfortably in the present. Toni Morrison's (1987) great novel *Beloved* is the quintessential statement of this, widely referenced in the literature on cultural haunting (e.g. Gordon, 1997) and central to the narrative and imagery of *In the Wake*. I will not re-describe this novel here, except to note its foundation in the historically attested event (attended to closely by Sharpe) of Margaret Garner, who killed her child to protect her from re-enslavement; *Beloved* may be a ghost story, but it is not 'just' fiction. The broader and more psychoanalytic point is how the wake is translatable into the familiar awareness of a past that will not go away, specifically the past of trauma with its intergenerational consequences. The principal issues here are not restricted to *Nachträglichkeit*, so-called 'afterwardsness', which in many ways is taken to be definitional of psychoanalytic temporality (the present remaking the past; the past working its way into the present), though there is an element of this in how the supposed 'pastness' of slavery is now revealed to be a fantasy: that is, slavery never died. We may not be as aware as we should be of how this corpse still moves around amongst us, as lively as ever; but in making it more visible we might begin to see how these past events (Jim Crow; the compensation to slave owners) are ever more traumatic in their social and psychic effects. Additionally, however, what *In the Wake* foregrounds is the way injustice perpetuates ghostliness, and how haunted our societies consequently become. This is precisely invoked by *Beloved*, and what Sharpe's analysis discerns is how it is specifically anti-Black *violence* that erupts as a destructive ghost through the gaps in awareness in which we so often live. We have seen this in the response to Black Lives Matter, which can be understood as a way of registering the unthought and denied murderousness of racism: the violence has come out in the open for a while, been seen for what it is. Will this last? Slavery was embedded, systematic, structural violence; it framed the modern world and formed the basis of its technological, political and economic power; and there it remains, denied and repressed both as knowledge and as impulse, yet breaking through. Can psychoanalysis acknowledge this in its own practices of constraint and control, its own normalizing activities and its neglect of these structures of violence as it goes along its day-by-day way? What price a psychoanalysis that might instead reveal the way these hauntings are not solely individual or family secrets, but social ones too? Violence everywhere: 'Wake; in the line of recoil of (a gun)' (*Wake*, p.97).

There is another point here about the unconscious. In the aside by Otto Fenichel (1940) on the dynamics of antisemitism mentioned briefly in Chapter 1, an association between the unconscious and the Jew was formulated: 'It can be expressed in one sentence: one's own unconscious is also foreign. Foreignness is the quality which the Jews and one's own instincts have in common' (p.31). Anti-Black racism has a parallel dynamic, which Joel Kovel (1995) and Sheldon George (2018), in different ways, have argued is constituted through the splitting off of the corporeality of the white subject into the fantasied 'non-human' of slavery. As noted in Chapter 5, for Hortense Spillers (1996), referencing the centrality of the Oedipus complex as a marker of human subjecthood for both Freud and Lacan, 'The riddle of origin that the Oedipus is supposed to constitute, first, as a crisis, then as a resolution of order and degree, was essentially cancelled by the Atlantic trade, as the "crisis," for all intents and purposes, has continued on the other side' (p.732). The exclusion of people of colour from the 'human' continues, which is why they can be so easily subjected to violence and why they also become the fantasized *embodiment* of violence. The rawness of what has been projected into them and institutionalized in slavery – the 'hold', in Sharpe's terms – makes them available as the psychic repository for violence itself. This operates in various ways, as Judith Butler (2020) demonstrates in her analysis of how it can be that unarmed Black men shot whilst running away from police are cast as threats.

> So, when unarmed black men or women, or queer and transgendered people, have their backs turned to police and are walking or running away, and they are still gunned down by police – an action often defended later as self-defense, even as a defense of society – how are we to understand this? [...] The violence that the policeman is about to do, the violence he then commits, has already moved toward him in a figure, a racialized ghost, condensing and inverting his own aggression, wielding his own aggression against himself, acting in advance of his own plans to act, and legitimating and elaborating, as if in a dream, his later argument of self-defense.
>
> (p.118)

'Phantasmatic' is the term Butler uses, emphasizing the phantasm, the ghost; she too is alert to the recurrence of slavery, even though she is also more explicitly referencing psychoanalysis in her rendering of how violence is projected onto the Black body and then returns. For Sharpe, this is a routine phenomenon in racism, that the one to whom violence is done comes to embody violence and then be experienced as a threat, but she asks too about the impact of this on Black people, and especially on Black women who are mothers. As she writes, 'What kind of mother/ing is it if one must always be prepared with knowledge of the possibility of the violent and quotidian death of one's child? Is it mothering if one knows that one's child might be killed at any time in the hold, in the wake by the state no matter who wields the gun?' (*Wake*, p.78). This is the precise reverberation of the notion of precarity that Butler (2004) has previously developed and recurs in her more recent vocabulary of grievability, registering the idea that some lives matter (are potentially grievable) and some lives matter less, or not at all. Indeed, Butler's first mention of grievability in *The Force of Nonviolence* (2020) is in the context of racism: 'One cannot explain this form of inequality, which accords measures of grievability to groups across the global spectrum, without taking account of the racial schemes that make such grotesque distinctions between which lives are valuable (and potentially grievable, if lost) and those which are not' (p.11). 'Racial schemes', racism, slavery; these structure the marking of lives in violence, between those that count as human and those (the slaves and those who come after them) who do not. The phantasmatic component of this is clear: when confronted by a terrorizing ghost, white violence erupts, without recognizing that the source lies in itself.

Wake as mourning

The Black mother is just one figure of mourning in *In the Wake*; more generally, the second meaning of 'wake' is mourning and grief. A wake is something that mourners hold for a person who has died, both sad and celebratory, asserting the value of a life and sorrowing for its loss. A wake is not in essence a melancholic situation in the psychoanalytic sense because it is part of the process of accepting and working through the loss, an attribute shared with rituals of mourning in other groups, such as the shiva in Jewish culture. However, there are specificities to Black mourning in the wake of slavery which makes it appear melancholic because of its unworked-through nature. What Sharpe establishes is that this is not melancholic in the sense of intimating a denial of loss, but rather the lack of working through happens because the loss is *ongoing*. One cannot finish grieving if grief descends on us unabated.

> I want to distinguish what I am calling Black being in the wake and wake work from the work of melancholia and mourning. And though wake work is, at least in part, attentive to mourning and the mourning work that takes place on local and trans*local and global levels, and even as we know that mourning an event might be interminable, how does one mourn the interminable event?
>
> (*Wake*, p.19)

I will come back briefly to Sharpe's use of 'trans*'; here, the issue is about mourning and melancholia. Mourning the event might be interminable and this could be called melancholia under some situations (though of course not always – for instance, the death of a child might be interminably mourned, and is so in many families); but mourning the *interminable event* is impossible because there is never an end to new losses. Sharpe takes this up in relation to how museums and memorials try to respond to trauma, a set of issues that trouble all monumentalizing and pedagogic memorializations. Her point is that there is an intrinsic contradiction at work in such efforts: 'how does one memorialize chattel slavery and its afterlives, which are unfolding still? How do we memorialize an event that is still ongoing?' (*Wake*, p.20). There is no final 'coming to terms with' continuing atrocity – an issue that has been of practical concern in many contexts and amongst other things has given rise to truth and reconciliation commissions in various places and to a large psychoanalytically informed literature on recognition and forgiveness (e.g. Wale et al., 2020).

Dealing with ongoing violence is also a challenge for psychoanalysis because psychoanalysis commonly operates with a model of putting the past in its place, of finding ways to articulate trauma so that it becomes comprehensible and can be worked through. I have argued elsewhere (Frosh, 2019) that the assumption that trauma is constituted as an inability to speak of something is too limited (though trauma can certainly be *hard* to speak of) and that, as with Thomas Trezise's judgement on Holocaust testimony, the claim that trauma 'is unrepresentable or unspeakable appears to stand in for a refusal to listen' (Trezise, 2013, p.211). The ethical necessity is to respond to suffering through a process of listening; the issue is not that usually trauma is *unspoken*, but that it is commonly *unheard*. This implies that there are two things wrong with an approach to racial trauma that positions it as an unsymbolized impingement in need of articulation. First, it is not in fact unsymbolized; there are innumerable articulations of the reality and effects of slavery and of racism. The problem is that these articulations are not listened to, recognized or acknowledged. There has been no solid reception 'that is not confined to the mere registration of traumatic narrative but encompasses a response to it' (Trezise, 2013, p.59). Secondly, as I have been emphasizing, what is being testified to is an *ongoing* trauma, an endless repetition – something that psychoanalysis should be attuned to (what is psychoanalysis if not the most developed discipline of repetition we have?). To try to be clear again: I am not suggesting that no psychoanalyst recognizes the continuing reality of racism, only that the challenge to psychoanalysis is to develop a way of integrating this fully into its theoretical and clinical practice. How can mourning occur, or trauma be resolved, in this locus of endless suffering? Can psychoanalysis speak to this problem with a more elaborated vocabulary than that of 'holding' or 'containing' the pain? Holding – the hold – is powerfully critiqued by Sharpe as an index of constraint over, and regulation of, Black lives, as it is bound to be in a society characterized by a racist carceral regime. The wake for a person who has died is a communal event; mourning is most complete when it is shared; and solidarity is key both for the acknowledgement of trauma and the action needed to prevent its recurrence. This suggests the need for an active rather than an interpretive stance in relation to racism on the part of psychoanalysis, perhaps even a campaigning approach – something for which the recent statements of support by several psychoanalytic societies for Black Lives Matter might act as a precursor.

Awakening

This leads into the third sense of 'wake' in *In the Wake*: wake as awakening, as waking up to the reality of racism, but also as awakening to possibility, despite everything, despite the ongoing disaster. '*Wake; the state of wakefulness; consciousness.* It was with this sense of wakefulness as consciousness that most of my family lived an awareness of itself as, and in, the wake of the unfinished project of emancipation' (*Wake*, pp.4–5). Wake work of this kind allows the presence of the past to appear, so that the reality of continuing racism, the everlasting wake of slavery, is not belittled or denied; but it also tries to take hold of this to push forward the possibility of the awakening being *to something else*. There are echoes here of Cathy Caruth's (1996) reading of Freud's (1900, pp.509–10) report of the 'Father, I'm burning' dream, in which she emphasizes the difficulty of waking up to something as the central problem of trauma. The father in the dream could not absorb his child's death and had to wake up to it retrospectively, always too late. '*Awakening* [...] *is itself the site of a trauma*, the trauma of the necessity and the impossibility of responding to another's death' (p.100). This seems potentially to be a call to all of us, including psychoanalysts: can we face the trauma of awakening both to the realization of the damage done, the deaths and to the challenge of what needs to be done, the change and recuperation?

Sharpe has an extended account of what wake work involves, which includes the disruption of academic disciplines that position Blackness as unknown otherness and instead questions 'how to live in the wake of slavery, in slavery's afterlives, the afterlife of property, how, in short, to inhabit and rupture this episteme with their, with our, knowable lives' (*Wake*, p.50). Veena Das's (2007) insistence on the 'ordinary' comes to mind, the way particular (singular) lives express opportunities for what we can call resistance as well as for suffering, for care alongside violence. Treating racism predominantly as a response to otherness, which has been one tendency in psychoanalysis when it has struggled with the question of the derogated 'other', participates in the exclusion of Blackness from the social norm, and therefore in the marginalizing of Black lives. It merges, we might say, into *othering*. Opening out to Black experience means relating to the quotidian and the possibilities this generates amongst those that have always been denied; that is, it de-mystifies otherness by allowing it to take up its place in the 'human'. For Sharpe, some of this potential openness of Black experience is symbolized by the asterisk in trans*:

> The asterisk speaks to a range of configurations of Black being that take the form of translation, transatlantic, transgression, transgender, transformation, transmogrification, transcontinental, transfixed, trans-Mediterranean, transubstantiation (by which process we might understand the making of bodies into flesh and then into fungible commodities while retaining the appearance of flesh and blood), transmigration, and more.
>
> (*Wake*, p.30)

Several of these trans* affiliations resonate with negations of life (for instance, 'transatlantic', as in the slave ship; 'trans-Mediterranean', as in contemporary flows of refugees); but they also leave something open. 'The asterisk after the prefix "trans" holds the place open for thinking' (*Wake*, p.30), signalling new possibilities in relation to the old versions of trans- that marked the slave trade. This is not to be too resolutely optimistic as a way of closing down the viscerality of Sharpe's portrait of Black suffering; that too would be an easy route for denial and also a psychoanalytic truism. Being open to possibility is a therapeutic goal, but the conditions for the redemption of that possibility have to be available and, given what has been written here, this is not the case with racism. Psychoanalysis needs to recognize this in its practices, in what it holds out as a route for psychic and social change.

But Sharpe's wake work is more precise than this and circulates around a notion of care. Again, we need to be cautious: the 'culture of care' is an important topic in contemporary social thought, and rightly so, but this has to be more than binding up each other's wounds if it is to effect the kinds of changes needed to offset the continuing disaster of racism. Laying out the ground at the start of her book, Sharpe (*Wake*, p.5) states, '*In the Wake: On Blackness and Being* is a work that insists and performs that thinking needs care ("all thought is Black thought") and that thinking and care need to stay in the wake.' Near the end, she fills this out as follows:

> Living as I have argued we do in the wake of slavery, in spaces where we were never meant to survive, or have been punished for surviving and for daring to claim or make spaces of something like freedom, we yet reimagine and transform spaces for and practices of an ethics of care (as in repair, maintenance, attention), an ethics of seeing, and of being in the wake as consciousness; as a way of remembering and observance that started with the door of no return, continued in the hold of the ship and on the shore.
>
> (*Wake*, pp.130–1)

Thinking and care run together, as do survival and imagination. 'Repair, maintenance, attention' echo the 'enduring time' elaborated by Lisa Baraitser (2017), a time of slowness and focused thought, indeed of endurance, so that wakefulness becomes not a sudden release from trauma, but a slow process of uncovering the way the past directs the present. In Baraitser's text, care always signifies something intersubjective; even self-care, as we know from Winnicott (1958), requires an other to care about one first. It happens as a background, a new turn in the weather, in the interstices of ordinary time; yet it is always a showing of solidarity, an acceptance of the basic principles of each person's life. Psychoanalysis again has, potentially, a lot to offer here. Its slowness and willingness to stay with someone over an extended period, to wait for something to happen and not to press when it fails to come; its capacity to confront and value repetitions – these attributes go against the run-of-the-mill therapies of neoliberalism (quick, short, 'efficient') to preserve a vision of care sustained over time. Sharpe's challenge to it is to bind this psychoanalytic ethic with *all* the elements of the wake: the enduring violence of slavery and anti-Black racism; the endless mourning for this enduring state; the endurance required to *think otherwise*.

Conclusion

Christina Sharpe's *In the Wake* is an especially potent expression of Black awareness of the kind signified politically by Black Lives Matter. It presents a challenge to everyone, but here my interest has been in what it speaks back to psychoanalysis. Psychoanalysis has largely ignored the 'weather' of ongoing racism, positioning slavery at worst as denied and forgotten, at best as past. In this regard, psychoanalysis remains a colonial discipline and one that fails its truth-seeking ethics by neglecting the actuality of Black experience. This is not to belittle the creative work of psychoanalytic thinkers on racism and the attempts by some institutes of psychoanalysis to respond honestly to racism in general and the Black Lives Matter movement in particular. Yet what *In the Wake* might alert us to is how psychoanalysis needs to address some of its own theoretical and practical assumptions if it is to rise to the challenge of wake awareness and wake work. This goes further than critiquing some of the more egregious elements of the theory, for example, Freud's use of the civilized-savage divide, or some of the interpretations of 'other' cultures promulgated in the mid-twentieth century, or even the perpetuation of the racialized vocabulary and imagery of 'cannibalism' in some psychoanalytic thought (Vyrgioti, 2022). It is additionally to require of psychoanalysis that it notices and makes explicit the real conditions of Black lives and how they – as well as society as a whole – are haunted by the legacy of slavery in the way ghosts haunt an unsettled body. This means acknowledging that slavery is still with us and that Black experience needs to be understood in the light of that fact. This is the ground and backdrop for psychoanalytic activity, the *weather* in which it takes place. Psychoanalysis cannot isolate itself from this, either in terms of who constitutes its practitioners and patients or how it speaks on a public stage about the persistence and effects of anti-Black racism. This may mean a re-examination of its focus on interpretive practice, not because the unconscious ceases to be its concern (that concern is of course the essence of psychoanalysis), but because the unconscious has an exterior structure, derived from the sociality in which it is embedded and actualized by the introjection of 'messages' from this sociality through processes of the kind that Laplanche (1999), amongst others, has so beautifully delineated.

There are many complexities entangled in this idea that the unconscious has an exterior structure, but for the moment the key point is to acknowledge the indivisibility of what we experience as our 'subjective' selves – our 'inner lives' – and what we participate in as social beings, both in relation to the encounters we have with other people and to the larger social forces around which the world is organized. These larger social forces can be thought of as 'entering into' us because they determine the ways in which we can live – who has access to what resources, who has power over whom, who we can engage with and who we might trust and love. But even this is too crude a way to think of things: it is not that we exist pre-formed as individuals and the social world then has its impact; it is rather that the way in which our subjectivity emerges is part and parcel of our social being. For Laplanche (1999), this is constituted in the process whereby the unconscious desires of the 'other' are transmitted to the subject (the infant) as a set of untranslatable messages that form the kernel of the infant's own unconscious life precisely because they cannot be fully known. Read more broadly, we are faced here with a psychosocial phenomenon in which social forces provide the 'exoskeleton' around the experience of interiority. In the divided world in which we live, a major form that this exterior structure takes is that of racism. The oppositions of Black and white, Jew and non-Jew, around which sociality is so powerfully organized, create both conscious beliefs and unconscious ideas that are continuously reproduced in action and in fantasy. Acknowledging this at every moment – not reducing it to psychological disturbance or bracketing it out as a sociological appendix or irrelevance but making it the centre of analytic interest – will not be a proposal that is universally acceptable to psychoanalysts, because it appears to turn attention away from the proper locus of psychoanalytic expertise, the 'individual' unconscious. But the manner in which this supposedly 'inner' entity is bound up with these presumed 'external' social forces is such that one cannot be examined without the other; and attempting to do so, to separate individual and social in the way that has sometimes been characteristic of psychoanalytic practice, can be argued to be a defence against recognizing the implication of psychoanalysis itself in the perpetuation of racialized divides.

The emphasis in this chapter has been on the challenge to psychoanalysis coming from contemporary Black thought, and how this might begin to be responded to. I have not particularly taken up the question of antisemitism here, but it is worth looping back to it as a final turn for this book. My intention throughout has been to explore a three-way relationship which contests both antisemitism and anti-Black racism through the prism of psychoanalysis, creating what we might call a psychosocial encounter that places racialized social oppression in the foreground whilst also acknowledging the unconscious resonance and implications of this. Psychoanalysis has its own history of implication in colonialist thought and it is has struggled to respond adequately to discrimination within its institutions. Yet it also offers powerful concepts and practices that can be drawn on when confronting the racism that is embedded in the wider social arena and that impacts on us all, including those who seek psychoanalytic help. Part of my argument has been that a contribution to this anti-oppressive practice can emerge from psychoanalysis's Jewish heritage. This is both because this Jewish heritage carries with it the deeply engrained experience of antisemitism, so in principle alerting psychoanalysts to the workings of racism more generally; and because there is a Jewish ethic that whilst being rooted in the singularities of Jewish life also pushes towards a more universalistic encounter with 'others'. I advanced this idea in the first part of this book and then looked in more detail at psychoanalysis in the context of a possible Black-Jewish alliance aimed at opposing racism. The difficulty of creating such an alliance came more into view in some subsequent chapters, where I was concerned with the effects of the construction of Jewishness as opposed to, or at least separate from, antiracist and decolonial practices. My approach to this has been to advocate for an understanding of Jewish identities as separate from a universalizing notion of 'whiteness' and instead to explore the potential for a new kind of 'barbarism' that confronts the colonial world – specifically that of Europe and North America – with its own barbaric history and its continuation into the present. This oppositional stance, coded as the 'solidarity of the oppressed', notes the connection between antisemitism and other forms of racism and uses this to spur mutual identification with the struggle against them both. Psychoanalysis helps here as a set of ideas about how racism and antisemitism are perpetuated as lived experiences and it offers its own ethic of responsibility, building on relational connections that in principle, if not always in practice, emphasize links and open encounters rather than repudiation and, indeed, 'othering'. This is an aid in creating alliances, though it does not in itself mean that the political and historical tensions between different racialized and minoritized groups can easily be overcome, especially when these are maintained in the interests of dominant groups. But if there is to be a forceful response to the menace of racism and antisemitism, a menace that seems only to grow, alliances across oppressed groups, especially including for my purposes Jewish-Black alliances, are going to be of central significance. We have to find ways to belong with one another, however complex and at times fractious that belonging may turn out to be.

BIBLIOGRAPHY

Abel, E. (ed.) (1997) *Female Subjects in Black and White: Race, Psychoanalysis, Feminism.* Berkely: University of California Press.

Ahad, B. (2010) *Freud Upside Down: African American Literature and Psychoanalytic Culture.* Chicago: University of Illinois Press.

Akhtar, S. (2014) The Mental Pain of Minorities. *British Journal of Psychotherapy,* 30, 136–53.

Alford, C.F. (2007) Levinas, Winnicott, and Therapy. *Psychoanalytic Review,* 9, 529–51.

Altman, N. (2006) Whiteness. *Psychoanalytic Quarterly,* 75, 45–72.

Anderson, W., Jenson, D. and Keller, R. (2011) Introduction: Globalizing the Unconscious. In: W. Anderson, D. Jenson and R. Keller (eds) *Unconscious Dominions: Psychoanalysis, Colonial Trauma and Global Sovereignties.* Durham: Duke University Press, pp. 1–18.

Anderson, W., Jenson, D. and Keller, R. (eds) (2011) *Unconscious Dominions: Psychoanalysis, Colonial Trauma, and Global Sovereignties.* Durham: Duke University Press.

Andrade, O. (1928) Manifesto Antropofágico. *Revista de Antropofagia,* 1, 1.

Arendt, H. (1943/2007) We Refugees. In: J. Kohn and R. Feldman (eds) *Hannah Arendt: The Jewish Writings.* New York: Schocken, pp. 264–74.

Arendt, H. (1944/2007) The Jew as Pariah: A Hidden Tradition. In: J. Kohn and R. Feldman (eds) *Hannah Arendt: The Jewish Writings.* New York: Schocken, pp. 275–97.

Aronowicz, A. (1990) Introduction. In: E. Levinas (ed.) *Nine Talmudic Readings.* Bloomington, IN: Indiana University Press, pp. ix–xxxix.

Baddiel, D. (2021) *Jews Don't Count.* London: TLS Books.

Badenhorst, P. (2021) Predatory White Racism. *Psychoanalysis, Culture & Society,* 26, 284–303.

Bakan, D. (1958) *Sigmund Freud and the Jewish Mystical Tradition.* London: Free Association Books, 1990.

Baraitser, L. (2017) *Enduring Time.* London: Bloomsbury.

Baum, D. (2017) *Feeling Jewish.* New Haven: Yale.

Benjamin, J. (2016) Non-Violence as Respect for All Suffering: Thoughts Inspired by Eyad El Sarraj. *Psychoanalysis, Culture & Society,* 21(1), 5–20.

Benjamin, J. (2018) *Beyond Doer and Done to: Recognition Theory, Intersubjectivity and the Third.* London: Routledge.

Berke, J. (2015) *The Hidden Freud.* London: Routledge.

Bhabha, H. (1991) *The Location of Culture.* London: Routledge.

Blass, R.B. (2004) Beyond Illusion. *International Journal of Psycho-Analysis,* 85, 615–34.

Brickman, C. (2003) *Aboriginal Populations in the Mind*. New York: Columbia University Press.

Brickman, C. (2009) Psychoanalysis and Judaism in Context. In: L. Aron and L. Henik (eds) *Answering a Question with a Question: Contemporary Psychoanalysis and Jewish Thought*. Boston: Academic Studies Press, pp. 25–54.

Bullard, A. (2005) L'Oedipe Africain, A Retrospective. *Transcultural Psychiatry*, 42(2), 171–203.

Bush, S. (2021) *Commission on Racial Inclusivity in the Jewish Community*. London: Board of Deputies of British Jews.

Butler, J. (1997) *The Psychic Life of Power*. Stanford: Stanford University Press.

Butler, J. (2004) *Precarious Life*. London: Verso.

Butler, J. (2005) *Giving an Account of Oneself*. New York: Fordham University Press.

Butler, J. (2009) *Frames of War*. London: Verso.

Butler, J. (2012) *Parting Ways*. New York: Columbia University Press.

Butler, J. (2020) *The Force of Nonviolence*. London: Verso.

Caruth, C. (1996) *Unclaimed Experience: Trauma, Narrative and History*. London: Johns Hopkins University Press.

Caygill, H. (2002) *Levinas and the Political*. London: Routledge.

Cheyette, B. (2013) *Diasporas of the Mind: Jewish and Postcolonial Writing and the Nightmare of History*. New Haven: Yale University Press.

Cheyette, B. (2017) Against Supersessionist Thinking: Old and New, Jews and Postcolonialism, the Ghetto and Diaspora. *The Cambridge Journal of Postcolonial Literary Inquiry*, 4, 424–39.

Cohen, S. and Kahn-Harris, K. (2004) *Beyond Belonging: The Jewish Identities of Moderately Engaged British Jews*. London: Profile Books.

Community Security Trust (2020) *Antisemitic Incidents Report*. https://cst.org.uk/data/file/7/2/Incidents%20Report%202020.1615559608.pdf.

Cushman, P. (2007) A Burning World, an Absent God. *Contemporary Psychoanalysis*, 43(1), 47–88.

Dalal, F. (2002) *Race, Colour and the Processes of Racialization: New Perspectives from Group Analysis, Psychoanalysis and Sociology*. London: Routledge.

Damousi, J. and Plotkin, M. (eds) (2012) *Psychoanalysis and Politics: Histories of Psychoanalysis under Conditions of Restricted Political Freedom*. Oxford: Oxford University Press.

Danto, E. (2005) *Freud's Free Clinics: Psychoanalysis and Social Justice*. New York: Columbia University Press.

Das, V. (2007) *Life and Words: Violence and the Descent into the Ordinary*. Berkeley: University of California Press.

Davids, F. (2011) *Internal Racism: A Psychoanalytic Approach to Race and Difference*. London: Macmillan.

Deutscher, I. (1968/2017) *The Non-Jewish Jew and Other Essays*. London: Verso.

Diller, J. (1991) *Freud's Jewish Identity: A Case Study in the Impact of Ethnicity*. London: Associated University Presses.

Du Bois, W. (1902) *The Souls of Black Folk*. New York: Dover.

Eng, D.L. and Han, S. (2000) A Dialogue on Racial Melancholia. *Psychoanalytic Dialogues*, 10, 667–700.

Ernst, S. and Maguire, M. (1987) *Living with the Sphinx – Papers from the Women's Therapy Centre*. London: Women's Press.

Evans Holmes, D. (2016) Culturally Imposed Trauma: The Sleeping Dog Has Awakened. Will Psychoanalysis Take Heed? *Psychoanalytic Dialogues*, 26, 641–54.

Fanon, F. (1952/1967) *Black Skin, White Masks*. Translated by C.L. Markmann. London: Pluto.

Fanon, F. (1970) *Toward the African Revolution*. New York: Grove Press.

Fenichel, O. (1940) Psychoanalysis of Antisemitism. *American Imago 1B*, 24–39.

Fenichel, O. (1946) Elements of a Psychoanalytic Theory of Anti-Semitism. In: E. Simmel (ed.) *Anti-Semitism: A Social Disease*. New York: International Universities Press, pp. 11–35.

Fletcher, J. (1999) Psychoanalysis and the Question of the Other. Introduction to J. Laplanche, *Essays on Otherness*. London: Routledge, pp. 1–51.

Fletcher, J. (2013) *Freud and the Scene of Trauma*. New York: Fordham.

Freud, S. (1883) Letter from Sigmund Freud to Martha Bernays, November 15, 1883. *Letters of Sigmund Freud 1873–1939*, 51, 74–6.

Freud, S. (1900) The Interpretation of Dreams. *The Standard Edition of the Complete Psychological Works of Sigmund Freud, Volume IV (1900): The Interpretation of Dreams (First Part)*, ix–627.

Freud, S. (1913/1930) Totem and Taboo. *The Standard Edition of the Complete Psychological Works of Sigmund Freud, Volume XIII (1913–1914): Totem and Taboo and Other Works*, vii–162.

Freud, S. (1919) The 'Uncanny'. *The Standard Edition of the Complete Psychological Works of Sigmund Freud, Volume XVII (1917–1919): An Infantile Neurosis and Other Works*, 217–56.

Freud, S. (1920) Beyond the Pleasure Principle. *The Standard Edition of the Complete Psychological Works of Sigmund Freud, Volume XVIII (1920–1922): Beyond the Pleasure Principle, Group Psychology and Other Works*, 1–64.

Freud, S. (1921) Group Psychology and the Analysis of the Ego. *The Standard Edition of the Complete Psychological Works of Sigmund Freud, Volume XVIII (1920–1922): Beyond the Pleasure Principle, Group Psychology and Other Works*, 65–144.

Freud, S. (1923) The Ego and the Id. *The Standard Edition of the Complete Psychological Works of Sigmund Freud, Volume XIX (1923–1925): The Ego and the Id and Other Works*, 1–66.

Freud, S. (1924) Letter from Sigmund Freud to Karl Abraham, 4 June 1924. *The Complete Correspondence of Sigmund Freud and Karl Abraham 1907–1925*, 5, 507.

Freud, S. (1925) Some Psychical Consequences of the Anatomical Distinction between the Sexes. *The Standard Edition of the Complete Psychological Works of Sigmund Freud Volume XIX (1923–1925): The Ego and the Id and Other Works*, 241–58.

Freud, S. (1926) Letter from Sigmund Freud to Members of The B'nai B'rith Lodge, 6 May 1926. *Letters of Sigmund Freud 1873–1939*, 51, 366–7.

Freud, S. (1927) The Future of an Illusion. *The Standard Edition of the Complete Psychological Works of Sigmund Freud, Volume XXI (1927–1931): The Future of an Illusion, Civilization and Its Discontents, and Other Works*, 1–56.

Freud, S. (1930) Civilization and Its Discontents. *The Standard Edition of the Complete Psychological Works of Sigmund Freud, Volume XXI (1927–1931): The Future of an Illusion, Civilization and Its Discontents, and Other Works*, 57–146.

Freud, S. (1939) Moses and Monotheism. *The Standard Edition of the Complete Psychological Works of Sigmund Freud, Volume XXIII (1937–1939): Moses and Monotheism, An Outline of Psycho-Analysis and Other Works*, 1–138.

Frosh, S. (1989) *Psychoanalysis and Psychology: Minding the Gap*. London: Macmillan; New York: New York University Press.

Frosh, S. (1991) *Identity Crisis: Modernity, Psychoanalysis and the Self*. London: Macmillan; New York: Routledge.

Frosh, S. (1999) *The Politics of Psychoanalysis*. London: Macmillan.

Frosh, S. (2005a) *Hate and the Jewish Science Anti-Semitism, Nazism and Psychoanalysis*. London: Palgrave.

Frosh, S. (2005b) Fragments of Jewish Identity. *American Imago*, 62, 179–92.

Frosh, S. (2006a) Psychoanalysis and Judaism. In: D. Black (ed.) *Psychoanalysis and Religion in the Twenty-First Century*. London: Routledge.

Frosh, S. (2006b) *For and against Psychoanalysis*. London: Routledge.

Frosh, S. (2010) *Psychoanalysis outside the Clinic*. London: Palgrave.

Frosh, S. (2011) Psychoanalysis, Antisemitism and the Miser. *New Formations*, 72, 94–106.

Frosh, S. (2012) The Re-enactment of Denial. In: A. Gulerce (ed.) *Re(con)figuring Psychoanalysis: Critical Juxtapositions of the Philosophical, the Sociohistorical and the Political*. London: Palgrave.

Frosh, S. (2013a) Psychoanalysis, Colonialism, Racism. *Journal of Theoretical and Philosophical Psychology*, 33, 141–54.

Frosh, S. (2013b) *Hauntings: Psychoanalysis and Ghostly Transmissions*. London: Palgrave.

Frosh, S. (2018) Psychoanalysis, Politics and Society: What Remains Radical in Psychoanalysis? In: R. Gipps and M. Lacewing (eds) *The Oxford Handbook of Philosophy and Psychoanalysis*. Oxford: Oxford University Press, 667–86.

Frosh, S. (2019) *Those Who Come After: Postmemory, Acknowledgement and Forgiveness*. London: Palgrave.

Frosh, S. and Mandelbaum, B. (2017) 'Like Kings in Their Kingdoms': Conservatism in Brazilian Psychoanalysis during the Dictatorship. *Political Psychology*, 38, 591–604.

Gay, P. (1988) *Freud: A Life for Our Time*. London: Dent.

Gaztambide, D. (2019) *A People's History of Psychoanalysis: From Freud to Liberation Psychology*. Lanham: Lexington Books.

Gaztambide, D. (2022) Entre Negros, Blancos y Judios: Revisiting Claudia Tate's 'Freud and His Negro' with Puerto Rican Eyes. *Psychoanalysis, Culture and Society*. https://doi.org/10.1057/s41282-022-00304-1.

George, S. (2018) *Jouissance* and Discontent: A Meeting of Psychoanalysis, Race and American Slavery. *Psychoanalysis, Culture & Society*, 23, 267–89.

Gidley, B., McGeever, B. and Feldman, D. (2020) Labour and Antisemitism: A Crisis Misunderstood. *The Political Quarterly*, 91, 413–21.

Gilman, S. (1991) *The Jew's Body*. London: Routledge.

Gilman, S. (1993) *Freud, Race and Gender*. Princeton: Princeton University Press.

Gilroy, P. (1993) *The Black Atlantic: Modernity and Double Consciousness*. Cambridge, MA: Harvard University Press.

Ginsburg, L. (1999) Sigmund Freud's Racial Vocabulary and Related Fragments from the Analyses of Clarence P. Oberndorf and Smiley Blanton. *International Forum of Psychoanalysis*, 8(3–4), 243–8.

Goldstein, R. (1992) Looking Back at Lot's Wife. *Commentary*, 34, 37–41.

Gordimer, N. (2003) Introduction to A. Memmi. *The Colonizer and the Colonized*. London: Earthscan.

Gordon, A. (1997) *Ghostly Matters: Haunting and the Sociological Imagination*. Minneapolis: University of Minnesota Press.

Greedharry, M. (2008) *Postcolonial Theory and Psychoanalysis*. London: Palgrave.

Gregory, J. (2022) Whiteness and/as War. Psychoanalysis, Culture and Society. https://doi-org.ezproxy.lib.bbk.ac.uk/10.1057/s41282-022-00305-0.

Hall, C., Draper, N., McClelland, K. and Donington, K. (2016) *Legacies of British Slave-Ownership*. Cambridge, UK: Cambridge University Press.

Harris, A. (2012) The House of Difference, or White Silence. *Studies in Gender and Sexuality*, 13, 197–216.

Hartman, S. (2019) *Wayward Lives, Beautiful Experiments*. London: Serpent's Tail.

Hartnack, C. (2011) Colonial Dominions and the Psychoanalytic Couch: Synergies of Freudian Theory with Bengali Hindu Thought and Practices in British India. In: W. Anderson, D. Jenson and R. Keller (eds) *Unconscious Dominions: Psychoanalysis, Colonial Trauma, and Global Sovereignties*. Durham: Duke University Press.

Herzog, A. (2005) Levinas, Memory and the Art of Writing. *The Philosophical Forum*, 36(3), 333–43.

Herzog, D. (2017) *Cold War Freud*. Cambridge: Cambridge University Press.

Hirst, P. and Woolley, P. (1982) *Social Relations and Human Attributes*. London: Tavistock Press.

Holman, C. and Holman, N. (2002) *Torah, Worship and Acts of Loving Kindness: Baseline Indicators for the Charedi Community in Stamford Hill*. Leicester: De Montfort University.

Hook, D. (2013) *(Post)apartheid Conditions*. London: Palgrave.

Hook, D. (2018) Racism and Jouissance: Evaluating the 'Racism as (the theft of) Enjoyment' Hypothesis. *Psychoanalysis, Culture & Society*, 23, 244–66.

Hook, D. (2022) Jouissance as Tool of Psychosocial Analysis. In: S. Frosh, J. Walsh and M. Vyrgioti (eds) *The Palgrave Handbook of Psychosocial Studies*. Cham: Palgrave/Springer.

Jacobs, J. (2015) *The Frankfurt School, Jewish Lives and Antisemitism*. Cambridge: Cambridge University Press.

Kahn-Harris, K. and Gidley, B. (2010) *Turbulent Times: The British Jewish Community Today*. London: Continuum.

Kahn-Harris, K. and Stothard, R. (2022) *What Does a Jew Look Like?* London: Five Leaves.

Khanna, R. (2004) *Dark Continents: Psychoanalysis and Colonialism*. Durham: Duke University Press.

Khanna, R. (2011) Hope, Demand and the Perpetual. In: W. Anderson, D. Jenson and R. Keller (eds) *Unconscious Dominions: Psychoanalysis, Colonial Trauma and Global Sovereignties*. Durham: Duke University Press, pp. 247–64.

Klein, D. (1985) *Jewish Origins of the Psychoanalytic Movement*. Chicago: Chicago University Press.

Klein, M. (1952) On Observing the Behaviour of Young Infants. In: M. Klein (1975) (ed.) *Envy and Gratitude and Other Works 1946–1963*. London: The Hogarth Press and the Institute of Psycho-Analysis, pp. 94–121.

Klein, M. (1957) Envy and Gratitude. In: M. Klein (1975) (ed.) *Envy and Gratitude and Other Works 1946–1963*. London: The Hogarth Press and the Institute of Psycho-Analysis, pp. 176–235.

Kovel, J. (1995) On Racism and Psychoanalysis. In: A. Elliott and S. Frosh (eds) *Psychoanalysis in Contexts*. London: Routledge, pp. 205–22.

Lacan, J. (1991/2007) *The Other Side of Psychoanalysis: The Seminar of Jacques Lacan Book XVII*. New York: Norton.

Laplanche, J. (1989) *New Foundations for Psychoanalysis*. Oxford: Basil Blackwell.

Laplanche, J. (1999) *Essays on Otherness*. London: Routledge.

Laubscher, L., Hook, D. and Desai, M. (eds) (2022) *Fanon, Phenomenology and Psychology*. London and New York: Routledge.

Leary, K. (2007) Racial Insult and Repair. *Psychoanalytic Dialogues*, 17, 539–49.

Leary, K. (2012) Race as an Adaptive Challenge. *Psychoanalytic Psychology*, 29, 279–91.

Lentin, A. (2020) *Why Race Still Matters*. Cambridge: Polity.

Levinas, E. (1963/1990) *Difficult Freedom: Essays on Judaism*. Baltimore: Johns Hopkins Press.

Levinas, E. (1978/1999) *Otherwise than Being or beyond Essence*. Translated by A. Lingis. Pittsburgh: Duquesne UP.

Levinas, E. (1985) *Ethics and Infinity*. Pittsburgh, PA: Duquesne University Press.

Levinas, E. (1990) *Nine Talmudic Readings*. Bloomington: Indiana University Press.

Levinas, E. (1991) *Entre Nous: On Thinking of the Other*. London: Athlone, 1998.

Mahler, A. (1946/1968) *Gustav Mahler: Memories and Letters*. Edited by D. Mitchell. Rev. edn. London: John Murray.

Malamed, C. (2022) Does Your Institute Have an Anti-racism Commitment? Interrogating Anti-racism Commitments in Psychoanalytic Institutes. *Psychoanalysis, Culture and Society*, 27, 375–85.

Malone, K. and Jackson, T. (2022) Dereliction: Afropessimism, Anti-Blackness, and Lacanian Psychoanalysis. In: S. George and D. Hook (eds) *Lacan and Race: Racism, Identity, and Psychoanalytic Theory*. London: Routledge.

Mandelbaum, B., Frosh, S. and Lima, R. (eds) (2021) *Brazilian Psychosocial Histories of Psychoanalysis*. London: Palgrave.

Mannoni, O. (1956) *Prospero and Caliban: The Psychology of Colonization*. London: Methuen.

Marcus, P. (2007) 'You are, therefore I am': Emmanuel Levinas and Psychoanalysis. *Psychoanalytic Review*, 94, 515–27.

McIvor, D.W. (2020) Clad in Mourning: Psychoanalysis and Race in Contemporary America. *Journal of Psychosocial Studies*, 13(1), 35–48.

Memmi, A. (1953/1955) *The Pillar of Salt*. Boston: Beacon Press.

Memmi, A. (1957/1965) *The Colonizer and the Colonized*. London: Earthscan, 2003.

Memmi, A. (1962) *Portrait of a Jew*. New York: Orino Press.

Mignolo, W. (2000) *Local Histories/Global Designs: Coloniality, Subaltern Knowledges and Border Thinking*. Princeton: Princeton University Press.

Mitchell, J. (2000) *Mad Men and Medusas: Reclaiming Hysteria and the Effect of Sibling Relationships on the Human Condition*. London: Allen Lane.

Morgan, H. (2021) *The Work of Whiteness: A Psychoanalytic Perspective*. London: Routledge.

Morrison, T. (1987) *Beloved*. London: Picador.

Moten, F. (2013) Blackness and Nothingness (Mysticism in the Flesh). *South Atlantic Quarterly*, 112(4), 737–80.

Nancy, J. L. (2020) *Excluding the Jew within Us*. Cambridge: Polity.

Nirenberg, D. (2013) *Anti-Judaism*. New York: Norton.

O'Loughlin, M. and Voela, A. (2021) Editorial Comment. *Psychoanalysis, Culture & Society*, 26, 411–13.

Oliver, K. (2004) *The Colonization of Psychic Space*. Minneapolis: University of Minnesota Press.

Oliveira, C. (2003) *História da psicanálise. São Paulo 1920–1969*. São Paulo: Escuta/ FAPESP.

Ortigues, M.C. and Ortigues, E. (1966) *L'Oedipe Africain*. Paris: Plon.

Osserman, J. (2022) *Circumcision on the Couch: The Cultural, Psychological, and Gendered Dimensions of the World's Oldest Surgery*. London: Bloomsbury.

Palacios, M. (2013) *Radical Sociality: On Disobedience, Violence and Belonging*. London: Palgrave.

Pick, D. (2000) *Svengali's Web: The Alien Enchanter in Modern Culture*. New Haven: Yale University Press.

Pick, D. (2022) *Brainwashed*. London: Profile Books.

Plotkin, M. (2012) The Diffusion of Psychoanalysis under Conditions of Political Authoritarianism: The Case of Argentina, 1960s and 1970s. In: J. Damousi and M. Plotkin (eds) *Psychoanalysis and Politics: Histories of Psychoanalysis under Conditions of Restricted Political Freedom*. Oxford: Oxford University Press, pp. 185–211.

Plotkin, M. (2021) 'Global' Psychoanalysis in Latin America: Some Reflections. In: B. Mandelbaum, S. Frosh and R. Lima (eds) *Brazilian Psychosocial Histories of Psychoanalysis*. London: Palgrave, pp. 21–37.

Rankine, C. (2015) *Citizen: An American Lyric*. Harmondsworth: Penguin.

Rieff, P. (1959) *Freud: The Mind of the Moralist*. Chicago: University of Chicago Press.

Robert, M. (1974) *From Oedipus to Moses: Freud's Jewish Identity*. New York: Anchor Books.

Rose, J. (2003) Response to Edward Said. In: E. Said (ed.) *Freud and the Non-European*. London: Verso.

Rose, J. (2011) *Proust among the Nations: From Dreyfus to the Middle East*. Chicago: University of Chicago Press.

Rubin, A., Mandelbaum, B. and Frosh, S. (2016) 'No memory, no desire': Psychoanalysis in Brazil during Repressive Times. *Psychoanalysis and History*, 18, 93–118.

Russo, J. (2012a) Brazilian Psychiatrists and Psychoanalysis at the Beginning of the 20th Century: A Quest for National Identity. *Psychoanalysis and History*, 14, 297–312.

Russo, J. (2012b) The Social Diffusion of Psychoanalysis during the Brazilian Military Regime: Psychological Awareness in an Age of Political Repression. In: J. Damousi and M. Plotkin (eds) *Psychoanalysis and Politics: Histories of Psychoanalysis under Conditions of Restricted Political Freedom*. Oxford: Oxford University Press.

Rustin, M. (1991) *The Good Society and the Inner World*. London: Verso.

Said, E. (1978) *Orientalism*. London: Pantheon.

Said, E. (1979) Zionism from the Standpoint of Its Victims. In: M. Bayoumi and A. Rubin (eds) (2001). *The Edward Said Reader*. London: Granta, pp. 114–68.

Said, E. (2003) *Freud and the Non-European*. London: Verso.

Scholem, G. (1941) *Major Trends in Jewish Mysticism*. New York: Schocken.

Schraub, D. (2019) White Jews: An Intersectional Approach. *AJS Review*, 43, 379–407.

Seshadri-Crooks, K. (1994) The Primitive as Analyst: Postcolonial Feminism's Access to Psychoanalysis. *Cultural Critique*, 28, 175–218.

Seshadri-Crooks, K. (2000) *Desiring Whiteness: A Lacanian Analysis of Race*. London: Routledge.

Sharit, A. (2000) An interview with Edward Said. https://politicsandculture. org/2010/08/10/an-interview-with-edward-said-2/, accessed 2 January 2020.

Sharpe, C. (2016) *In the Wake: On Blackness and Being*. Durham: Duke University Press.

Shatz, A. (2020) On Albert Memmi. *London Review of Books*, 42(16). https://www.lrb.co.uk/the-paper/v42/n16, accessed 12 January 2023.

Sheldon, R. (2019). On Learning from the Margins: Jewish Nonreligious Grammars within a Secular-Protestant Landscape. *Secularism and Non-Religion*, 8, 1–6.

Simmel, E. (1946) Anti-Semitism and Mass Psychopathology. In: E. Simmel (ed.) *Anti-Semitism: A Social Disease*. New York: International Universities Press.

Singh, A. (2018) *The Talking Cure in the Tropics*. Unpublished PhD thesis, Queen Mary University of London.

Slabodsky, S. (2014) *Decolonial Judaism: Triumphal Failures of Barbaric Thinking*. London: Palgrave.

Slavet, E. (2009) *Racial Fever: Freud and the Jewish Question*. New York: Fordham.

Spillers, H. (1996) All the Things You Could Be by Now if Sigmund Freud's Wife Was Your Mother: Psychoanalysis and Race. *Critical Inquiry*, 22, 710–34.

Staetsky, L.D. (2022) *Haredi Jews around the World: Population Trends and Estimates*. London: Institute of Jewish Policy Research.

Steele, J. (2021) Fear of Blackness: Understanding White Supremacy as an Inverted Relationship to Oppression. *Psychoanalysis, Culture & Society*, 26, 388–404.

Stonebridge, L. (1998) *The Destructive Element: British Psychoanalysis and Modernism*. London: Macmillan.

Stonebridge, L. (2019) *Placeless People: Writing, Rights and Refugees*. Oxford: Oxford University Press.

Tate, C. (1996) Freud and His 'Negro': Psychoanalysis as Ally and Enemy of African Americans. *Journal for the Psychoanalysis of Culture & Society*, 1, 53–62.

Traverso, E. (2016) *The End of Jewish Modernity*. London: Pluto Press.

Trezise, T. (2013) *Witnessing Witnessing: On the Reception of Holocaust Survivor Testimony*. New York: Fordham.

Vyrgioti, M. (2018) *The Cannibal Trope: A Psychosocial Critique of Psychoanalysis' Colonial Fantasies*. Unpublished PhD thesis. Birkbeck, University of London.

Vyrgioti, M. (2022) *Freud and the Cannibal: Vignettes from psychoanalysis' Colonial History*. In: S. Bar-Haim, E. Coles and H. Tyson (eds) *Wild Analysis: From the Couch to Cultural and Political Life*. London: Routledge.

Wale, K., Gobodo-Madikizela, P. and Prager, J. (eds) (2020) *Post-Conflict Hauntings: Transforming Memories of Historical Trauma*. London: Palgrave.

White, K.P. (2002). Surviving Hating and Being Hated. *Contemporary Psychoanalysis*, 38, 401–22.

Wilderson, F. (2010) *Red, White, and Black: Cinema and the Structure of U.S. Antagonisms*. Durham: Duke University Press.

Winnicott, D.W. (1958) The Capacity to Be Alone. *International Journal of Psychoanalysis*, 39, 416–20.

Winnicott, D.W. (1960) The Theory of the Parent-Infant Relationship. *International Journal of Psychoanalysis*, 41, 585–95.

Winnicott, D.W. (1969) The Use of an Object. *International Journal of Psychoanalysis*, 50, 711–16.

Winograd, B. (2014) *Black Psychoanalysts Speak*. PEP Video Grants 1 (1):1.

Young-Bruehl, E. (1996) *The Anatomy of Prejudices*. Cambridge, MA: Harvard University Press.

Zaretsky, E. (2015) *Political Freud: A History*. New York: Columbia University Press.

Zeavin, H. (2022) Unfree Associations: Parasitic Whiteness on and off the Couch. *N+1*, 42. https://www.nplusonemag.com/issue-42/essays/unfree-associations/.

Žižek, S. (1993) *Tarrying with the Negative*. Durham: Duke University Press.

Žižek, S. (1994) *The Metastases of Enjoyment*. London: Verso.

Žižek, S. (1997) *The Plague of Fantasies*. London: Verso.

Žižek, S. (2009) *The Fragile Absolute: Or, Why Is the Christian Legacy Worth Fighting For?* London: Verso.

Zornberg, A. (1995) *The Beginning of Desire: Reflections on Genesis*. London: Doubleday.

Zornberg, A. (2009) *The Murmuring Deep: Reflections on the Biblical Unconscious*. New York: Schocken.

INDEX